Economic Development: Strategies for State and Local Practice

Economic Development: Strategies for State and Local Practice

Steven G. Koven

Thomas S. Lyons

International
City/County
ICMA
Management
Association
icma.org

The International City/County Management Association (ICMA) is the professional and educational organization for appointed administrators and assistant administrators in local government. The mission of ICMA is to create excellence in local governance by developing and fostering professional local government management worldwide. To further this mission, ICMA develops and disseminates new approaches to management through training programs, information services, and publications.

ICMA's interests and activities include public management education; voluntary credentialing and standards of ethics for members; an information clearinghouse; local government research and development; data collection and dissemination; technical assistance; and a wide array of publications, including *Public Management* magazine, newsletters, management reports, and texts. ICMA's efforts toward the improvement of local government—as represented by this book—are offered for all local governments and educational institutions.

For further information about the publications or services for local governments offered by ICMA, write to Publications Department, ICMA, 777 North Capitol St., N.E., Suite 500, Washington, D.C. 20002. To order publications, call 800/745-8780 (outside the United States, call 770/442-8631, ext. 377) or visit the ICMA Bookstore online at http://bookstore.icma.org.

Text design by Will Kemp.

Library of Congress Cataloging-in-Publication Data

Koven, Steven G.
   Economic development : strategies for state and local practice / by
Steven G. Koven, Thomas S. Lyons.
      p. cm.
   ISBN 0-87326-134-8 (paper)
   1.   Economic development projects—United States. 2. Local
government—United States. 3. State governments—United States. I.
Lyons, Thomas S. II. Title.
   HC110.E44.K68 2003
   338.973—dc21
                                        2002156223

Printed in the United States of America.

08 07 06 05 04 03
5 4 3 2 1

This book is dedicated to our families,
Debra, Dylan, Andrea, Eli, and Faye.

Contents

Acknowledgments

A book is always the product of a collaborative effort that extends well beyond the authors themselves. We would like to acknowledge all those who contributed their time, effort, and expertise toward making this book possible.

In particular, we would like to thank Nicole DeVaughn, Songmei Li, Marcus Lourenco, Stuart Strother, and Biqui Zhao for their excellent background research. We also wish to extend our gratitude to CAP Services of Stevens Point, Wisconsin, and the staff of the CAPsell Center in Wautoma, Wisconsin, for allowing us an insider's view of their business incubator operations. We would also like to thank the Aspen Institute, which funded the development of that case study. Thanks, also, to Greater Louisville, Inc., United Parcel Service, and the University of Louisville for sharing with us the story of Metropolitan College.

We are also indebted to the School of Urban and Public Affairs at the University of Louisville for its support throughout the research and writing of this book. A supportive environment in which to work is too often undervalued.

We offer our heartfelt thanks to our editors, Christine Ulrich and Mary Marik, at the International City/County Management Association. Their helpful suggestions, eye for detail, and insightful probing greatly enhanced the quality of the final product.

Finally, we would like to acknowledge the hard work and creativity of all the practitioners and scholars in the field of economic development whose contributions to this field are reflected in the pages of this book.

Introduction

Governments across the United States seek to invigorate and sustain their local economies through programs of economic development. Governments pursue growth and improvements in terms of population, tax base, per capita income, investments, jobs, and the overall well-being of citizens. Although policymakers cannot wave a magic wand to create growth, deliberate choices of one strategy or another can have profound implications for the overall development of jurisdictions as well as for the basic quality of life of residents.

This book explains how economic development is promoted in state and local jurisdictions, and it assesses various development strategies. The authors' objectives are to increase awareness of different economic development theories and show how these theories can be put into practice through descriptions of various tools of development, discussion of relevant literature, and review of economic development cases. The overall objective of this book is to help current and future leaders identify and capitalize on opportunities for economic development that will benefit citizens of the jurisdiction and the business community.

To attain these objectives, the book describes both broad theories and specific tools of development. Chapter 1 addresses theories of development. For example, one theory is the notion that wealth will be maximized when people are free to make their own economic decisions. Another idea of development focuses on the need to develop social capital in communities. Other broad development ideas look at the ability to innovate and create new products, the need to export products, and the synergies that can be generated from existing production.

Chapter 2 shifts focus to narrower concepts of development. At this level, various economic development techniques—sometimes called the tools of economic development—are explained. These tools include the use of financial incentives (such as loans and tax-exempt bonds), tax incentives (such as tax exemptions and tax abatements), and nonfinancial assistance (such as site development and customized education).

An understanding of these specific tools of development is essential for leaders who hope to protect and expand their tax base. City and county leaders need both a strategic vision and tactical knowledge of how to pursue that vision. Understanding of broad concepts can help to generate long-term, major strategies for communities. Not all communities, however, are able to follow the same strategies. Some communities may face better options than others because they have a better-educated citizenry, a critical mass of development in an industry, a wealth of natural resources, or established infrastructure. Leaders can make strategic choices after realistically assessing threats and opportunities in a given environment. After strategic decisions are made, having a broad vision can help in applying specific techniques that can be pulled from the economic development toolbox.

This book does not endorse specific strategies or plans of development but presents theories of development, techniques of development, and descriptive cases in an attempt to instruct future decision makers. No one concept will guarantee economic growth for a community, but knowledge of theories and an awareness of developmental techniques can help public officials assess their environment and make good choices. A comprehensive glossary is presented at the back of the book. Awareness of terminology is a basic prerequisite for those who wish to become accomplished at the economic development game.

Chapters 3, 4, and 5 look at the connections between economic development theory and economic development tools. Case studies describe how diverse public sector actors have adopted different strategies in pursuit of economic development. These studies provide rich detail on the application of economic development visions to specific settings. The case studies bring to life the abstract concepts of development. Cases include the creation of small businesses in rural America, the preservation of jobs in a large package-handling company, the legitimization of previously banned activity, and the expansion of high-tech industry. Insights from these cases should be useful to public officials evaluating their own alternatives for protecting or strengthening their economic base.

Critical choices for policymakers

Successful policymakers rarely wait passively for external forces to affect their communities; they actively seek to shape their environments. How successfully they interpret and reinvent those environments will influence their success or failure at economic development. Many local and state officials seek to create an across-the-board climate favorable to business. Some officials may target certain companies or industries for special tax or financial incentives. Some jurisdictions may try to tap into federal programs that allocate funds for encouraging the development of low-income neighborhoods, the training of specific categories of dislocated workers, the building of infrastructure, or other development activities.

Policymakers may choose to focus on bottom-up strategies—assisting lower-income neighborhoods—or top-down strategies—aiding companies that are already prosperous and have the highest potential for growth. Policymakers may create new types of relationships and partnerships between private sector and public sector actors. They may legalize previously banned behavior such as gambling. Economic development policymakers may carefully plan strategies that will build on identified strengths of their jurisdiction. For example, economic development policymakers may try to attract firms in one industry rather than another industry. They may "go the extra mile" in saving jobs, or strongly resist a company's development plans. Or they may do nothing, ignoring signs of economic decline. Policymakers may choose strategies that focus on specific goals: improving higher education, attracting tourists, helping low-income neighborhoods, attracting white-collar jobs, or capitalizing on a local surplus of low-wage earners.

At the operational level, the techniques, or tools, that have been used to reach these goals are many and varied. Governments have provided grants to local jurisdictions as well as to private sector firms. Governments have made loans available to businesses that could not raise money from the private sector. Governments have underwritten or subsidized the cost of borrowing. They have given tax breaks to companies that promised to relocate to a new area or remain in a given jurisdiction. These tax breaks have taken a variety of forms, including agreements to forgo assessing taxes for a period of time (tax abatement), reductions in assessments of property (tax exemption), direct reductions in tax obligation (tax credit), and financing improvements with future tax revenues expected after successful economic development (tax increment financing). Public sector leaders may choose to reduce taxes or shift the tax burden from one group to another. Some state and local policymakers offer tax and financial incentives. These incentives are relatively straightforward and are dependent on the political power of the various interest groups in the community.

In addition to their tax and financial policies, communities can implement other strategies to improve prospects for economic development. Communities can improve their infrastructure, develop sites for businesses, and assist with training. Communities can build roads, acquire parcels of land for development, cut red tape in enterprise zones, and improve local education systems. Each technique has led to success.

Implications of economic development strategies

Economic development strategies are not neutral in terms of economic, political, or social consequences. Some communities are more accommodating than others to residential builders; some communities accept low-wage businesses that others shun; some jurisdictions place a high priority on maintaining the natural beauty of their environment; others seem to seek out growth at any cost. Public sector leaders shape the economic direction of the community by actively pursuing job retention, attraction, or creation strategies. Development choices—even a do-nothing strategy is a choice—will influence the long-term economic health of a community.

Political power may also shift as a consequence of development strategies. For example, attraction of low-wage industries may alter the political as well as social consensus of a jurisdiction. Public officials therefore should carefully weigh the strategies they choose to pursue. These strategies should be consistent with the values and desires of constituents.

Case studies presented later in this book illustrate the consequences of various types of development. Case Study 3–1 (United Parcel Service and Metropolitan College: Retaining jobs in Louisville, Kentucky) illustrates that public sector assets (universities) may be leveraged to create business environments that are more attractive to employers. Research Case 3–1 (Attracting jobs: Is gambling a good economic development bet?) identifies social implications of development choices. Case Study 3–2 (Luring Mercedes to Alabama) describes how a relatively small state in the South was able to attract a high-quality automobile manufacturer. Case Study 4–1 (Business creation in rural America: The CAPsell Center business incubator) identifies the possibility for an expansive, targeted, public sector role in job creation. Research Case 5–1 (Testing the link between education and economic development) tests empirical linkages between education and economic development. Finally, Case Study 5–1 (Austin, Texas, and the Dell Computer Company) illustrates how the general milieu of an economic environment (an environment not targeted to specific individuals or companies) can facilitate growth in new high-tech industries.

Case studies can be an effective learning tool for students of economic development. The nuances and detail of public policies help the reader understand the environment in which economic development strategies are implemented. Because there is no one solution—no magic wand—for economic development, carefully investigating policies that have been applied in different settings and considering the results can lead to assessments of whether those policies will work in another community, under other circumstances.

Cases as reflections of alternative strategies for development

How can we foster prosperity? That is what this book is about. Various perspectives on this question—including the role of government, the best targets for development, and the importance of innovation—will be reviewed in Chapter 1.

Although prescriptions for economic development vary, there is general agreement that prosperity is desirable. Because of their culture, geography, history, and demographics, communities pursue different strategies to reach a common end. Some jurisdictions choose higher taxes and place greater emphasis on the quality of public services, while other jurisdictions focus on keeping taxes low to encourage business investment. Some jurisdictions subsidize corporate expansion, other communities encourage community and neighborhood empowerment, and still others promote education and technological advancement as an overall economic development strategy.

Case studies in this book demonstrate why communities and government leaders follow different strategies for development. Leaders in Austin, Texas, a relatively prosperous community, could afford to foster an environment of innovation and entrepreneurship. On the other hand, officials in Atlantic City, New Jersey; Detroit, Michigan; and Tunica, Mississippi, were far less sanguine about their communities' economic prospects, and these communities chose to relax gambling restrictions as a way to foster investment.

Many jurisdictions recognize that attracting white-collar, nonpolluting, and immensely profitable corporations is not feasible. These jurisdictions must carefully assess their options and pursue those within their reach. Wautoma, Wisconsin, a rural community profiled in Chapter 4, chose to encourage the creation of small, locally based enterprises. Wautoma's government program creates value where none existed by helping citizens open small, mom-and-pop businesses. Even if only a few survive, economic value in the locality is enhanced. Other small communities choose to create jobs or revenues by promoting environmental or historical tourism or by offering services other jurisdictions need—a prison or a refuse disposal plant, for example.

The prospect of gaining (or losing) a large corporation puts pressure on public officials, who may anticipate huge tax-base benefits from the new investment (or fear severe losses). Public officials realize that they will be blamed when the local economy is weak and praised when it is strong. This pressure, as well as the desire to improve their communities, is a great motivator.

1 Theories of economic development

Learning objectives

You should be able to:

- Describe two broad theories of economic development that affect state and local economic development in the United States today

- Describe three classical theories of the role of government in enhancing or inhibiting economic growth

- Describe the major theoretical difference between top-down and bottom-up government economic strategies; provide two examples of government activities for each approach

- Describe two ways that state and local governments foster innovations that enhance local economic development.

Theories of economic development

It is generally agreed that the economic well-being of citizens requires productivity, profits, and wages. Dissent arises over how to attain those goals.

The role of government in economic development

Experts disagree about the role government should play in economic development. Does government help sustain growth or does it inhibit vibrant economies? Likewise, there is no consensus on when or how government should intervene in the private sector, or if government should intervene at all. Different conceptual images of the role of government will lead to contrasting answers.

Another major issue is the proper target or appropriate focus of government intervention. Who should the government assist? Should it assist producers of goods and profits, or should it assist consumers? Is it necessary to help declining communities and lower-income groups, or is public sector assistance better targeted to those who have the greatest ability to succeed? Will a rising economy help all to achieve their economic goals? Should government programs strive to be as neutral as possible, giving no group special benefits and forcing everyone to compete under the same rules? What is the role of government in protecting citizens from the unintended consequences of economic development? These and related questions are addressed in this chapter.

Laissez-faire model of economic development

In the latter part of the twentieth century, it became quite popular for politicians to decry government as not only ineffective but detrimental to social and economic development. "Government is not the solution; government is the problem" became the mantra of such politicians as Newt Gingrich, Phil Gramm, Jack Kemp and the most famous advocate of limited government, Ronald Reagan. Even "new Democrat" Bill Clinton felt obliged to declare that the era of big government was over. The minimalist-government view is neatly summarized in the statement that "government is best that governs least."

Antipathy toward government did not arise in an intellectual vacuum. For much of the nation's history, leaders have warned against the danger of concentrating power in a few hands. The Founders, particularly James Madison, built into the U.S. Constitution safeguards to protect citizens against the dangers of concentrated power. Institutional structures such as the system of checks and balances, separation of powers, federalism, and popular elections all were developed with the intent of fragmenting power and making it more difficult for the few to dominate the many.

Madison's views of the virtues of limited government were consistent with the writings of the Scottish moral philosopher, Adam Smith, and the French political philosopher, Baron de Montesquieu.[1] Adam Smith's book, *An Inquiry into the Nature and Causes of the Wealth of Nations*, published in

> ### Federal, state, and local economic development programs
>
> Federal, state, and local governments are interrelated in the federal system of governance in the United States. This form of government attempts to create a workable national authority while retaining relatively autonomous units known as states. With its strong resource base, the national government is better able to address major issues such as how to enhance economic development. The national level of government often supplies the funding and defines the rules, but it relies upon the state and local levels to implement the policy.
>
> For example, the national government may allocate money to train displaced workers. National government officials, however, do not directly train the workers but instead rely on cities to set up their own programs. The idea that one level of government can raise money and pass resources through to lower levels of government is essential to federalism. Major decisions are made at the federal level, and implementation is decentralized to other levels.
>
> Decentralizing decision making for a host of programs has gained in popularity in recent years as enthusiasm for an expansive national government has declined. Local leaders want to capture resources from the federal government. Decentralizing resources to the local level is consistent with the view that those working most closely with citizens can best identify and respond to citizen needs.

1776, provided an intellectual justification for the doctrine of limited government. Smith's classic work helped to end the economic system known as mercantilism and brought acceptance of an entirely new economic framework. According to Smith, government controls could be harmful to economic development and could lead to less wealth creation. Maximization of wealth for both individuals and for the nation would occur when individuals were free to make their own decisions about how they should pursue their economic well-being. Smith concluded that concentrations of power in the system of mercantilism had the effect of raising the price of consumer goods and channeling capital, as well as labor, away from industries where demand was great. Concentrated power directed capital and labor into industries where legal restrictions kept profits artificially high.

One of Smith's key insights was his assertion that a market structured without restrictions would bring about the sale of commodities at the lowest price possible at any given level of economic development. Smith described an "invisible hand" directing free and "unfettered" markets toward the goal of maximizing wealth. Smith noted that each individual seeks personal gain but is led by "an invisible hand to promote an end which was no part of his intentions . . . by pursuing his own interest he frequently promotes that of the society more effectually than when he really intends to promote it."[2]

According to Smith, the profit motive channels self-interest into collective interest. Profits are kept to a minimum by competition, and every commodity is believed to have a natural price that is determined by its costs of production. When the market price of a commodity differs from its natural price, market forces move it back into conformity. If prices are too high, competitors enter the market, thereby driving prices down; if prices are too low, firms go out of business, allowing others to raise prices. This theory of a self-adjusting marketplace does not require an external body (such as a government) to control prices and wages.

Smith advocated only three essential duties for the state: defense, the administration of justice, and the maintenance of public works. Smith thought government should not be actively involved in the control or direction of economic activity. Smith's ideas are associated with modern-day capitalism and the general philosophy of laissez-faire, or the view that government should leave the economy alone.

Politicians, authors, and policymakers who advocate lower taxes, less regulation of business, and smaller government champion Smith's basic concepts. Theorists such as the Harvard University business professor Michael E. Porter place a high priority on market solutions to economic problems. Echoing ideas expressed by David Ricardo in his famous law of comparative advantage, Porter advocates identifying one's economic strength and specializing in that area of strength.[3] Porter believes that focusing attention on existing strengths could enhance the wealth of entire regions.

Porter has applied his theories of economic development to all levels of government, including the inner city. According to Porter, inner cities can attract private, for-profit investment by appealing to economic self-interest and competitive advantage. Porter does not call for an end to social pro-

---

Ricardo's law of comparative advantage

The law of comparative advantage was first presented in 1817 in the writings of the British economist, David Ricardo. To justify free trade between nations, Ricardo contended in *Principles of Political Economy and Taxation* that trade would lead to greater specialization in production. He believed that each nation could produce certain commodities more efficiently than other nations. Costs would be less in some nations for certain products because of various differences: natural resources, labor force skills, and technological capabilities.

Ricardo felt that if all countries specialized in the commodities in which they possessed a comparative advantage (could produce relatively more efficiently) and also traded with other nations, then a more efficient allocation of world resources would result. Free trade would drive down prices of some domestically produced goods because it would allow consumers to purchase less-expensive goods produced in foreign countries.

As a country successfully specializes in producing specific goods, however, its costs of production often increase because of administrative growth, division of labor, declining productivity, and inflation. When the costs of production rise to a specific level, the country's goods can no longer compete with other nations' goods. At this point the country's production shifts to other goods.

Ricardo postulated that the welfare of individual countries—as well as the welfare of the world—is maximized through free trade. He thought that efforts to protect a domestic economy (by imposing tariffs or restricting trade) are inefficient and reduce potential standards of living. However, some groups—textile workers in the United States and computer producers in Japan who cannot effectively compete with foreign producers, for example—gain in the short term from protectionist policies that prevent foreign countries from competing with them.

Ricardo and his followers are known for applying his law of comparative advantage to the international economic system. Their general ideas about free trade are widely endorsed by mainstream economists today.

grams for poor urban residents but, consistent with the market model, claims that social programs alone cannot revitalize declining areas. To achieve successful economic development, Porter recommends that inner cities exploit advantages such as their strategic location close to highways or rail lines, the demand of residents for retail trade, a ready labor force, and the potential for connecting with regional clusters.[4]

Mixed-market model of economic development

Market solutions to problems of economic stagnation remain popular, but critics of the pure laissez-faire theory of development cite the need for public intervention in the market to address problems that fall in the category of market failure. Market failure occurs when the pursuit of private interest leads to an inefficient use of society's resources, or when unfettered pursuit of private interest leads to an unacceptable distribution of society's goods. Collective goods, externalities, natural monopolies, and information asymmetries are four commonly recognized areas in which pure market principles may not be most beneficial—market failure, in other words.[5] When the government intervenes to remedy market failure, a mixed market results.

Collective goods   Collective goods, or public goods, are goods that are not provided by the marketplace because their acquisition cannot be confined to a particular group.[6] They are termed "nonexcludable" because no one can be excluded easily from using them. National defense is an example of a collective good that is nonexcludable and benefits many people. Because access to collective goods cannot be limited to paying consumers, private market interests have no incentive to provide them. Collective goods and services that are considered necessary to a healthy society are generally supplied through government intervention.

Whether a good is considered excludable or nonexcludable is determined by the cost of enforcing the exclusion. For example, fish in the ocean and fireworks displays are typically viewed as nonexcludable goods. Although it is technically possible to place controls on fishing and to charge people who want to see a fireworks show, placing strict limits on the ability of individual people to obtain these goods (fish in the sea and observation of a fireworks show) is exceedingly difficult. The cost of excluding users in all probability will exceed any gain from sale of the good. Another example of a nonexcludable good is a lighthouse that shines its beacon to help seafarers navigate treacherous waters. Without payment, these seafarers can take advantage of the illumination. It would be quite difficult to exclude users since the cost of patrolling the seas for those who did not pay a user fee would be prohibitive, far exceeding reasonable payments from ship owners.

On the other hand, exclusion is relatively simple for "individual" goods such as food, clothing, private automobiles, housing, and other items sold in the marketplace. For example, if a customer does not have the money to purchase a hamburger at McDonald's, the worker at the counter can simply refuse to deliver the burger. Similarly, a store sells clothing only to customers with money or a valid credit card. These easily excludable goods are provided through the mechanism of the free market: consumers demand goods; entrepreneurs recognize the demand, produce the goods in demand, and sell them to buyers at mutually acceptable prices. The government rarely intervenes to provide individual goods, but government oversight may be necessary to assure product safety (typically for food, drugs, airplanes, and buildings), honest reporting (for example, on labels and in media advertising), and contract enforcement. In short, the government acts to prevent harmful effects of market activities on the community at large.

Some goods are consumed by more than one person at the same time. Many viewers can watch a television program. One individual viewing a television program in no way limits its "consumption," or viewing, by someone else. The program is available to all for consumption, and its quality is not diminished by an individual's use. National defense is another example of a jointly consumed good. All citizens enjoy this good at the same time without detracting from its benefit to others. Other government-provided services that are jointly consumed include air pollution control, mosquito abatement, and disaster warning systems.

Public roads and highways and public parks are also used jointly, that is, many people can use them at the same time. If the total number of city street users or park visitors approaches the capacity of the street or park, however, the quality of the good (city street or park) may be diminished. When a public good is subject to congestion (i.e., when it is "contestable"), it is not a pure joint-consumption good like television broadcasting. Air pollution control is a pure joint-consumption good because citizens cannot be deprived of air, and all people benefit from its purity. Police protection is an example of a collective good that is "contestable" because police who are busy responding to crime in one part of a city may be unavailable to protect another area.[7]

Some goods fit the criteria of individual goods but are provided by the public sector because the larger society suffers if every individual does not have them. For example, in theory, individuals with communicable diseases such as smallpox, typhoid, and diphtheria can be denied medical care if they lack the ability to pay. Denying them care, however, poses a grave danger to society at large. People who do not pay for fire protection can be denied access to fire department services, but it is clearly recognized that putting out fires, like treating people with communicable diseases, benefits the community. These services therefore are treated as collective goods.

E. S. Savas, one of the country's leading proponents of privatization, has noted that because no one can be excluded from using collective goods, everyone has an economic incentive to become a "free rider." Free riders use collective goods without paying for them or sharing in the effort required to supply them. Savas concluded that collective goods must be provided through voluntary or coerced contributions such as taxes.

In many of America's communities, volunteers do provide fire protection, and they collect contributions from neighbors to cover the cost of supplies and equipment. Philanthropists provide parks, local merchant groups provide street lighting, and neighborhood associations patrol the streets. Voluntary action may fall short of community needs, however. When voluntary action does not meet community needs, government action is necessary:

> [I]f voluntary action fails to provide an adequate supply of collective goods, for example, where the social unit is large and diverse, contributions must be obtained by legally sanctioned coercion, such as tax collection and compulsory military service. This transforms free riders into forced riders. This is where government is needed, a government, one hopes, that is democratically created and which, therefore, can itself be considered the result of voluntary action.[8]

Externalities Another reason for a public role in the economy is the need to control externalities. An externality is an impact on someone who did not consent to the impact through participation in a voluntary exchange. Familiar negative externalities include air and water pollution generated by industrial plants and the unsightliness of dilapidated houses in a well-kept neighborhood. In a pure free-market model (absent government controls), private firms can easily transfer the cost of negative externalities to others.

There are various public remedies to the problem of negative externalities.[9] Most economists favor the use of fines. For example, a pollution charge can be imposed on companies that pollute the air or water. Fines must be high enough to encourage companies to spend money on pollution abatement—in other words, fines have to approach or exceed the cost of abatement measures. Alternatively, instead of taxing pollution, the government can subsidize pollution abatement expenditures, helping companies cover the costs required to clean up their operations.

A third public sector strategy to remedy negative externalities is regulation. Government today regulates many industries. To limit pollution, the government sets emission standards for automobiles; requires industrial firms to employ scrubbers or other pollution abatement devices; mandates smokestacks of a given height; and prohibits the use of low-grade, polluting coal. Governments designate certain areas for nonsmokers and put forward detailed regulations for the disposal of toxic chemicals.

Finally, the legal system deals with negative externalities. Individuals or groups of individuals who believe that they have been harmed can sue for damages. A class-action lawsuit can be filed on behalf of an entire class of injured individuals. In recent years, major industries such as the tobacco industry have been subject to large class-action suits. Critics of class-action litigation contend that the awards are excessive and largely benefit lawyers for the plaintiffs. Proponents argue that damages awarded as a result of class-action litigation are a useful check on potential abuses by large corporations and that such suits are an avenue for the expression of the legitimate complaints of average citizens.

In instances of positive externalities, an individual's actions confer a benefit on others. If a man plants a flower garden in front of his house, the neighbors' view is improved. A beekeeper confers a positive externality on the owner of a neighboring apple orchard. The apple orchard also confers a positive externality on the beekeeper since the more trees in the apple orchard, the more honey the bees can produce. Someone who rehabilitates a house in an older neighborhood increases the desirability of the neighborhood and enhances neighbors' property values. Government may encourage positive externalities by, for example, granting favorable tax treatment to people who rehabilitate homes or restore historic buildings.

Natural monopolies   The market may not work in the situation of a natural monopoly. Natural monopolies occur when increased production of some good or service results in continually decreasing average costs. In other words, the greater the level of output, the lower the cost per unit. Economists refer to this as increasing returns to scale. Supply of electricity is an example of a natural monopoly. Because of increasing returns to scale, it is less expensive to have one large electrical generator serve a region than to put a generator in every neighborhood. Similarly, it may be efficient to have only one telephone company serving a local market, or one water company. Great duplication would exist in water lines and power lines if every other house used a different water or electric company. Because of the increasing returns to scale in these industries, it is expected that monopolies will arise in the absence of regulation.

Problems in electricity deregulation—for example, recent rationing and sharp price increases in California—have led to a renewed recognition that the realities of natural monopoly persist and that creating a genuinely competitive market for electricity is likely to be a challenge. By 2001, it appeared that the deregulation of electricity would follow the pattern of other deregulated industries such as airlines and railroads. In these industries, an initial burst of competition and price cutting gave way to what economists call oligopoly markets—markets in which a few companies dominate, manipulate supply, keep out competitors, and avoid price wars. In 2002, fewer than a dozen companies consolidated their hold on most of the nation's privately owned generating capacity.[10]

In the United States, natural monopolies are regulated. Regulation prevents these companies from charging exorbitant prices for goods and services. Examples of regulated monopolies include telephone and electric service. Other natural monopolies are run directly by the government. Many water companies are publicly owned. Postal delivery is public throughout the world although there has been rapid growth in the private provision of postal services.[11]

Information asymmetries   Finally, information asymmetries, or imperfect information, can illustrate how the market is not always the best answer. Buyers and sellers may not have equal access to information and therefore cannot properly assess their options. For example, workers may not be well informed about the health risk of industrial chemicals that employers know are potentially dangerous. Because they are unaware of the risk, workers are not able to place an appropriate monetary value on their labor. Employers therefore can have an unfair advantage and may pay less for workers in a free marketplace than they would have to pay if workers had full information concerning hazards.

Government activism in the United States

A mixed-market economy has grown up in the United States in response not only to specific instances of the failure of the pure laissez-faire market but also to a common wish to stimulate economic development.

Response to specific issues   In the early years of the American republic, economic regulation and economic development were undertaken mainly by individual states. States tried to stimulate growth through public works projects, subsidies to railroads, and licensing of programs. In contrast with this fairly activist role in economic development at the state level, the national government defined its economic function more narrowly, essentially confining itself to collecting tariffs, funding public improvements, and regulating interstate commerce.

Over time, concerns about equity led the public sector to become more involved in private sector activities. In 1887, Congress passed the Interstate Commerce Act to protect small farmers from discriminatory charges by the large and powerful railroad industry. Government began to be viewed as an institution that could defend the economic welfare of average citizens and control the abuses of the massive corporations (commonly known as trusts) that were created in the latter part of the nineteenth century. The Sherman Antitrust Act, passed in 1890, prohibited attempts to monopolize industries and reflected the rejection of the pure laissez-faire model of economic development. Major monopolies such as the oil monopoly (identified with John D. Rockefeller's Standard Oil Company) were restructured following antitrust legislation.

During the Progressive Era of 1901–1917, consumer protections were introduced into the economy. Congress passed laws such as the Pure Food and Drug Act of 1906 to regulate products that could be harmful to unwary consumers. In 1933, responding to the need to guarantee the economic viability of average citizens ravaged by the effects of the Great Depression, Franklin Roosevelt introduced his New Deal and, with it, the interventionist state. In the interventionist state, the government plays an active role in guiding and regulating the private economy instead of leaving the private sector alone to operate under a framework of general rules.[12]

Providing worthy goods   Increasingly in the United States, government intervenes in the market to provide "worthy goods," goods deemed so worthy that their consumption is to be encouraged regardless of the consumer's ability to pay. These goods are either subsidized by government or produced directly by the public sector and supplied to everyone or to a broad group of people who are eligible. Market goods can become worthy goods if government decides that they are so essential that they should be provided to all citizens.

Examples of market goods that have been transformed into worthy goods include education, food, housing, and medical care. Education was once considered to be an individual good because exclusion was clearly possible. Today in the United States (and in many other nations) education not only is freely available but is mandatory up to a certain age. Food, housing, and medical care are available to individuals whose incomes fall below a minimum level. The justification for government provision of these goods is that deficiencies in the areas of education and health pose dangers to society, which needs a well-educated, healthy work force. If education is limited to those who can pay for it, talented citizens lose opportunities, productivity suffers, and economic growth is constrained. Worthy goods include not only social services such as public housing, health care, and job training, but also sports arenas, cultural centers, and agriculture.[13]

Ongoing debate   Although the public sector has grown significantly in recent decades, disagreements continue concerning its appropriate size and scope. Some contend that the best way to promote economic development is to follow a laissez-faire market model and leave the private sector alone to work its "magic." Others contend that the notion of a pure, free-market economy in the United States is a myth—it never existed and is far off the mark in describing contemporary America. Those who doubt the free-market magic assume government should be involved in the economy but debate how its extensive involvement should be channeled.

The level of government involvement in the economy is well documented. Despite the rhetoric of the Reagan and Bush administrations, federal government outlays grew from 31.4 percent of gross domestic product in 1980 to 33.3 percent in 1996,[14] not including off-budget spending such as outstanding federal loans, guaranteed loans, and borrowing from federally sponsored enterprises.

Factors contributing to the growth of government in recent decades include an increased demand for government services by recipients such as the elderly, pressure from suppliers such as defense contractors to increase government goods or services, and inefficiency in the public sector.[15] Citizens clamor for still more public sector goods and services. In recent years various levels of government have been asked to subsidize the cost of drugs, provide health care guarantees for the uninsured, provide day care for children, protect the population against terrorism, and supply other protections from life's uncertainties.

The marketplace could provide many goods that are demanded by citizens—whether or not a service or product is considered a worthy good is usually determined by the political process. Even at the local level, public sector policymakers can try to move a mixed market closer to a pure market model with:

• **Deregulation**   Regulation is a constant balancing of public and private interests. Conditions that justify regulation may erode over time. For example, in recent years there has been a concerted effort to reduce the extent of federal regulations in a number of industries. The airline industry was deregulated with the elimination of the Civil Aeronautics Board in 1984. Subsequently the natural gas, trucking, electricity, and banking industries were deregulated. However, events at the beginning of the millennium led to demands for more regulation in some areas. Government leaders called for better regulation of airport security in the aftermath of the September 11, 2001, World Trade Center and Pentagon attacks and more oversight of financial reporting techniques following the bankruptcy in 2001 of the large energy trading company, Enron.

Local communities also get involved in regulation and deregulation. For example, communities have recently been successful in regulating the growth of unsightly transmitters and antennas that are necessary for continuous cell phone reception. In Spartanburg, South Carolina, the city council placed a moratorium on the construction of transmitters to give officials time to review placement. Following the moratorium, in 1999, the city approved an ordinance that included setback requirements for transmitters in residential areas. Palm Beach, Florida, successfully prevented transmitter construction and was even able to receive a fee for permission to install hidden antennae on the roof of the Palm Beach town hall. Cities have been aided by the language of the Telecommunications Act of 1996 that supported the rights of local governments in tower-siting disputes.[16]

- **Legalization**   Legalization for economic development purposes applies mainly to casino gambling, although other activity previously prohibited—horse racing, drinking, and sexually oriented businesses—may be legalized in order to attract dollars into the local economy.

- **Privatization**   Many jurisdictions have privatized government services ranging from garbage collection to management of prisons, resulting in various mixes of private and public sector activity.

Supply-side and demand-side economics

The public sector can stimulate markets through either supply-side or demand-side subsidies. In general, supply-side strategies assist producers and the free-enterprise market rewards the efficient. Supply-siders believe that benefits to producers and suppliers will eventually benefit all others in the economy as well. In contrast, a demand-side focus targets consumers, and the ultimate aim is increasing economic activity by encouraging greater consumption of goods or services. The theory behind demand-side strategies, which are generally associated with public sector activism and aimed at lower-income groups, is that increasing the purchasing capacity of consumers will lead to more spending and economic growth. Tax-break proposals, although they appeal to both high- and low-income groups, often benefit higher-income groups disproportionately.

Top-down development strategies

In general, supply-side economics is grounded in neoclassical economic thought, specifically in the ideas of the French economist Jean-Baptiste Say (1766–1834). Say argued that the goal of government should not be to encourage consumption but to stimulate production, and government's role should be to remove impediments to the effective use of factors of production (labor, land, and capital). According to supply-side theory, a large government sector acts as a drag on the economy. A smaller government and a lower tax burden stimulate the economy by allowing individuals to keep and spend more of their money.

The supply-side view is that high taxes act as a disincentive to both workers (causing them to reduce their efforts) and investors (encouraging them to hide their money in nonproductive tax shelters). Supply-siders argue that lower taxes encourage work and discourage leisure. They believe that if taxes are low workers will keep a larger proportion of their wages and owners will keep a larger proportion of their company's profits. Investors (both big and small) are thought to be more likely to invest in speculative ventures if they believe they can retain high after-tax returns. The supply-side view sees high tax rates as clear impediments to investment, work, and economic growth. Some supply-siders also believe that incentives should be targeted to upper-income individuals who are more likely to invest in enterprises that will improve the economy.

A fundamental tenet of supply-side economics is that the propensity to invest and take risks is inversely related to the tax rate (in other words, the lower the tax rate the higher the willingness to take risks). Economist Arthur Laffer helped to popularize the notion that if taxes rise above a given percentage rate, total tax revenue falls. This view attained great popularity in the early 1980s when it was adopted by the Reagan administration, and it is often referred to as Reaganomics or trickle-down economics. Critics of the supply-side view claim that it enriches the wealthy and that very little wealth actually trickles down to the masses.

In theory, supply-side economic development policies promote growth by increasing potential returns on investment. If before-tax profits are the same magnitude, lowering the rate of taxation will increase after-tax returns. Investors should be more willing to put their money into projects if they can keep more of the earnings; the rate of interest (cost of business borrowing) should therefore fall. The supply-side view holds that the government should take a hands-off (laissez-faire) approach to the free enterprise system and should allow investors to choose for themselves where to place their money. The role for government, then, is to allow the marketplace to operate freely. Only from time to time can the government act as a referee in disputes, but it should not actively try to shape investment decisions. The supply-side approach represents a distinct alternative to Keynesian economic prescriptions—which advocate government activism—that dominated economic thought before the 1980s.

Supply-siders contend that businesses should not be held hostage to job creation mandates or mandates to remain in a specific location. Supply-siders believe that inducements (such as lower taxes) should be provided with few strings attached. They argue that governments should keep taxes low in order to attract or retain businesses, and governments should not tie the hands of companies by placing needless restrictions on them or by preventing money from flowing to areas of greatest opportunity. In this way, the supply-side world view is consistent with classical economic thought. The primary mandate of business from the supply-side perspective is to earn profits for stockholders. In the course of earning profits, businesses produce jobs and economic prosperity.

Specific supply-side inducements to business are reviewed in this book. Grants (money given), loans (money lent to new or small firms that do not possess established lines of credit), interest subsidies (loans at below-market rates), equity financing (money given for a stake in future profits), tax incentives, and nonfinancial assistance are examples of supply-side inducements.[17] Tax incentives can include abatements (agreements not to tax for a period of time), exemptions (reductions in the property tax base), credits (direct reductions in tax liabilities), cuts in equipment and inventory taxes,

---

Keynesian economic theory

The Keynesian theory of economics makes a strong case for federal government intervention into economic activity. The Keynesian view focuses on the need to stimulate
demand and avoid lengthy periods of suboptimal economic performance (that is, avoid
economic depressions).

The economist John Maynard Keynes rejected the classical economic notion that
labor markets are self-regulating—that in times of recession, wages fall, more workers
are therefore hired, and unemployment falls. Keynes contended that capitalist
economies might actually drive unemployment higher. To prevent high unemployment,
Keynes advocated proactive government measures.

Keynes suggested that governments could manipulate aggregate levels of public
sector spending (in other words, increase government spending), cut taxes, or lower
interest rates in efforts to reduce unemployment. Effective management of economies,
Keynes believed, could produce stable prices and steady growth. Keynesian economists
(believers in Keynes's theory) contend that the federal government can fine-tune the
economy by stimulating the economy during times of slow growth and dampening the
economy when growth rates are too high, thereby minimizing boom-and-bust cycles.

Keynes is recognized as one of the most important economic thinkers of the twentieth century. Tools advocated by Keynes, known today as fiscal and monetary policy,
have become widely accepted by economists. However, the election of Ronald Reagan
in 1980 and the popularization of supply-side economics somewhat tarnished the view
that government could manage economic growth.

---

lower sales taxes, and reductions in license fees. Nonfinancial assistance can
include customized training for workers, regulatory relief, or customized
research. Jurisdictions can also encourage development on the basis of anticipated increases in property taxes (tax increment financing). Each of these
supply-side strategies is consistent with the general philosophy of fostering
a favorable business climate for investment.

In practice, however, many of the inducements that governments offer to
business are intended to influence business decisions, as will be seen in later
chapters. Chapter 2 describes specific inducements to businesses in greater
detail and shows how policymakers use inducements to promote economic
development in general as well as influence business decisions.

Bottom-up development strategies

In contrast with the top-down, supply-side strategy that targets benefits to
producers (including increasing available investment capital), the demand-
side perspective focuses on stimulating demand from consumers in the
belief that if lower-wage earners earn more they will spend more and stimulate economic growth. Demand-side development does this by increasing
the economic value and purchasing power of individuals.

People who advocate demand-side policies often view the distribution of
income and wealth in the United States as in need of some alteration. Data
show that the gap between top earners and others has increased in recent
years. In 1999, the 20 percent of U.S. households with the highest incomes
earned more than 50 percent of all income earned in the United States. In
1977, this group earned approximately 44 percent of all income. In contrast,
the bottom 40 percent of households earned about 15 percent of all income

earned in 1999 and about 17 percent in 1977.[18] Between 1980 and 2000, income inequality increased in 45 out of the 50 states. New York experienced the greatest increase in income inequality over the 20-year period. Suggested strategies to decrease income inequality include raising the minimum wage, strengthening unemployment insurance, removing barriers to unionization, and reforming regressive state tax systems.[19]

Demand-side strategy may also include helping local businesses find markets, helping entrepreneurs create new businesses, helping existing businesses expand, and nurturing indigenous talent. The bottom-up approach implicitly accepts the view that government's role is to help identify investment opportunities that the private sector may overlook or decline to pursue.[20]

Public-private partnerships   Local governments often partner with the private sector to develop opportunities for citizens to participate in the economy. These partnerships can go beyond project-specific collaborations to include long-term interactive relationships between governmental and private sector parties. Partnerships can help private entrepreneurs identify new opportunities, new products, and new markets. The implementation of a public-private partnership strategy is described in detail in Case study 3–1.

Subsidies   Demand-side development uses subsidies to reduce the price of goods or services to final consumers. Tax expenditures and vouchers are two basic methods of providing demand-side subsidies. Tax expenditures (or specific tax breaks) allow taxpayers to keep and spend more of their income; they have the effect of lowering the after-tax price of specific goods such as housing, education, and child care. For example, tax deductions for interest payments on home mortgages lower the after-tax price of home ownership; lower housing prices, in turn, stimulate demand for houses. Increased demand leads to greater production.

Vouchers allow consumers to purchase market goods they might not otherwise be able to afford. The largest voucher program in the United States is the food stamp program, under which eligible low-income individuals receive vouchers (food stamps) that enable them to buy food from private sector food stores. Voucher advocates have proposed expanding vouchers to the areas of education, day care, and housing. Vouchers remain highly controversial, however. For example, teachers' unions claim that subsidizing private education through vouchers would lead to a mass exodus of the most able students from public schools.

Social capital   Bottom-up development strategies are consistent with the belief that "social capital" contributes to economic prosperity. Building social capital involves linking individuals and organizations into networks that enhance a community's ability to achieve goals by pooling resources, skills, and risks.[21] According to this popular concept, social capital and civic engagement are necessary prerequisites for successful economic development.

Recent discussions of social-capital building and civic engagement have spawned a renewed interest in what is commonly termed civil society and community building. Civil society has been defined as "the space of uncoerced human associations and also the set of relational networks—formed for the sake of family, faith, interest, and ideology—that fill this space."[22] These associations help to create and sustain livable communities. Many feel there is a general yearning in our society for a new kind of community, one that is permeated by a sense of connectedness and life-sustaining linkages, a community with a great deal of social capital. Public policies such as fostering neighborhood watch programs can build social capital; neighbors get a sense of working together for the common good of reducing crime.

The concepts of community and neighborhood are closely related. Neighborhood organizations try to build social capital by identifying the neighborhood as a distinct place that is involved in assisting businesses, developing commercial space, and training local residents.[23] Neighborhoods can adopt a bottom-up approach to development by supporting family-owned businesses and working to prevent corporate disinvestment from the community. Neighborhoods can develop a sense of place that can foster growth.[24] Neighborhood development can also foster positive mind-sets and deter the formation of cultural pathologies.

Human capital   Another popular bottom-up strategy is labor force development. Improved skills usually lead to better wages for workers and to the creation of businesses that add greater value to the local economy. In general, a well-trained labor force is linked to higher levels of productivity and the development of new goods and services. Many growing companies recognize that the presence of a well-trained workforce is the most important factor in their future success, and they are attracted to places where they know they can secure well-trained, educated workers. An absence of such a pool of workers is likely to discourage investment.

More generally, development of human capital enhances productivity and economic growth. Better education leads to innovation and creation of products that will be in high demand in the global marketplace. Creation of high-demand products produces wealth for individuals who hold the patents or intellectual property rights. Specialized skills enhance the wealth and security of workers. Skills and education, therefore, should increase both the collective wealth of society and individual incomes. At the individual level, data clearly indicate a strong association between education and earnings. At the national level, higher education levels are linked to income in advanced industrial nations.[25] At the local level, it is apparent that the surrounding areas of Boston and the San Francisco Bay area have benefited from their proximity to educational institutions such as the Massachusetts Institute of Technology, Harvard University, Stanford University, and the University of California at Berkeley.

Building social capital—Tupelo, Mississippi

Well-known for employing the concepts of social-capital building and civic engagement for achieving economic development is the city of Tupelo, Mississippi. Between 1940 and the 1990s, Tupelo and Lee County went from being one of the poorest communities in Mississippi and the nation to having the second highest per capita income in the state. In the 1990s, Tupelo and Lee County generated an average of more than 1,000 new jobs per year and were home to eighteen Fortune 500 manufacturing companies. Visionary leadership and a long-term process of community building are given credit.

Tupelo engaged its citizens in both identifying and solving community problems. This was accomplished through a variety of top-down and bottom-up approaches to developing awareness. A special focus was given to citizen empowerment. Community- and region-wide coordinating organizations drove the overall process.

Source: Vaughn L. Grisham, *Tupelo: The Evolution of a Community* (Dayton, Ohio: Kettering Foundation Press, 1999), 2.

American education—An economic deficit?

Economists have raised concerns about the quality of the U.S. education system. According to a 1998 study of math and science education in more than 40 countries, the longer American students stayed in school, the worse they did by international comparisons. While American fourth graders recorded above-average scores in math and were second in science, by the eighth grade American students had fallen to below average in math and had dropped to the middle of the group in science. By the twelfth grade, American students' math scores had dropped close to the bottom of the pack.

Source: Darla Carter, "Expert: Middle Schools Need Tough Courses," *Louisville Courier Journal*, 20 February 1999, 1B.

In the future, the role of knowledge may become even more important. Economists have documented the dominant role of knowledge-based industries in job creation and economic growth. In the past the basis of success has been controlling natural resources, but in the future economic success will depend on creating and improving knowledge-based products. The development of new products and the creation of an adaptable workforce have been identified as two viable strategies for maintaining America's standard of living.[26]

Location, export, and innovation models

Together with the market and mixed-market models, a few other models—location, export, and innovation models—have endured over time. They also are able to explain aspects of economic development.

Location model

Consistent with the market model, economists have often looked at location to explain why development occurred in one place instead of another. Studies indicate that, before 1960, costs of transportation; access to natural resources and natural harbors; and the availability (as well as cost) of labor were influential in channeling growth. For example, New York benefited by its deep-water natural harbor; Pittsburgh by its access to raw materials that were needed for producing iron and steel; Louisville, Kentucky, by its location on the Ohio River near rapids that could not be navigated by riverboats.

Transportation costs have traditionally been considered an important factor in explaining why a business locates in one particular area rather than another.[27] If the inputs to production were heavier, bulkier, and more expensive to transport, the best location for the business was the one closest to the sources of its inputs. If, however, the final product was bulkier and more expensive to transport, proximity to the market was paramount.[28] This made business attraction and retention strategies fairly simple—market your community as a source of production inputs or as a market for products, depending upon the nature of the firm being courted.

The need to minimize transportation costs has also been used to explain the location of retail businesses. For example, because retail outlets need to consider customers' transportation costs, they tend to locate near their customer base;[29] recently this has been in the suburbs, away from the inner city.

With changes in the technology of transportation and the globalization of markets, the old considerations of industrial location have faded in importance. A new list of location factors includes six important factors:

- Labor costs
- Labor unionization
- Proximity to markets
- Proximity to supplies and resources
- Proximity to other company facilities
- Quality of life.[30]

Thus, in addition to transportation costs, labor costs and the availability of an adequate supply of labor are now important concerns in business location decisions (see Case study 3–1). Some companies look for areas with an ample supply of potential workers. Some companies avoid areas where there are militant labor unions.[31] In the low-unemployment environment of the 1990s, communities that did not have a critical mass of high-skill workers were at a distinct disadvantage. Knowledge-intensive businesses in fields such as computer software design felt compelled to locate in areas where they were more likely to find high-tech workers or to induce highly skilled workers to live. During the 1990s, highly skilled workers flocked to areas—Silicon Valley in California, the Research Triangle in North Carolina, the Boston area, northern Virginia, and Austin, Texas—with desirable amenities and an existing base of high-tech production.

State and local governments often try to influence firms' location decisions by adjusting the mix of local public services and their costs (taxes).[32] According to the Tiebout model, given a number of assumptions such as equal access to information and willingness to move, individuals will migrate to jurisdictions that offer more efficient "bundles" of taxes and services.

Universal agreement about the importance of taxes does not exist, however. Some analysts claim that taxes play a significant role in location decisions while others feel that the influence of taxes on location decisions is not critical.[33] A number of studies suggest that as the economy becomes more complex, noneconomic factors (such as the technological competence of the labor force and the quality of life in the area) become more important.

With the decline in manufacturing-based industries (where transportation costs are important) and the rise of knowledge-based industries, location models appear to be less relevant today. Transportation costs have diminished in importance, and amenities and the labor force have become more important. Amenities of an area may include good rapid transit or an active airport with links to international cities. Transportation is important in terms of general quality of life of a community and its ability to attract or retain knowledge-based, information-age workers. Communities often try to match their inherent strengths with the needs of businesses they seek to attract to their area. Case study 3–1 shows how public sector organizations can institute changes in order to accommodate business interests. Large firms no longer simply investigate the advantages of various areas; they seek to create advantages through negotiations with public leaders. Large businesses in particular often partner with government to alter the local environment.

Export model

As the location model has declined in importance, one perspective that still holds logical and intuitive appeal is the theory that economic development is linked to the ability of local businesses to produce goods that are wanted by residents of other locations.[34] The export model holds that a region's growth is a function of its interregional and international export performance. Performance is based on increasing the value of existing exports or developing new exports. To enhance economic development, state and local policymakers can support programs that expand the export sector; export-based jobs will then fuel growth in other areas of the local economy.

Export-producing industries are believed to be critical to a region's growth for a variety of reasons.

First, export industries attract income from other regions. This income can then be used to finance imports of goods and services.

Second, export industries tend to be technologically advanced and tend to operate at comparatively high levels of productivity. They need to be supplied and supported by lower-tech industries and service businesses and therefore help spur the development of nonexport industries. Economists refer to the creation of nonbasic jobs that serve the needs of workers in the export sector as the multiplier effect—one export job can multiply into more than one job for the community as workers in support industries (such as real estate, restaurants, and barber shops) are hired.

Third, since export industries are often linked to other regions and industries, they encourage the integration of a region within the national economy. Greater integration with the national and international economies (such as the linkage of new factories in Alabama with the global automobile industry) can produce more opportunities for local businesses and economically benefit citizens of the state. This can lead to further growth and development as money from outside the state finds its way to local citizens.

Fourth, a strong export sector allows a region to shift part of its tax burden to residents of other areas.[35] Costs for local services can be shifted to outsiders by passing taxes (placed on business inventories, business profits, or business property) on to others. For example, states and local jurisdictions may place taxes on multinational corporations doing business in those localities; the multinationals can then pass these taxes on to purchasers of their products throughout the world.

Innovation model

Consistent with the theory that exports are essential for the maintenance of economic prosperity is the theory that innovation and the creation of unique products will lead to economic growth. For example, Great Britain, as an early innovator and pioneer of the Industrial Revolution, significantly increased its wealth in the eighteenth century. In the nineteenth century large economic gains were made by other technologically advanced nations such as the United States, Germany, and Japan. Less-developed countries that have been slow to adapt to the technological revolution remain mired in poverty. Numerous studies have identified relationships between technological innovation and economic development.[36]

Consumer products have life cycles. Technological sophistication, rarity, and demand determine a product's value and price in the free market.[37] Companies that can innovate and secure patents (intellectual property rights) on new products that are in high demand can reap high profits. If only one company can produce a cool computer game, better access to the Internet, or a high-speed jet aircraft, it can charge a high price and possibly generate large profits. Technology, therefore, is inextricably linked to the creation of profits, jobs, and economic growth.

The concept of innovation can be applied to individuals and to communities. Individuals who possess technological skills are in high demand and short supply, and can command high wages in the marketplace. Likewise,

---

Creative destruction

The phenomenon of displacement (out with the old and in with the new) was termed the process of "creative destruction" by economist Joseph Schumpeter. Schumpeter stated that the opening of new markets represented a process of industrial mutation that revolutionized economies from within. According to Schumpeter, the system of capitalism incessantly destroyed old products and old economic processes while it continuously created new ones. Schumpeter maintained that this represented an essential feature of capitalism.

Joseph Schumpeter, *Capitalism, Socialism and Democracy,* 5th ed. (London: Allen & Unwin, 1976), 83.

---

communities that foster innovation and the development of new high-demand products should prosper. Consistent with classical economic thought, the displacement of the obsolete by the novel is not an aberration but an essential component of capitalism and monopoly creation.

In the 1930s, the economist Joseph Schumpeter described various clusters of innovation that sparked cycles of economic development. He contended that industrial cycles begin as entrepreneurs introduce basic innovations into the economy (for example, the introduction of iron smelting in the 1780s, steel-making processes and the steam engine in the 1840s, and the internal combustion engine in the 1890s were innovations that sparked development). Innovations create the environment for large profits as innovators build monopoly positions. Eventually, profits and growth slow because imitators enter the market and compete for market share. Over time the market becomes saturated, profits disappear, and the overall economy turns downward.[38]

Drawing upon the insights of Schumpeter, economist Raymond Vernon applied the concept of technological development to a single product's life cycle in the economies of both developed and developing nations. Vernon hypothesized that products move through three phases of development (new, mature, and standardized). Each phase is associated with different markets and production processes.

In the initial phase, a product is unfamiliar to the general public. As the product matures, demand for it increases and producers adopt mass production techniques in order to exploit economies of scale. As the product becomes cheaper and more standardized, demand for it grows in external (foreign) as well as domestic markets. In response to external demand, producers begin to move some production facilities to foreign locations, reducing costs and preventing foreign entrepreneurs from setting up their own production facilities. As the product moves to the final stage of complete standardization, production is concentrated in the foreign markets because those markets have a cost advantage over home production. The production cycle is complete when production in foreign countries forces the closure of domestic production facilities.[39]

Many new products—stealth bombers, video games, and computer software are recent examples—that make use of state-of-the-art technology cannot be duplicated easily and therefore command high prices in the open marketplace. However, more mature products such as steel, automobiles, and tires rely on processes that can be transferred more easily to other locations. According to the product-life-cycle theory, these products will command lower prices in the marketplace. Labor-intensive products such as

---

Technology and prosperity

Even the most casual reading of history indicates that technological development is linked to security and prosperity. The classical economist David Ricardo noted that Britain prospered because technological breakthroughs facilitated the mass production of goods and a concomitant generation of large profits. History also suggests that economic advancement is not a permanent condition but varies over time. At given periods of time, China, Egypt, Persia, Greece, Babylon, and Rome all enjoyed great wealth and power. Gunpowder and paper were both invented in China during a period when Europe was considered to be in the dark ages and there was little evidence of development in the Americas. While China declined, Russia and Japan enhanced their wealth after they adopted modern technologies from the West.

In the United States, businesses recognize the aphorism that education is expensive but ignorance is even more costly. Firms in the emerging information-based industries know that they must be at the forefront of innovation or they will die. Boston's Golden Horseshoe and California's Silicon Valley show that a critical mass of knowledge workers can foster tremendous advancement. It is probably not a coincidence that areas of the United States (such as Appalachia) with relatively low levels of educational attainment remain poor while areas of the country (such as around Boston and San Francisco) possessing higher-quality elementary, secondary, and post-secondary educational institutions prosper.

---

clothing, footwear, toys, and basic electronic assembly (products not reliant on sophisticated technologies or high levels of skill) can be produced in the undeveloped regions of the globe where labor costs are minuscule compared with labor costs in advanced industrial nations.

In the global marketplace of today, workers with high-tech skills can command relatively high wages even if they live in poorer regions of the world. In an example of the linkage between higher wages and global technological expertise, some workers in India can now earn relatively high wages (by their national income standards) by working for computer companies in more developed countries. Technologically sophisticated citizens of the world can now send the output of their work to their home companies almost instantly through the Internet. On the other hand, those without skills (wherever they live) may suffer declines in their wages, especially if the goods or services they produce can be produced less expensively in other regions of the world.

State and local governments as well as nations subscribe to the export and innovation models of economic development. As the twenty-first century begins, nearly every urban region in the Western world has a technology park, a high-tech economic development plan, or a program of some type to lure high-tech enterprises. Universities often become partners in attempts to incubate firms with specialized technologies. Many cities have prospered as a result of attracting high-tech development. Cities or groups of cities that have been relatively successful in attracting high-tech industry include San Jose, Emeryville-Oakland, and San Diego in California; Cambridge, Massachusetts; Ogden, Utah; Austin, Texas (discussed in Chapter 5); and Chapel Hill-Durham-Raleigh (the Research Triangle), North Carolina.[40]

At the federal level, in 1999 a presidential advisory committee called for a doubling of federal financing for information technology research. The committee noted that businesses that produce computers, semiconductors, software, and communications equipment accounted for significant increases in total job growth during the 1990s. Keeping pace with technological advances in other advanced industrial nations was perceived to be critical for assuring future job growth.[41] The idea that innovative products lead to a stronger economy is consistent with the market view of development.

Summary

This chapter has presented various perspectives on economic development. Neoclassical thinkers have advocated market approaches to development: lower taxes, less regulation, and the creation of environments where profits can be maximized. In short, they endorse an economic development strategy that follows the laws of supply and demand. If demand exists, producers will arise to supply the desired goods and services. Competition will ensure efficiency in production, quality, and customer satisfaction.

Other analysts note that because of market failure and other reasons, the idea of a small, unobtrusive public sector is an anachronism. Government is a major part of the modern economy and will remain so. The salient questions relate to the nature of government's role and who will benefit from that role. Government programs run the gamut from assisting large corporations to helping small businesses, aiding displaced workers, subsidizing farmers, paying for medical care, and supporting the impoverished. Which people and programs should receive assistance is the focus of heated debate. Policymakers strive to see their visions implemented. Lobbyists tirelessly pursue politicians in efforts to acquire benefits for their clients. Leaders often must pursue innovative development solutions such as those that encourage collaboration between the private and the public sectors.

Study questions

- How did the Founders influence economic development in the United States?

- What was Adam Smith's greatest contribution to our understanding of wealth creation?

- What appears to be Michael Porter's contribution in the debate over identifying viable options to revitalize declining areas?

- Why does government intervention in the economy appear to be necessary?

- How do collective goods differ from private goods?

- What goods do you think should be considered worthy goods? Which goods should not qualify? Why?

- Describe the basic logic of supply-side economics. Do you agree with its fundamental propositions? Do you think this strategy works? Why or why not?

- How might bottom-up development strategies enhance economic development? Do you think these strategies lead to economic growth? Why or why not?

- What is the life cycle of a product? Could the theory of a product life cycle be applied to explain both individual and national economic development? How?

- Describe export theory. How is export theory related to Schumpeter's conception of creative destruction and Vernon's product life cycle? How might a community plan an economic development strategy that is based on export theory, Schumpeter's view of creative destruction, and Vernon's product life cycle?

1 Steven G. Koven, *Public Budgeting in the United States: The Cultural and Ideological Setting* (Washington, D.C.: Georgetown University Press, 1999), 32.

2 Jerry Z. Muller, *Adam Smith in His Time and Ours: Designing the Decent Society* (New York: Free Press, 1993).

3 Michael E. Porter, *Competitive Advantage: Creating and Sustaining Superior Performance* (New York: Free Press, 1985); Porter, *The Competitive Advantage of Nations* (New York: Free Press, 1990); Porter, "The Competitive Advantage of the Inner City," *Harvard Business Review* (May-June 1995): 56–71.

4 Porter, "The Competitive Advantage of the Inner City."

5 David L. Weimer and Aidan R. Vining, *Policy Analysis: Concepts and Practices*, 3d ed. (Upper Saddle River, N.J.: Prentice Hall, 1999), 74.

6 E. S. Savas, *Privatization and Public-Private Partnerships* (New York: Chatham House, 2000), 53.

7 Ibid., 46.

8 Ibid., 53.

9 Joseph E. Stiglitz, *Economics of the Public Sector,* 2d ed. (New York: W.W. Norton, 1988), 220–234.

10 Steven Pearlstein, "On California Stage, A Cautionary Tale; Prices, Blackouts Spotlight Deregulation's Risks," *Washington Post,* 21 August 2001, A1.

11 Stiglitz, *Economics of the Public Sector,* 73.

12 Karen O'Connor and Larry J. Sabato, *American Government: Continuity and Change* (Boston: Allyn and Bacon, 1999), 716.

13 Savas, *Privatization and Public-Private Partnerships*, 58.

14 Ibid., 20.

15 Ibid., 21–22.

16 Christina Couret, "Solving the Problem of Cell Tower Placement," *American City and County* (September 1999): 45–54.

17 Deborah Matz and Larry Ledebur, "The State Role in Economic Development," in

Financing Economic Development in the 1980s: Issues and Trends, 2d ed., eds. Norman Walzer and David L. Chicoine (New York: Praeger, 1986), 85–102; Weimer and Vining, *Policy Analysis.*

18 Kevin Phillips, *Wealth and Democracy* (New York: Broadway Books, 2002), 129.

19 Economic Policy Institute and Center on Budget and Policy Priorities, "Despite Past Boom Times Income Gaps Have Widened in 45 States Over the Past Twenty Years," April 23, 2002, www.cbpp.org/4-23-02sfp.htm.

20 Peter Eisinger, *The Rise of the Entrepreneurial State: State and Local Economic Development Policy in the United States* (Madison: University of Wisconsin Press, 1988), 12.

21 James S. Coleman, "Social Capital in the Creation of Human Capital," *American Journal of Sociology* (1988 Supplement): S95–S119; Alejandro Portes and Julia Sensenbrenner, "Embeddedness and Immigration: Notes on the Social Determinants of Economic Action," *American Journal of Sociology* 98 (1993): 1320–1350; Jan L. Flora, "Social Capital and Communities of Place," *Rural Sociology* 63 (1998): 481–506; Robert D. Putnam, *Bowling Alone: The Collapse and Revival of American Community* (New York: Simon & Schuster, 2000); Francis Fukuyama, *Trust: The Social Virtues and the Creation of Prosperity* (New York: Free Press, 1995).

22 Michael Walzer, "The Idea of Civil Society," *Kettering Review* (Winter 1997): 8–22.

23 Wim Wiewel, Michael Tietz, and Robert Giloth, "The Economic Development of Neighborhoods and Localities," in *Theories of Local Economic Development: Perspectives from across the Disciplines,* 2d ed., eds. Richard D. Bingham and Robert Mier (Newbury Park, Calif.: Sage Publications, 1993), 81.

24 Roger Bolton, "'Place Prosperity' vs. 'People Prosperity' Revisited: An Old Issue with a New Angle," *Urban Studies* (1992): 192–193.

25 Derek H. Aldcroft, *Education, Training, and Economic Performance* (New York: St. Martin's Press, 1992).

26 Robert B. Reich, *The Work of Nations: Preparing Ourselves for 21st Century Capitalism* (New York: A. A. Knopf, 1991).

27 Jacques-François Thisse, "Location Theory, Regional Science and Economics," *Journal of Regional Science* 27 (1987): 519–528.

28 David M. Smith, *Industrial Location: An Economic Geographical Analysis,* 2d ed. (New York: Wiley, 1981); and Michael J. Webber, *Industrial Location* (Beverly Hills, Calif.: Sage, 1984).

29 Brian J. L. Berry, *Geography of Market Centers and Retail Distribution* (Englewood Cliffs, N.J.: Prentice Hall, 1967).

30 Roger W. Schmenner, *Making Business Location Decisions* (Englewood Cliffs, N.J.: Prentice-Hall, 1982), 37–38.

31 Ibid.

32 Charles M. Tiebout, "A Pure Theory of Local Expenditures," *Journal of Political Economy* 64 (1956): 416–424; Steven Koven and Mack Shelley, "Public Policy Effects on Net Urban Migration," *Policy Studies Journal* 17 (1989): 705–718; Mack Shelley and Steven Koven, "Interstate Migration: A Test of Competing Interpretations," *Policy Studies Journal* 21 (1993): 243–261.

33 John P. Blair and Robert Premus, "Location Theory," in *Theories of Local Economic Development,* 3–26; Barry Rubin and C. Kurt Zorn, "Sensible State and Local Economic Development," *Public Administration Review* 45 (1985): 333–339.

34 John Rees, "Theories of Regional Growth and Industrial Location: The Relevance for Understanding High-Technology Complexes," in *Technology, Regions and Policy,* 2d ed., ed. John Rees (Totowa, N.J.: Rowman & Littlefield, 1986), 23–50; Bernard L. Weinstein, Harold T. Gross, and John Rees, *Regional Growth and Decline in the United States,* 2d ed. (New York: Praeger, 1985).

35 Weinstein et al., *Regional Growth and Decline in the United States,* 47.

36 Edward J. Malecki, *Technology and Economic Development: The Dynamics of Local, Regional and National Competitiveness,* 2d ed. (Edinburgh Gate, U.K.: Addison, Wesley Longman Limited, 1997); Robert B. Reich, *The Work of Nations* (New York: Vintage Books, 1992).

37 Raymond Vernon, "International Investment and International Trade in the Product Cycle," *Quarterly Journal of Economics* (May 1966): 190–207.

38 Joseph A. Schumpeter, *Business Cycles: A Theoretical, Historical, and Statistical Analysis of the Capitalist Process* (New York: McGraw-Hill, 1939).

39 Vernon, "International Investment and International Trade in the Product Cycle," 195–203.

40 Edward J. Blakely, *Planning Local Economic Development: Theory and Practice*, 2d ed. (Newbury Park, Calif.: Sage Publications, 1994).

41 Steve Lohr, "Panel to Urge Big U.S. Effort in Technology," *New York Times*, 24 February 1999, C1.

2 Tools of economic development

Learning objectives

You should be able to:

- Name four main financial incentives and describe how each is used to attract or retain businesses

- Name three tax policies that governments commonly use to influence business location decisions

- Identify four nonfinancial incentives and describe the role each plays in enhancing economic growth

- Assess which incentives are appropriate for specific development strategies

Tools of economic development

P ublic sector officials need to be informed about various economic development concepts in order to understand the role they can play in shaping growth or halting decline. On a pragmatic level, however, state and local officials need to understand theoretical frameworks for viewing development and also need to possess a working knowledge of the tools of development. This chapter describes tools available to policymakers: What tools are available? How are the tools used? What is their impact? Officials with knowledge of these techniques will be better prepared to address the economic challenges in their own jurisdictions.

Severe economic downturns, a decline in manufacturing jobs, and federal efforts to decentralize governance have forced local leaders to make aggressive efforts to stabilize and enlarge local tax bases. Local initiatives to enhance growth include a variety of fiscal, tax, and nonfinancial tools that have been applied to attract, retain, and create jobs.

Chapter 1 explained that the pure market model of development exists more as a theoretical construct than as a description of reality. The public sector plays a large role in stabilizing the economy and assuring economic growth. Through fiscal and monetary policy, the federal government attempts to create an environment of low inflation, low unemployment, and steady growth in gross national product. The federal government intervenes on the macroeconomic level in the sense that it tries to establish broad goals (in terms of inflation, unemployment, and growth rates) for the economy.

Within these broad parameters, state and local governments compete with each other to retain companies, attract firms, and create new jobs. In this post-laissez-faire world, public-private collaborations are an essential feature of the landscape. The desirability of economic development is accepted by local politicians who want the goodwill of constituents as well as local business leaders. Both business and labor leaders view government intervention as vital to fostering their agendas of greater profit or high-paying jobs.[1]

In pursuit of stability and economic growth, state and local officials try to provide inducements to businesses that threaten to relocate to other jurisdictions, that promise to expand existing employment, or that agree to build new facilities. Inducements include three broad categories of tools: financial incentives, tax policies and nonfinancial assistance.[2]

Financial incentives

States and localities typically offer various types of financial incentives. Common incentives that are presented to businesses to attract or retain jobs include grants, loans, tax-exempt bonds, and equity and near-equity financing.[3] These are useful aids to encourage economic development at all levels of government. Each of these tools possesses various advantages and disadvantages.

Grants

Grants are a highly desirable type of assistance because businesses are under no obligation to repay the grants. Grants are by no means a novel invention and have been used in the United States to a greater extent than champions of laissez-faire philosophies are willing to admit. Land grants to railroads and homesteading helped open up land in America's West. The Morrill Act of 1862 established and subsidized land-grant schools that offered instruction in the agricultural and mechanical arts. All these initiatives facilitated economic development. The Great Depression of the 1930s set the stage for the acceptance of other public sector responsibilities in addition to education and infrastructure.

In the past half century, federal, state, and local governments have implemented programs that deal with job security, agriculture, public works, health services, income support for families, business loans, and a multitude of other activities. Contemporary examples of federal grant programs include urban renewal, support for small businesses, programs in the U.S. Economic Development Administration, community development block grants, and urban development action grants.[4]

The Economic Development Administration (EDA, part of the U.S. Department of Commerce) was set up to promote development in distressed areas. Established under the Public Works and Economic Act of 1965, the EDA provides federal resources for public works construction, economic development planning at the local level, and capital subsidies for industry. Congress hoped that these activities would lead to private investment in areas of high unemployment.

Initially the EDA program was targeted to depressed rural communities, but after the mid-1970s, programs were directed to urban areas as well. Public works grants, business loans, technical assistance grants, and grants to assist communities affected by economic dislocations are the four main programs administered by EDA. Communities adept at marketing their needs were more likely than others to gain access to these programs. EDA operates two programs of assistance to localities: a basic loan program (Title II) and the Special Economic Development and Adjustment Assistance program (Title IX). The Title IX program aids workers affected by economic dislocation such as plant closings and steady, long-term capital disinvestments.[5]

States also provide grants for rural development, building construction, equipment, land, and public infrastructure. Growth in state economic development grants coincides with reduced levels of grant support from the federal government. States target grants to activities expected to bring direct economic payoffs, and they try to put together attractive packages of benefits—these can include loans at below-market rates and loans to higher-risk businesses—to attract investment.

Loans

Loans are a popular financial-incentive tool available to public officials. EDA's Title II Business Development Loan program provides loans and loan guarantees to both for-profit and nonprofit organizations in an effort to spur commercial and industrial expansion. State and local authorities also supply loans to enterprises that promise to enhance the economic development of an area.

Public loans permit firms that have difficulty borrowing from the private sector to obtain funding at market or below-market rates. Such loans are especially beneficial to new or small firms that do not possess established

---

State loan funds

States have devised various methods for establishing loan funds. For example, Ohio repays tax-exempt bonds with a fixed amount of state profits from state-owned liquor stores. Pennsylvania and Kentucky both use legislative appropriations and bond issues for their loan funds. California employed a one-time legislative appropriation to establish a revolving loan fund.

Most states target loans to firms that meet certain specifications. Kentucky targets loans to small firms with high-growth potential in the areas of tourism, agriculture, or manufacturing. New Jersey and Pennsylvania give priority to firms that promise to locate in communities or rural areas with high unemployment and low income. Pennsylvania targets a proportion of its loans to firms that deal with advanced technology. Ohio gives priority to businesses already operating in the state. Both Hawaii and Alaska offer loans to owners of fishing vessels who are unable to secure conventional financing.

Source: Peter Eisinger, *The Rise of the Entrepreneurial State: State and Local Economic Development Policy in the United States* (Madison: University of Wisconsin Press, 1988), 154–156.

---

lines of credit. Firms engaged in promising but highly speculative ventures can borrow from public programs. Rewards to individual companies (through future profits) as well as to communities (through the creation of jobs) may be significant.

Public loan programs also carry the risk of default and financial loss to taxpayers, however. By definition, loans to businesses that cannot secure loans from the private sector carry high risk. Companies with good credit ratings and adequate collateral do not need to borrow from public entities and can instead go to the local bank. Community leaders, however, may judge that the potential reward in terms of economic growth outweighs the risk of making questionable loans. Elected officials are sometimes more worried about reelection and being perceived as "not doing much" than they are about the credit quality of loans, especially when an election is imminent and defaults are farther in the future.

Usually the state or local departments of economic development or separate industrial development authorities make direct loans. Revolving loan funds recycle repayments of outstanding loans to make loans to other businesses. In theory, once they are established, revolving loan funds provide a self-renewing pool of funds. As long as default rates and administrative costs are relatively low, revolving loan funds can be a self-financing tool for development.

Public sector revolving loan funds face the same questions as any loan fund: Who is eligible for loans? How large should loans be? Eligibility criteria can be broad or narrow. Broad standards allow almost any business to apply for a loan, but narrow criteria permit only certain kinds of businesses or companies in selected neighborhoods to qualify. Commercial or industrial businesses that show particular promise may be given preference. Minority applicants for loans, applicants located in high-poverty areas, or applicants with other specified characteristics may be given special consideration when projects are assessed.[6]

State and local governments can charge interest rates that are linked to rates on state industrial development bonds, to the federal discount rate, or

---

Tax-exempt bonds

What does it mean to purchasers of bonds when the federal government subsidizes the cost of state and local borrowing?

An investor deciding what kind of bond to purchase will of course consider the amount of profit on the bond purchase.

If corporate bonds are paying interest at 10 percent, it means that a $1,000 corporate bond will pay $100 in interest. However, the federal government will tax this interest income. For example—this is a simplified scenario—if the purchaser is in the 36 percent tax bracket, $36 of that $100 will be paid to the government in taxes. That leaves $64—a 6.4 percent yield on $1,000—for the purchaser of the bond.

But the federal government does not tax the interest on many local government bonds. Thus, jurisdictions can offer a lower interest rate on these bonds because purchasers will keep all interest paid. In our example, local governments need to offer only 6.4 percent interest to compete with 10 percent interest on corporate (taxable) bonds to attract customers in the 36 percent tax bracket. If the potential investor is in a lower tax bracket, the savings offered by tax-exempt bonds will be less.

Many people criticize tax-exempt bonds:

- The tax exemption on local bonds can create a bias that leads communities to spend more for capital construction and less for operating expenses.

- Tax-exempt bonds provide the greatest advantage to those in the highest tax bracket who are trying to shelter their income, thereby undermining the equity of the federal income tax.

- Because of competition among communities, benefits can accrue to industries that pressure communities to make infrastructure improvements. Costs for the improvements to help the private sector are borne by the federal government, which loses money in the form of lower income tax revenues. Those who depend on federal spending may suffer from the loss of federal revenue.

- Revenue lost by the federal government from the tax exemption exceeds the benefits received by communities in terms of lower borrowing costs. Some of the benefits go to wealthy individuals who purchase state and local bonds.

- Tax-exemptions can divert resources from their best use to the use that gains the biggest subsidy. This is economically inefficient and can produce lower levels of growth.

- State and local governments can abuse their tax-exempt privileges by transferring funds from federal government coffers to private companies (through inappropriate use of tax-exempt bonds) or to state and local treasuries (through arbitrage). These abuses were curtailed in 1986 with passage of the Tax Reform Act.

---

to Treasury bill rates. All these rates are below market, lower even than the rates for companies with very good credit. Other loan inducements include extended amortization schedules (borrowers can extend the repayment time period) and balloon payments (minimal repayment of principal is required until a specified time when the entire principal becomes due).[7] The sale of industrial development bonds is typically used to allow private businesses to borrow at below-market rates. How these bonds and other tax-exempts

For almost 200 years, questions have been raised about the constitutional authority of the federal government to impose a tax on income of state and local governments. Beginning with the case of *McCulloch v. Maryland* (1819), the Supreme Court held that both the states and the federal government were immune from tax interference by the other. The Sixteenth Amendment to the U.S. Constitution altered this interpretation when it established the right of the national government to collect taxes on income "from whatever source derived."

Even after the passage of the Sixteenth Amendment, however, Congress did not impose taxes on interest from state and local bonds. The ability of Congress to impose such a tax remained a question mark until 1988, when the Supreme Court clarified the issue by ruling in *South Carolina v. Baker* that state and local governments had no constitutional right to borrow at tax-exempt rates. This ruling was in line with others that firmly established the supremacy of the national body.

In response to the Supreme Court ruling, political support for the exemption mobilized. State and local officials organized to protect the tax-exempt status of their bonds. In 1988 the Public Finance Network (PFN), a broadly based coalition of groups, was created to protect state and local borrowing from federal taxation and unnecessary regulation.

The combination of lobbying by state and local officials and curbing the most egregious abuses of tax exemptions (through implementation of the Tax Reform Act of 1986) removed pressure to eliminate the tax-free exemption. State and local officials are committed to the exemption and have resisted efforts to change the exemption to a direct subsidy or outlay by the federal government. Investment banking houses that specialize in tax-exempt bonds have also lobbied to preserve the exemption.

Before 1986, public borrowing was used to finance questionable activities such as liquor stores, luxury sky boxes at stadiums, and discount-store expansion. After 1986 this type of financing was disavowed. Localities were forced to return to their traditional pattern of borrowing for basic infrastructure development, not for projects such as most sports stadiums and parking facilities.

Some local officials and investment bankers have been able to avoid restrictions, however. Local officials have circumvented Tax Reform Act restrictions on funding convention centers by issuing "governmental" bonds that can be used to fund convention centers if the centers are largely involved in activities that benefit the public. Nevertheless, the Tax Reform Act largely accomplished the goals of Congress and limited the use of tax-exempt bonds. After passage of the act in 1986, the use of industrial development bonds declined sharply.

Sources: Ronald Fisher, *State and Local Public Finance* (Glenview, Ill.: Scott Foresman and Company, 1988); Alberta M. Sbragia, *Debt Wish: Entrepreneurial Cities, U.S. Federalism, and Economic Development* (Pittsburgh: University of Pittsburgh Press, 1996).

have been used to stimulate state and local economic development is discussed beginning on page 32.

Leveraging, or using public sector resources to get the private sector to commit resources to development activity, has become increasingly useful and popular. Leveraging reduces the potential costs to the public sector and engages the private sector in evaluating business risks. Leveraging can include direct loans as well as other activities to encourage development.

- **Loan guarantees**   Loan guarantees are one type of leveraging that can promote development by reducing the risk private banks take when they make loans: a governmental unit assures payment of a large portion of a private bank loan in case the borrower company defaults. Loans that the private sector normally would not make (because of risk of default) suddenly become feasible when repayment is guaranteed by the government. Typically, guarantees stipulate that in the event of default, the public entity must repay 90 percent of the loan. Potential public sector costs (for administration and loan guarantees) are lowered when private firms are responsible for payment of at least a small portion of these loans.[8] Banks are more cautious about making loans when all costs are not guaranteed.

- **Loan pooling**   Loan pooling represents another economic development technique that can involve leveraging. Two or more lenders contribute to a fund from which loans are made. A publicly chartered, privately funded corporation can be established to pool the resources of various lenders such as banks or nonprofit philanthropic organizations. For example, several banks may agree to provide a line of credit to a development credit corporation. The development corporation may also sell stock to investors who are looking for dividends and an increase in the value of the stock.

Tax-exempt bonds

The federal government allows state and local jurisdictions to issue bonds that pay interest. Traditionally, this interest has not been taxed by the federal government. In effect, therefore, the federal government has subsidized the cost of state and local borrowing. State and local governments have clearly benefited financially from the tax-exempt status of their bonds.

This tax-exempt status has led to some problems, however. In the 1980s, this benefit came under scrutiny as it became evident that jurisdictions were misusing their tax-exempt privilege and issuing tax-exempt bonds for certain purposes—such as financing industrial parks and sports facilities—that were not originally intended. In essence, these arrangements resulted in the federal government subsidizing private ventures through state and city bonds. In addition, state and local governments were able to reinvest their borrowed funds—borrowed at lower rates due to their bonds' tax-exempt status—in private securities that paid a higher rate. This practice, known as arbitrage, funneled more and more money to state and local governments but shielded the money from federal taxation.

Abuses and complaints about the misuse of tax-exempt bonds were addressed in the Tax Reform Act of 1986, which restricted the use of state and local bonds and arbitrage practices. The new law required state and local jurisdictions to send arbitrage profits to the federal government. Bonds used for construction of facilities or infrastructure to provide "essential" services were still tax-exempt under the Tax Reform Act, and bonds for the construction of airports, docks and wharves, hazardous waste treatment plants, and water supply facilities also retained tax-exempt status; however, earned interest from these bonds was included in calculating a federal minimum tax. The tax-exempt status of bonds for the construction of industrial parks, parking garages, sports facilities, and convention facilities was eliminated, which significantly reduced the appeal of these types of bonds.[9] Without tax-exempt status, borrowing of this type has to compete with corporate borrowing and has to pay higher interest rates. Cities and states still pay lower interest rates for basic infrastructure financing, the traditional focus of tax-exempt bonds, however.

Equity and near-equity financing

Equity financing gives government entities part ownership of an enterprise in return for their financial support. Recovery of funds and profits depends on the success of the enterprise. Equity financing is used to foster particular types of industry or commerce, usually businesses with a good potential to create jobs. Equity financing is not a typical tool of the public sector; reluctance to accept too great an expansion of public sector ownership may constrain its use.

- **Stock**   Governments can acquire equity in three ways: the purchase of common stock, the purchase of preferred stock, and the purchase of convertible debt. Owners of both common and preferred stock receive dividends, in other words, a percentage of the firm's earnings. Owners of common stock can vote to accept or reject recommendations made by a company's board of directors; owners of preferred stock have no vote. Owners of preferred stock will be paid before owners of common stock if the company declares bankruptcy and company assets are liquidated. Convertible debt permits the conversion of a debt to common stock. Following conversion to common stock, owners of the stock enjoy all the benefits of any other owner of common stock.

- **Royalty agreements**   Royalty agreements provide that in return for an investment, investors will receive a proportion of future sales revenue. Royalties are usually paid up to some predetermined amount, at which time the pay-back obligation is satisfied.

- **Warrants**   Warrants are contracts giving the investor the option to purchase a certain number of shares of a company's stock at a given price. Individual state statutes determine the legal use of warrants, such as whether warrants can be sold to a third party. Under the provisions of a warrant, the option to purchase stock is available only for a stated period of time. The option price of a warrant is typically higher than the market price of shares at the time the warrant is issued, and the option or exercise period is typically a substantial number of years. If stock prices rise above the warrant price during that time period, the holder of the warrant may exercise the option and purchase stock shares at the lower option price. If stock prices never exceed the option price, the option has no monetary value because investors would place no value on the right to purchase something at a cost higher than its market price. Because warrants do not carry voting rights in the company, warrants can be an attractive alternative for a government that wishes to support a local company but does not want to possess a direct ownership stake in the firm.[10]

Governments purchase equity stakes to provide funding in return for future payments if the company earns profits. In the appropriate situation, injecting equity capital into a company can be an effective mechanism for inducing development. For companies, equity stakes are less onerous than debt because debt must be repaid from operating funds, forcing some marginal companies into bankruptcy.[11]

Some equity schemes are controversial. Government ownership of enterprises remains anathema to free-market economists who blame stagnant economies on the intrusive and/or expansive nature of the public sector. In such a political environment, many public sector leaders are reluctant to advocate policies that interfere with the free marketplace, preferring to rely on accepted Keynesian tools of development such as tax incentives and government spending.

Tax policies

Tax policy and business location

Tax issues often fall within the broader category of general business climate. All other things being equal, high taxes are associated with a negative business environment while low taxes are associated with a more positive environment. Some theories of business location assign an important role to taxes because businesses prefer to locate in areas where they can maximize after-tax earnings.[12] Others contend that, at most, taxes are one of many factors businesses consider when they contemplate expansion or relocation.[13] Professional studies indicate that taxes can act as a tiebreaker in business location decisions when other factors are more or less equal.[14]

Nearly every state offers some type of tax incentive to attract and retain business. These incentives are often targeted to certain types of firms or to certain areas. In general, corporations have been relatively successful in limiting their tax obligations. Since World War II, as a result of the supply-side strategy of creating conditions favorable to business, the proportion of total U.S. taxes paid by corporations has fallen compared with the proportion paid by individuals through sales, payroll, and personal income taxes.

Differences in state and local taxes affect industry location in two ways. First, all other things being equal, higher taxes will reduce after-tax profits. Lower taxes result in higher profits if the lower business cost (taxes) is not passed on to consumers in the form of lower prices, shifted to workers in the form of higher pay, or transferred to landlords in the form of higher rents. Taxes are more relevant to the location choices of capital-intensive manufacturing and wholesale businesses; they are less important for labor-intensive businesses. Second, relatively high taxes in a specific jurisdiction can hurt a firm's ability to attract workers. As rational economic actors, many workers choose to work in areas where their personal after-tax earnings are greater.

Widely held perceptions of the impact of taxes on local development are summarized in the box on page 35. When a firm is beginning its location decision process, taxes have little bearing; taxes become more important as location choices are narrowed. In the long run, local taxes that are too high compared with other similar areas can lead to relocations, declines in property values, and a downward economic spiral.[15]

A number of studies in the early 1980s linked taxes to overall economic conditions and found that high taxes tended to adversely affect employment and reduced the likelihood of attracting capital-intensive businesses. The impact of high taxes was not always immediate, but over the long term it hurt community economies.[16]

Many development planners are not convinced that lowering taxes will lead to economic prosperity. However, state and local governments are inclined to provide tax incentives for two reasons. First, governments fear that if they don't offer tax incentives, neighboring jurisdictions will capture the economic growth. Second, governments want to project a friendly image to businesses. Local governments tend to adopt tax policies that resemble those of other jurisdictions in the region. To the business community, a jurisdiction's decision to lower taxes is more important for the message it sends than for the difference it makes in the cost of production. There is general consensus that taxes and other financial inducements are not by themselves determinants of business location, but they can influence companies that are indifferent to other location factors.

Common tax incentives

Commonly used tax incentives include abatements, exemptions, and tax increment financing.

Perceptions of tax impact on local development

- During a company's initial search for possible business sites, taxes have virtually no bearing on location decisions. After a firm has narrowed its location choices or is equally disposed toward two or more sites, a local government's tax burden becomes more important.
- Nontax factors such as labor supplies, labor costs, energy costs, transportation networks, space availability, and the skills and education level of the workforce are more central than tax-related factors to location decisions of a firm.
- The effect of local taxes on business investment decisions varies by business. Manufacturing and wholesale businesses are more sensitive to property tax rates. Firms in other industries are more sensitive to other types of taxes.
- Very high local tax burdens may promote migration of skilled labor from high-tax areas to low-tax areas. Manufacturers, followed by retail and service industries, may then follow in an effort to be close to their labor supply. On the other hand, highly skilled labor may choose to cluster in specific areas because of desired amenities and better opportunities for professional advancement. Aspiring actors and actresses may gravitate to Hollywood and Los Angeles while stock analysts and investment bankers flock to Wall Street and New York City. Many ambitious individuals choose the chance to attain high levels of pay; their desire for success far outweighs the bite that the local government may take out of their earnings.
- In the long term, all other things being equal, above-average property tax burdens can lead to declines in property values as businesses and households favor relocating to lower-tax areas. If businesses and households start relocating to other areas, governments are then pressured to levy even higher taxes, which precipitates further declines in the local tax base and a possible downward spiral.

Source: Robert Bland, *A Revenue Guide for Local Government* (Washington, D.C.: ICMA, 1989).

Tax abatements   Tax abatements are legal agreements between a government entity and a property owner or real estate developer to forgo taxing some share of assessed real estate value for a certain period of time. It is expected that by the time the abatement expires, property values will have increased. When rates are reapplied, they will bring in increased tax money, linked to an appreciation in property values. In the long run, tax revenues should grow and the overall tax base should be strengthened.

Tax abatements are the most popular type of tax incentive and the least costly to administer. Under tax abatement plans, taxes are frozen at a specified (usually predevelopment) rate for a stated number of years (usually 10 to 15 years). Following this period, the property is reassessed and taxed at the jurisdiction's regular tax rate. In theory, tax abatements attract developers and, in return for the tax abatement, developers often agree to make physical improvements to an area. Tax abatement agreements between developers and public sector officials can specify the amount of tax exemption as well as the method of calculating the exemption. The agreement can also list promised improvements, specify types of activities permitted on the property, and allow for inspection by city personnel.[17]

In some states, residential property may qualify for tax abatements. In recent years most states have relaxed enterprise zone regulations to permit a broad range of uses and locations for abatement programs.[18] For example, in

1987 the Texas legislature amended the state's tax abatement law to include areas that would contribute to the retention or expansion of primary employment or attract major investment.

Tax abatement policies vary from state to state with respect to the time period, type of property eligible, and the amount of the abatement. Missouri allows firms a maximum abatement period of 25 years. Time periods in most other states vary from 10 to 15 years. Ohio has extended abatements to new buildings or improvements to existing buildings but has not extended abatements to the assessed value of land or personal property. In contrast, the state of Florida has extended abatements to improvements in real property and to all tangible personal property.

Many local governments use tax abatements to attract or retain economic development. Toledo, Ohio, for example, granted generous abatements to building-products maker Owens Corning and automobile manufacturer DaimlerChrysler. In 2001, city officials in Toledo granted DaimlerChrysler a 10-year tax abatement, estimated to save the company $8 million for that year. DaimlerChrysler was able to waive a prior agreement to pay 45 percent of Toledo's school taxes. In the new agreement, the Toledo school district received a one-time payment of $1.4 million, an amount roughly equal to the taxes that would have been paid over the 10 years by homes and businesses demolished for construction of DaimlerChrysler's new Jeep plant.[19]

Other localities that have used tax abatements for economic development include New York City; Jersey City, New Jersey; and Richardson, Texas. In New York City, developers were granted tax abatements on residential buildings in parts of Manhattan in return for contributions to low-income housing. In Jersey City, more than 30 buildings for which taxes were abated were constructed or were under construction in the period between 1980 and 2000. In the Dallas/Fort Worth metropolitan area, Richardson, Texas, credits much of its remarkable growth to offers of 10-year, 50 percent tax abatements. Richardson, with an area of 17 square miles, by 2001 was home to 700 technology companies, half of which were in telecommunications. Between 1990 and 2000, Richardson's property tax base doubled to $8 billion a year.

Despite these success stories not everyone is enthusiastic about granting tax abatements. In the late 1990s, San Antonio, Texas—in contrast with Dallas, Houston, and Austin—refused to grant tax abatements for real estate development. San Antonio guidelines focused on tax abatements for companies bringing jobs to the area, but officials in San Antonio noted that they were cautious about considering residential abatements because property taxes accounted for such a large proportion (between 65 percent and 75 percent) of the county's budget. Local economic developers asserted that the city already had many advantages in terms of restaurants, retail, and pleasant footpaths provided by the San Antonio Riverwalk, although a downtown housing component remained a missing piece of development.[20]

It is typical for tax abatement programs to abate taxes on the entire value of property but require some payment in lieu of taxes (PILOTs). These payments reflect the amount of taxes that would have been collected on the value of the property alone, without improvements. The PILOT amount is often negotiated between the jurisdiction and the developer. Some states allow abatements on only a portion of improvements rather than all improvements. For example, towns in Connecticut can abate 80 percent of property taxes for improvements on property. Maryland law grants tax abatements on a graduated scale: 80 percent of property tax abated in the first five years; 70 percent in the sixth year; 60 percent in the seventh year; and 50 percent, 40 percent, and 30 percent in years eight through ten.[21]

Tax abatements are often used to encourage economic development in depressed or blighted areas, and all types of firms (retail, service, warehousing, and manufacturing) that agree to locate in blighted areas will usually qualify for tax abatement. Abatements are often associated with enterprise zones and empowerment zones that are set up in many state and local jurisdictions to give tax breaks to businesses that locate in a specific geographical area. In theory, tax breaks will induce businesses to locate in depressed areas and people in those areas will benefit—more people will have jobs and the general economic vitality of the area will pick up.

The reality of the situation, however, does not support the hopes of enterprise zone proponents. Studies of the impact of enterprise zones in six states showed that zones did not have the anticipated impact on income and employment.[22] This finding has been supported by a study of Louisville, Kentucky, that found that a targeted enterprise zone area continued to decline compared with a similar area. Furthermore, a survey in Louisville revealed that most of the private investment that took place inside the enterprise zone would have occurred even without the program.[23] Another study compared New Jersey cities that were awarded enterprise zone status with New Jersey cities that applied for but did not receive zone status and also cities that qualified for zone status but did not apply to the program. This study found no evidence of job growth or increased real estate values as a result of the enterprise zone program.[24] By 2000, texts in urban economics were concluding that enterprise zones were not very effective in luring firms to central cities.[25]

Some analysts claim, therefore, that enterprise and empowerment zones are not the panacea described by early proponents.[26] Tax policies are only one of many factors in investment decisions. Other factors to be considered included available land, transportation infrastructure, utility costs, proximity to inputs, proximity to customers, cost of labor, availability of labor, and community amenities.

Tax exemptions   Tax-exempt state and local bonds, discussed on page 32, are forms of tax exemption. Another type of tax exemption can be found in reductions to the base upon which property is taxed: a specific number of dollars is subtracted from the assessed value of the property. In a simplified example, if a state or local jurisdiction decides to give each veteran an exemption of $10,000 on a personal home, a veteran whose home is assessed at a value of $80,000 will deduct $10,000 from the assessment and pay property taxes on $70,000. In this example, if the tax rate is $1.00 per $100 in assessed value (.01 of assessed value), the actual savings to the veteran would be $10,000 × .01, or $100.

Exemptions are often granted to individuals, institutions, or types of property. Types of property normally granted tax exemptions include government property; property held by religious, educational, charitable, or nonprofit organizations; and residential property held by owners who qualify for homestead, veterans', or old-age exemptions. Homestead exemptions, like veterans' exemptions, allow homeowners to deduct a specific amount from the assessed property value. The homestead exemption significantly reduces property taxes in many states. Tax exemptions may also be granted to induce desired activities such as the construction of new plants, the installation of pollution-control facilities, or a set-aside of land to preserve its natural beauty.[27]

States have authority to determine what to include in local property taxes. Complete exemption from local taxes has been accorded in various states for various kinds of property: motor vehicles, household personal property, agricultural personal property, business inventories, or all tangible and personal property.

Typical tax exemptions

- **Homestead exemption**   Deduction on the assessed value of one's residence
- **Old-age and veterans' exemptions**   Partial exemption or deduction from assessed values on property
- **Exemptions for religious, governmental, educational, and charitable organizations**   Tax relief for nonprofit organizations that benefit the community; the federal government sometimes makes payments to local governments to make up for the loss of revenue caused by these exemptions, but states rarely do
- **Special corporate income tax exemptions**   Exempts recipient firms from taxes on corporate profits; is often used to encourage employment of specified types or numbers of workers
- **Special personal income tax exemptions**   Exempts taxes on an individual's personal income, often directed at small-business entrepreneurs
- **Excise tax exemptions**   Intended to reduce operating costs for firms that use large amounts of commodities—such as gasoline and other fuels—normally subject to excise taxes
- **Inventory tax exemptions**   Concerns taxes on goods that are warehoused in a state that levies the inventory tax but that are intended for delivery in another jurisdiction
- **Manufacturers' inventory tax exemptions**   Releases firms that store items for use in production from paying personal property tax on these items
- **Tax exemptions on land, capital improvements, and equipment**   Specific incentives to encourage investment in land and capital equipment; firms are exempt from property taxes on these items, either permanently or for a specific period of time
- **Sales and use tax exemptions on new capital equipment**   Taxes are not imposed on purchase, use, consumption, or storage of new capital equipment; stimulates capital expansion
- **Tax exemptions to stimulate research and development**   Exemptions on property taxes, corporate income taxes, and sales and use taxes are given to firms that conduct research and development.

Sources: John Mikesell, *Fiscal Administration: Analysis and Applications for the Public Sector* 4th ed. (Belmont, Calif.: Wadsworth Publishing Company, 1995); and Roger Hamlin and Thomas Lyons, *Economy Without Walls: Managing Local Development in a Restructuring World* (Westport, Conn.: Praeger, 1996).

Personal property encompasses tangible personal property such as business inventories, machinery, jewelry, livestock, pets, and household furnishings. Intangible personal property consists of claims on real assets identified in corporate stocks and bonds, bank deposits, and mortgages. The main components of the property tax are land (residential, commercial, agricultural, and vacant) and capital improvements to the land. During the 1980s, most local jurisdictions moved away from taxes on personal property toward taxes on real property. This change combined with the expanded use of exemptions caused a nationwide decline in the personal property share of locally assessed taxable property, from 15.7 percent to 9.8 percent between 1961 and 1986.[28]

Tax increment financing   In recent years, economic development officials and political leaders have increasingly turned to tax increment financing (TIF) as a tool of economic development. Only local governments in states that have enacted specific enabling legislation can use TIF. With state sanction, a local government can establish a TIF district; prepare an inventory of land uses, zoning, and building stock; and formulate a redevelopment plan.[29] State laws vary in detail but all maintain the same basic approach: the local jurisdiction borrows money, uses it to make improvements to property or infrastructure, and repays the borrowed funds with increased tax revenue generated by the improvements and the resulting increases in property values. Robert Bland, in ICMA's *A Revenue Guide for Local Government,* summarized features of tax increment financing:

> Tax increment financing divides tax revenue from the areas into two categories: Taxes on the predevelopment value of the tax base (the tax increment base) are kept by each taxing body, while the taxes from the increased value of property resulting from redevelopment (the tax increment) are deposited by each jurisdiction in a tax increment fund, which is usually maintained by the city. Money in the tax increment fund is usually used to repay TIF-backed bonds that are issued to finance public improvements in the redevelopment area.[30]

Tax increment–backed bonds typically provide financing for the purchase and preparation of land in a designated district. Financing can be used by the district to make capital improvements such as street improvements, lighting, water and sewer lines, curbs, gutters, and landscaping—improvements that should make the land more desirable to developers. Once prepared, land is often sold to developers at a relatively inexpensive price, a price that is lower than the cost of preparing the site. These sales are often termed land write-downs. Land write-down costs are recovered through the tax increment fund over the life of the project.

Under TIF arrangements, municipalities reserve or set aside the increases in property taxes to pay for improvements. Increments (added taxes attributed to improvements) are designated for a period of time necessary to fully pay off debt incurred to make the improvements. When bonds are fully paid, the TIF district can be dissolved and the full share of the tax increment can be designated for the city's general revenue. The increased values of the land are taxed at the same rate as other properties.

TIF mechanics are relatively straightforward:

- Establish the predevelopment value of the property
- Borrow money for improving the property
- Make improvements
- Calculate the postdevelopment value of the property
- Calculate the difference between predevelopment and postdevelopment values
- Set aside additional tax revenues associated with increases in property values; use those revenues to repay the bonds.

TIF programs have been both praised and criticized in the public finance literature.[31] Supporters of TIF argue that:

- The jurisdiction does not incur out-of-pocket expenses
- The jurisdiction does not obligate itself to raise taxes
- Added obligations are not placed on property owners who reside outside the TIF zone

TIF economics

The table below is an example of tax increment financing. It shows developed-land values, tax rates, and projected increases in tax yields over a period of 10 years. In the example, land before development is valued at $50,000. Values (assessments) are estimated to increase to $100,000 in year one, to $150,000 in year two, to $200,00 in years three through five, and finally to $250,000 for years six through ten.

Assuming a constant tax rate of 5 percent, total tax yields are anticipated to be $5,000 in year one ($100,000 × .05), an increment of $2,500 over the predevelopment tax yield of $2,500 ($50,000 × .05). In year two the tax yield increases to $7,500 ($150,000 × .05), an increase of $5,000 over the predevelopment tax yield. By year six, the new tax yield is $12,500 ($250,000 × .05), an increase of $10,000 over the predevelopment tax yield. The total tax increment (adding the tax increments of years one through ten) that accrues following the improvements to the land is $80,000.

This sum of money can be set aside for payment of principal and interest on funds that were borrowed for the improvements. At the completion of an agreed period of time (such as 10, 20, or 30 years), bonds or borrowing can be completely repaid. At this time, the jurisdiction will reap the benefit of the higher property values (land assessed at $250,000 instead of the predevelopment assessment of $50,000) and will be able to enjoy the benefit of an enlarged tax base. Increased tax revenues will flow to the jurisdiction on the basis of its higher assessed values even if the jurisdiction maintains its tax rate of 5 percent.

Year	Value[a] ($)	Tax rate[b] (%)	Yield[c] ($)	Tax increment[c] ($)
Year 1	100,000	5	5,000	2,500
Year 2	150,000	5	7,500	5,000
Year 3	200,000	5	10,000	7,500
Year 4	200,000	5	10,000	7,500
Year 5	200,000	5	10,000	7,500
Year 6	250,000	5	12,500	10,000
Year 7	250,000	5	12,500	10,000
Year 8	250,000	5	12,500	10,000
Year 9	250,000	5	12,500	10,000
Year 10	250,000	5	12,500	10,000
Total Increment				80,000

[a] Value of predeveloped land calculated at $50,000
[b] Tax rate for predeveloped land is 5%
[c] Yield on predeveloped land, each year = $2,500

- TIF bonds are revenue bonds and are not included in a city's general obligation debt
- After the TIF bonds are retired, the city and all other affected taxing units (such as school districts) enjoy the advantage of the enhanced tax base
- The enhanced tax base can be used to pay for any additional services required by new development
- No voter approval is required for TIF bonds, and a local government council may act unilaterally to authorize them.

Critics of TIF plans counter that:

- Governments are not accountable to the voters
- Lack of accountability to the voters violates principles of democracy
- Development may increase the need for services such as police, fire, and schools; and taxpayers who reside outside the designated development zone must pay for these services
- The local government must find other sources of funds or let bonds go into default if the tax increment fails to materialize
- TIF borrowing is more expensive than general obligation debt
- Jurisdictions can allow use of TIF in areas that do not need publicly subsidized assistance
- TIFs subsidize big developers to help them carry out projects they would have undertaken with or without government assistance
- Other jurisdictions and districts will lose their proportional share of some taxes and therefore are subsidizing local government projects.

Other types of tax incentives

Tax abatement, tax exemption, and tax increment financing represent only a few of the many tax incentives that can be used by public officials who wish to protect or strengthen their economic base. Other tools of economic development, usually used in the name of promoting the business climate or promoting equity, can be used to fine-tune taxes. Circuit breakers, tax credits, tax deferrals, tax classifications, accelerated depreciation, and tax stabilization agreements are tax treatment options also available to state and local leaders.

Circuit breakers   Circuit breakers provide tax relief to low-income property holders. When property taxes as a proportion of an individual's income rise above a specified level, an overload is declared and tax relief measures are triggered. Circuit breaker measures are targeted to those most in need of tax relief: people on fixed incomes and low-income residents of neighborhoods where property values are increasing. The overload is easily identified and measured by the ratio of property taxes to current family income (total property taxes divided by total family income). When this ratio exceeds a threshold defined by law, the government returns some portion of the property taxes to the taxpayer. Because circuit breakers can be attractive to retirees who want to minimize their tax obligations, jurisdictions hoping to lure retirees can implement circuit breakers as part of an economic development strategy.

Many states limit circuit breaker relief to the elderly, a group that is especially susceptible to overload because their incomes are often fixed or lag behind increases in property values. By targeting tax breaks to lower-income individuals, governments exclude those who are simply overextended because they have taken on large mortgages or other debt. States define income broadly (they usually include transfer payments from Social Security and other sources) when they set triggers for a circuit breaker. Circuit breakers are associated with state policies that can provide relief in a variety of ways, including income tax credits or rebates, direct payments to qualified individuals, and state payments to local governments that lose tax revenue because of circuit breakers.

Circuit breakers represent an attempt to aid people on fixed incomes who are burdened by ever-increasing property taxes; they are progressive in the sense that they increase tax equity. As taxes increase in line with property values, property owners who do not upgrade their housing must still pay

---

Tax tools

- **Accelerated depreciation**   Allows firms to depreciate equipment at a faster rate in hopes that firms will reinvest tax savings in plant and equipment
- **Circuit breakers**   Property taxes that are tied to individual income levels; pinpoint property tax relief to those with high property tax payments compared with current family income
- **Tax abatement**   Agreement between a government and a property owner to forgo taxing some share of assessed real estate value for an agreed period of time
- **Tax classification**   Different tax rates applied to different types of property
- **Tax credit**   Subtracted from a tax bill after the liability has been calculated (differs from exemption, which is a reduction in value prior to calculation of a tax)
- **Tax deferral**   Delays the time by which the property tax has to be paid; deferred taxes represent a loan that creates a lien against the property
- **Tax exemption**   A reduction in assessed property values granted to specific groups such as veterans or for specific activities such as the construction of new plants
- **Tax increment financing**   Increase in property tax revenue resulting from government development of an area
- **Tax stabilization agreements**   Commitment by the government to limit fluctuations in the amount and type of taxation to be borne by businesses.

Source: Mikesell, *Fiscal Administration.*

---

higher taxes. Unless and until they sell their property, they are burdened by an unrealized capital appreciation. In communities where the population is aging, a circuit breaker may be triggered with increasing frequency and may retard the growth rate of total property tax collections.

Tax credits   Companies that invest in an area may significantly lower their tax burden if they receive a tax credit from the local jurisdiction. Tax credits differ from tax exemptions (a fixed amount is deducted from total assessed values) or tax abatements (the property tax rate is frozen for a specific period of time). Tax credits instead subtract specific amounts of money directly from tax bill obligations. For example, if the property tax credit is 10 percent and a tax obligation is $2,000, $200 (i.e., $2,000 × .10 = $200) would be subtracted from the entire tax bill of $2,000. The resulting tax obligation would then be $1,800 ($2,000 minus $200).

From a company's perspective, a tax credit is more desirable than a tax exemption or tax abatement because it directly reduces tax obligations instead of reducing taxable values or holding taxes at one rate for a given period of time. A tax credit reduces tax liability dollar for dollar. Deductions from taxable assets (as in tax exemptions) are worth only the value of the deduction multiplied by the marginal tax rate. For example, a $1,000 deduction to someone in the 32 percent tax bracket will be worth $320 (i.e., $1,000 × .32). Deductions from taxable assets have a greater dollar value for individuals in higher tax brackets.

Tax credits are often granted to encourage activity that will in the long term benefit the community. For example, the federal government gives tax credits for college tuition and new investment because the country will benefit from a better-educated workforce; and worker productivity, profits, and gross domestic product will benefit from investment in new plant and equipment. At the state and local levels, tax credits have been used to encourage land conservation, housing, and creation of renewable energy such as wind power.

Tax deferrals   Agreements to defer taxes for a given number of years can help companies in the early stages of their development and can increase their chances of survival. Assistance of this nature at the community level can stabilize areas threatened with decline. If property values have risen dramatically, deferrals also permit individuals or businesses to pay taxes on the basis of older values. Deferrals can be particularly relevant to farm owners on the fringe of development who have witnessed large increases in the value of their property. Records are kept on the difference between the deferral payment and the payment that would be owed in the absence of the deferral. Taxes that are deferred must still be paid at a later date. Deferred taxes are sometimes collected at the time of death, when taxes become a primary claim against the estate. Deferred taxes on agricultural land at the fringe of development often are collected when the land is sold and converted to a nonagricultural use. Taxpayers should view deferred taxes as loans to property owners rather than subsidies.

Tax classifications   Another tax tool used by policymakers is classification. Classification refers to categorizing properties to explain how they are used. Typical classification categories for property include

- Owner-occupied residential property
- Agricultural property
- Commercial and industrial property
- Property used by public utilities.

Tax classification systems assume that some categories of property are more valuable to the owners and that some owners have a greater ability to pay taxes. Principles of taxation assume that the value of property and ability of owners to pay should be related to tax rates. Conflict often exists in states or localities where one group of taxpayers (such as farmers) tries to shift the tax burden to other groups of taxpayers (such as homeowners). Classifications that lower business taxes by shifting them to others can increase a locality's attractiveness to business.

Accelerated depreciation   Accelerated depreciation, another method of altering tax payments, enables companies to write down the cost of plant and equipment more quickly than usual. Owners can then tie reinvestment to depreciation schedules, pay lower taxes, and modernize plant and equipment more frequently. Localities can benefit from new investment if the demand for workers increases and existing workers become more productive.

Tax stabilization   Agreements to maintain current tax rates are sometimes used to assure potential investors of a stable tax environment. Taxes can be frozen to assure investors who want to avoid sudden changes in taxation that tax rates, tax burdens, or assessed values on property will remain constant for a period of time. For example, city officials might guarantee a company that taxes on its inventory will remain at a certain rate for a specific number of years. Officials might also guarantee that the city will maintain a specified assessment on the company's factory for a certain number of years.

Nonfinancial assistance

In addition to financial inducements, government can also enhance economic growth with nonfinancial incentives that include efforts to create a favorable business climate. Private sector firms, all other things being equal, should be more inclined to invest in areas with site development assistance, regulatory relief through enterprise zones, adequate human resources, and a critical mass of research capacity.

Site development

Many economic development programs involve public efforts to acquire and improve sites for industrial or commercial use. The object of this strategy is to offer land to private firms at a reduced cost by subsidizing acquisition, preparation, infrastructure provision, and landscaping activities. The vast majority of states and many local governments either provide catalogues of available industrial sites or seek to match firms with appropriate sites. Two major types of site development include land banks and industrial parks.

Land banks   Land banking is the practice of acquiring and improving contiguous parcels of land to assemble sites suitable for development. Land bank sites can include surplus city-owned land, donated land, land acquired through condemnation, land purchased from private sources, former stockyards, and former military installations. To construct a land bank, public officials search for underused, underdeveloped, and/or misused properties. They catalogue the properties by size and location and keep the information up to date for quick reference. Geographic information system (GIS) computer programs are helpful for cataloguing and displaying information.

In declining neighborhoods, some owners who find themselves in tax arrears may abandon their property rather than pay back taxes. Government bodies may also purchase property in order to tear down vacant buildings that blight the community. Rather than resell properties acquired through default or purchase, a city may choose to retain ownership and create a land bank until it has assembled a parcel of land large enough for development. Usable structures in the land bank may be leased during the period of land accumulation.[32]

Land banking usually requires a substantial amount of capital (funds that are set aside for the purchase of land have also been called land banks). Potential sources of funds include surtaxes on local real estate and the sale of bonds. In 1998 voters in Cape Cod, Massachusetts, approved the creation of a fund (called a land bank) to preserve undeveloped land. A surtax of 3 percent was placed on real estate assessments in the Cape's 15 towns. With its share, the town of Sandwich, Massachusetts, planned to purchase 275 acres and block construction of 75 large houses. Each town's share of the land bank money was proportional to the amount of money the town raised through its real estate surtax. The state of Massachusetts made a one-time contribution to assist the land bank.[33]

An alternative approach to the direct purchase of land is to gain control of suitable parcels of property by purchasing an option on them and later selling the option to a private developer.[34] The Trust for Public Land offers technical and financial assistance to local governments that are trying to assemble parcels for use as open space.[35]

Industrial parks   Industrial parks, whose origins in the United States date back to 1899, are usually developed entirely by private interests, without public subsidies; however, cities, counties, and states can be involved in

---

Use of GIS for local land banking

Although the use of geographic information system (GIS) technology in local government has become increasingly common, the use of GIS for land banking is still relatively new. The city of Baton Rouge–parish of East Baton Rouge, Louisiana, recently won an award from the U.S. Department of Housing and Urban Development (HUD) for its land banking efforts using GIS technology. The city's office of community development (OCD) had been having problems locating land suitable for redevelopment from its pool of $63 million worth of parcels taken for nonpayment of taxes. This had become a barrier to inner-city revitalization. The OCD contracted with the Computer-Aided Design and Geographic Information Systems Laboratory at Louisiana State University to digitize parish parcel maps. This permitted OCD to create a land banking and disposition program involving over 6,000 properties. Now, OCD can rapidly locate land that can be redeveloped and can tell potential developers something about environmental conditions on these sites and surrounding sites as well. As a further service, OCD has put its maps on its Web site.

Source: HUD Blue Ribbon Practices in Housing and Community Development, John J. Gunther Awards, www.hud.gov/ptw/docs/la1598.html.

---

industrial park development. State participation is mostly limited to planning and development. States that have operated industrial parks include New Hampshire, Rhode Island, New Jersey, and Hawaii. Maryland has provided loans to local governments for the purchase of land, the planning of industrial parks, and the construction of "shell" buildings. The interiors of shell buildings are left largely unfinished until a tenant is found. They are marketing tools for attracting or retaining firms.

Industrial parks operated by local governments began to appear in the 1940s. Some parks were converted from wartime facilities and others were developed as parts of urban renewal projects. For example, in Norfolk, Virginia, 123 acres of slum housing were cleared in order to build a 35-acre industrial park.

A substantial portion of the annual growth in the number of industrial parks is fueled by public subsidies.[36] Private firms may benefit from public sector industrial parks because publicly owned industrial parks do not levy property taxes (though they may require payments in lieu of taxes) and the initial cost of facilities is borne mainly by the public sector.

Many towns and industrial development corporations have attempted to attract new companies or retain existing companies by investing in infrastructure and constructing industrial parks. Typical improvements include the installation of water lines, sewer lines, and street lights as well as the construction of access roads, sidewalks, schools, parks, recreational facilities, parking garages, and parking lots. Local governments make these improvements when a business promises to build a facility and hire workers. It is difficult to definitively compare benefits with costs for infrastructure investments, and disagreement exists about whether incentives given to business are cost effective (see Case study 4–2).

Recently the industrial park concept has evolved to include "smart parks" that provide high-tech telecommunications infrastructure to research-based and other technology-oriented firms. The size of many industrial parks has also increased substantially. For example, a few buildings were constructed in the early 1970s for the Hauppauge Industrial Park on Long Island in New York. By 2002 the Hauppauge Industrial Park was home to 1,300 companies and 55,000 employees.[37]

Enterprise zones

Enterprise zones, described earlier under tax abatement, are established to generate new investment and employment in declining neighborhoods. They provide tax incentives and regulatory relief to businesses that are willing to locate in the designated zone. Embracing the basic assumptions of supply-side economics, proponents of enterprise zones contend that reducing constraints on free enterprise (rules, regulations, and other red tape) and minimizing the cost of private investment (lowering the tax rate, for example) will lead to new development. The new private investment in turn will generate employment and increase public revenues.[38]

Governments that have used enterprise zones effectively have chosen their areas carefully to incorporate land that retains a stable economic base. The basic premise of enterprise and empowerment zones is that businesses can be induced to invest and create jobs in places they would not normally invest because of high costs. In theory, this can work if the benefit of the inducement is greater than the extra cost of the investment. For example, if $1,000 invested in one location will produce less profit than $1,000 invested at another site, the government must provide enough inducements to more than make up for the lower profit.

Many analysts believe that enterprise zones can unleash creative talents. A leading student of enterprise zones has stated:

> [Enterprise zones] would create, within the most depressed sections of the inner city, areas where there would be a conscious attempt to reduce regulation, and to reduce the stifling burden of tax. The zones would be areas where experiments could take place with the minimum of red tape, and where small enterprises could flourish. Not only would these zones bring the innovative power of the small entrepreneur and the neighborhood group to bear on the depressed area in which they were established, but they would also be laboratories which would provide tested ideas that might have more general application.[39]

The Housing and Community Development Act of 1987 allowed the U.S. Department of Housing and Urban Development (HUD) to designate up to 100 federal enterprise zones, but the act provided no real fiscal incentives and no designations ever took place. While little occurred at the national level, a majority of state governments adopted the enterprise zone concept in the 1980s. By 1995, 34 states had active enterprise zone programs. During the Clinton administration the federal government embraced and adopted the concept of enterprise zones, calling them "empowerment zones."

The federal Community Renewal Tax Relief Act of 2000 extended empowerment zones through 2009. The act provided additional tax benefits to businesses and authorized nine new zones. A principal tax incentive is the empowerment zone employment credit that is applied to wages paid to employees who work at least 90 days, live in the empowerment zone, work in the zone, and provide services in the zone.

Some analysts cite the benefits to localities of empowerment zones. The Baltimore empowerment zone was involved in a reverse-commuting program that brought West Baltimore residents to neighboring Howard County. A similar reverse-commuting program was successful for the East Baltimore empowerment zone that brought inner-city residents to neighboring counties.

Enterprise zones—Early champions

An early advocate of the concept of enterprise zones was Sir Geoffrey Howe, a British member of Parliament who was a spokesperson on economic issues for Britain's Conservative Party. In a 1978 speech, Howe vigorously promoted a set of policies that he labeled "enterprise zones." Howe believed that many of the problems experienced by depressed neighborhoods in central cities could be traced to governmental obstacles. He maintained that these obstacles stifled enterprise, inhibited business creation, and depressed creativity. To remove these external constraints, Howe proposed a radical reduction in taxes and cuts in regulation and envisioned a climate would be created that would encourage innovation, risk taking, job creation, and growth.

Although Howe championed the enterprise zone cause he did not originate the concept. Professor Peter Hall, an authority on urban planning and former chair of the Fabian Society (a group in Britain committed to democratic socialism), contributed greatly to crystallizing the enterprise zone idea. In the United States and Canada, the concept of enterprise zones can also be traced to writings of Jane Jacobs, who emphasized the virtues of entrepreneurship and social capital.

In an innovative private-public collaboration, Blimpie Subs and Salads franchisees who open shops in Detroit's empowerment zone (where nearly 100,000 people live) do not have to pay the $18,000 franchise fees. In New York City, the Upper Manhattan empowerment zone played a crucial role in establishing the Harlem USA retail development, which helped to open the first movie theaters in Harlem in more than 50 years as well as an Old Navy store.[40]

Other analysts claim that the benefits of empowerment zones are overstated. For example, biotech companies in the New Haven, Connecticut, empowerment zone reportedly contribute little to the city's tax base. A number of the companies that were spun off from Yale University pay royalties to the university for the right to commercialize its inventions but pay little in property taxes because they operate within the empowerment zone. Critics of New Haven's empowerment zone claim that when tax breaks for biotech companies are set to expire, the companies will move out of the city.[41] Residents of Harlem have expressed concerns that the empowerment program does more to help big developers and national retailers than small businesses.

Zones usually provide little assistance to small or labor-intensive firms and tend to transfer investment from one location to another instead of generating new business. In some zones, job losses outnumber job gains. Areas suffering from severe economic blight require more assistance than the relief provided by enterprise zones. Studies of the general effectiveness of enterprise zones show a mixed picture. Some studies indicate that regulatory relief has had little or no influence on business location decisions because regulations represent a very small portion of business costs.[42] These studies suggest that the entrepreneurs most likely to benefit from enterprise zones are large, capital-intensive firms that have high tax liabilities.

Most large corporations refuse to make significant investments in declining areas even though tax and regulatory relief are offered to them. Other concerns—the availability of a well-trained work force and crime rates—seem to counter the attraction of lower taxes and regulatory relief. Private industry will invest in enterprise zones only if it is convinced that the tax and regulatory benefits will outweigh other costs of making such investments. Some enterprises, however, such as Blimpie International, have been willing to expand their operations within empowerment zones. Other corporations have aided empowerment zones in various ways. Hewlett-Packard gave the East Baltimore empowerment zone millions of dollars worth of products, services, and social venture capital. Costco and Home Depot agreed to run their stores in the Upper Manhattan empowerment zone.

Enterprise and empowerment zones might be viewed as a worthy good in the sense that the benefit to the neighborhood of more jobs is so constructive that it should be done even if it is costly. The government will lose tax revenues from profits generated in zones; government may also subsidize employee wages in zones and allow companies to avoid costly regulation. All of this is often justified in the name of economic development.

Human resources

In his classic work, *The Wealth of Nations*, Adam Smith asserted that human capital was the principal resource of economic growth. Human capital, defined as a well-educated, well-trained workforce, is still considered essential to economic development:

> Economic development depends on human resources, and the post-industrial economy requires a work force that is increasingly technologically literate, adaptable to rapid market changes, capable of continuous relearning and retraining, and internationally oriented. Some states are far ahead of others in reacting to changing circumstances. Economic development depends mainly on people: engineers, scientists, and inventors; entrepreneurs and skilled state business managers; and skillful employees.... Human capital has become a key requirement of successful state economic development. State governments have a very important role in building a statewide human capital infrastructure and can significantly influence the human resource development process.[43]

Many experts are concerned about the quality of human capital in the United States. The 1983 study, *A Nation at Risk,* concluded that economic vitality and national survival were in danger because America's education system was not adapting to new challenges. A growing number of more recent reports have identified inadequacies in elementary, secondary, and postsecondary education.[44]

Top executives contend that the nation's businesses are not competing effectively in world markets because of workforce inadequacies and human capital problems. They observe that universities and secondary schools can play a role in reversing educational deficiencies and that economic development depends on human capital. Former secretary of labor Robert Reich is pessimistic:

> Unless America moves quickly into a new era in which upgrading and using our human capital becomes a central concern, however, our future wealth will come primarily from extracting coal, timber, and grain from our lands, from assembling advanced components that have been designed and fabricated elsewhere, and from distributing the resulting products to our own citizens. We will become a nation of extractors, assemblers, and retailers—poor by the standards of the rest of the world.[45]

In some areas of the United States, relatively low rates of high school graduation and relatively high rates of adult illiteracy create a mismatch between the skills of the workforce and the needs of technologically sophisticated employers.[46] This mismatch threatens to lead to a two-tier economy, in which some workers are paid high wages while others are left behind and, in essence, compete with workers in underdeveloped countries where wages are extremely low. Data indicate that while U.S. unemployment plunged in the 1990s the gap between the earnings of the rich and the poor grew. The differing market values of American citizens' skills no doubt contributed to this growing disparity. To minimize this disparity, some analysts advocate customized training and better education to improve the international market value of lower-paid U.S. workers.

Customized training   The concept of customized training is relatively simple; it is designed to meet particular employer needs and is typically provided at the employer's site or at a local community college. The clear objective of customized training is to use human resources to attract new business by underwriting staff development costs. Governments usually offer to provide customized training in order to attract a new employer; however, existing firms seeking to expand their operations have also taken advantage of customized training.

Customized training is the most common industrial incentive financed directly from state resources. Many state and local governments tailor training to the specific needs of the individual firm. Such training assures businesses a ready supply of trained workers, a key factor in business location decisions. Uncertainty over the availability of workers remains a major deterrent to both business expansion and relocation (see Case study 4–1).

Workforce concerns grew as the labor market tightened in the late 1990s. For example, United Parcel Service probably would not have retained major facilities in Louisville, Kentucky, if workforce concerns had not been allayed by government action. In a similar decision, Amazon.com chose to locate a new facility in an area of Kentucky where the company was assured of a large supply of low-wage workers who had recently been laid off by the textile industry. They turned out in large numbers to apply for minimum-wage positions.

A number of state and local governments have worked with educational institutions to meet retraining needs. For example, in California, a nonprofit, community-based agency was established to identify community colleges that were willing to set up flexible, custom-designed programs, and the agency acted as a catalyst or facilitator for these programs. Another example of linking business-retraining needs with universities is the Bay State Skills Corporation of Massachusetts, a state agency that awards grants to institutions willing to offer employee retraining in high-demand fields such as fiber optics, artificial intelligence, robotics, telecommunications, photovoltaics, and marine science.[47]

Local governments also have attempted to train or retrain workers. In 2001 New York City created several job centers to function as hubs where job referrals, counseling, training, and other services can be made available in a single place. In the Washington, D.C., metropolitan area, a group of laid-off employees formed a company to provide training in specialized fiber-optics fields. Training included instruction in electronic assembly, network repair, and equipment soldering. A class could be six hours long or a week long, depending on the material. This private training company was able to get business from local companies that had eliminated their own training departments because of budget constraints. The public sector became involved in fiber-optics training when Howard Community College in Howard County, Maryland, offered courses and on-site training.

Long Beach, California, operates a joint venture between the Long Beach school district and Long Beach City College to teach specific trades to students still in high school. Training is provided in the fields of sheet metal, construction, refrigeration, air conditioning, welding, and machine tool and aviation maintenance.[48] Similar training is offered in many local high schools countrywide.

Retraining becomes particularly relevant when large numbers of workers in specific fields are let go. In the United States in recent years, large numbers of workers laid off from high-paying blue-collar jobs have not been able to find other jobs at comparable salaries because their skills are not suited to knowledge-based jobs.

Retraining is likely to be in continuous demand because of the pace of technological development and because workers, to stay employed, must stay abreast of the latest developments in their fields. States and localities wanting to compete in national and international marketplaces must invest in continuous training, geared toward the industries of the future. It is likely that customized training will move away from instruction in entry-level skills and the performance of repetitive tasks and will move toward the concept of continuous retraining of workers. Local leaders should try to upgrade the skills of the workforce in order to keep their areas competitive in the national and international marketplaces.

Education   Formal education also plays a role in the development of human capital. For generations, education has been linked to economic progress for the individual and for society. In the late 1990s, education seemed to be valued more than ever. In 1999, it was estimated that suburban schools sent 70 to 80 percent of their students to college, and the total number of students enrolled in four-year institutions of higher education was 14.8 million, an all-time high. The proportion of high school students expected go to college expanded from 50 percent in 1977 to 67 percent in 1999. The number of high school seniors taking scholastic aptitude tests (SATs) also expanded in the 1990s. A strong economy, population growth, sophistication of the education industry, and a growing belief in the link between education and personal success contributed to the growing numbers of students enrolled in college.[49] Growing income disparity between college graduates and high school graduates supports the general perception that a college education is well worth the investment of time and resources.

State and local governments recognize the link between education and economic development as well as the growth of knowledge-intensive fields. Education is viewed as particularly relevant for emerging industries, which are placing new demands on the nation's workforce. In the past, production called for technical expertise, knowledge about local and regional markets, financial capital, a stable workforce, and skills that were slow to change. In the future, production will depend on knowledge of national and international markets, skill in learning how to learn, knowledge of information processing, flexibility, and skills that change frequently.[50]

Establishment and development of a knowledge infrastructure are seen as essential for local development in the twenty-first century:

> Just as a region needs a high-quality and efficient physical infrastructure—transportation and community facilities, and various utility systems—to have the capacity for future growth and development, so it needs a knowledge infrastructure to grow creative and innovative organizations and individuals that can lead to sustainable economic development.[51]

Today's universities serve as engines of economic development for states and localities. The best-known examples of university-industry linkages are Silicon Valley in California and the Route 128 corridor in Massachusetts, which have contributed greatly to economic growth in the San Jose and Boston metropolitan areas. Other localities have also benefited from their association with research universities. For example, Durham, Chapel Hill, and Raleigh, North Carolina; Salt Lake City, Utah; and Austin, Texas (see Case study 5–1), have all grown as a result of their access to research institutions. Institutions credited with assisting development in these localities include Duke University, the University of North Carolina at Chapel Hill, North Carolina State University, the University of Utah, and the University of Texas.[52] As mechanisms for development, universities have several advantages over private and nonprofit organizations:

- **Concentration of technical knowledge and expertise** Faculty at research universities are rewarded for not only creating new knowledge but also keeping abreast of technical advances

- **Credibility** University research is perceived to be nonpartisan and scientifically rigorous

- **Access to a pool of talented but inexpensive labor** Bright graduate students are willing to accept relatively low pay to gain experience and acquire prestigious and lucrative positions in the future.[53]

To assist local economic development, some universities customize their programs to fit the needs of major employers. For example, the University of Louisville provides flexible class scheduling for students who work the night shift at United Parcel Service, the largest employer in the Louisville metropolitan area. Other universities provide technical assistance to businesses and are able to supply high-tech firms with highly educated, skilled workers.

Research capacity

Specialized knowledge that leads to product improvements or creates new products with high market demand is and will continue to be a major determinant of wealth (see the page 18 discussion of the innovation model of economic development). Jurisdictions therefore have an incentive to acquire and maintain a knowledge-based advantage. Without a knowledge infrastructure, they risk decline in the standard of living. Therefore, local jurisdictions welcome a potential for research in their regions.

Some of the most technologically advanced companies have located near major universities where they have access to research expertise. Knowledge-based companies in the Boston area, Silicon Valley, and Austin, Texas, appear to have benefited greatly from access to university researchers who work on the cutting edge of their fields.

Fields such as microelectronics, biotechnology, health sciences, computer hardware, and computer software have grown rapidly as a consequence of adapting products to meet consumer demand. Companies with technological advantages usually earn high profits and are able to pay relatively high salaries. Workers with the technological sophistication to adapt products and develop new products are in high demand and command high salaries. This kind of expertise is cultivated most often in a university environment, and university-business linkages have played an important role in developing wealth and supporting high-tech businesses.

Many U.S. universities have become involved in extensive research collaborations with major corporations. Such relationships are perceived to be in keeping with the utilitarian and pragmatic strain that runs through the

---

Centers of excellence

Creating centers of excellence in universities has become a popular method of using research to foster economic development. Centers of excellence identify, strengthen, and ultimately apply whole areas of research to commercial activity. In the state of New York, centers of excellence were established at seven university campuses—each center reflected the host university's existing academic strength. The University of Rochester opened a center in the area of optics, Cornell University created agricultural and biotechnology centers, and Columbia University developed a computer center for excellence, for example.

Other states have adopted similar strategies. In Ohio, the University of Akron, building on the region's historical strength as the "rubber capital of the world," established the Edison Polymer Innovation Corporation to augment research in this area. The University of Akron was counseled to make use of the resources of local rubber and chemical companies in order to transform the area from the "tire capital" to the nation's "Polymer Valley."

Source: Jeffrey Luke, Curtiss Ventriss, B. J. Reed, and Christine Reed, *Managing Economic Development* (San Francisco: Jossey-Bass, 1988), 148.

---

history of U.S. higher education. Leaders from Thomas Jefferson to John Dewey, implicitly rejecting the European concept of pursuing knowledge for its own sake, argued that knowledge exists to be put to use.[54]

Universities can assist businesses at a number of different levels. The surge of interest in developing ideas, patenting products, and marketing technology represents only one indication of linkages that have developed between industry and higher education. On another level, universities have traditionally served to provide training for managerial- and professional-level business employees. Community colleges provide specialized training for technical positions.

Summary

Economic development is a complex and multidimensional concept. Tools of development described in this chapter, if used wisely, can benefit governments, residents, and businesses. Local governments often provide financial incentives in the form of grants, loans, and tax-exempt bonds; equity financing can be more controversial because some people object to government ownership of enterprises.

Local governments also look to tax incentives to attract businesses to their areas. Tax abatement plans are most popular, but tax exemptions are also granted to individuals, institutions, and specific types of property. Tax increment financing plans attract businesses and garner additional tax revenue for jurisdictions through increased tax yields from land prepared for development by the government. Other tax incentives include circuit breakers, tax credits, tax deferrals, tax classifications, accelerated depreciation, and tax stabilization.

Not all tools involve direct financial incentives for businesses. Governments—using land banks and industrial parks—sometimes acquire and improve land for industrial or commercial uses. Enterprise zones, although their benefits are debated, are supported by federal legislation.

Local governments, knowing that forward-looking employers need skilled employees, also work to improve the skills training and general education levels of their residents. Some jurisdictions even collaborate with local institutions of higher education to create research facilities that attract promising industries to their area.

Study questions

- Why do governments provide grants, and what are the obligations of businesses that receive grants?

- Should your community make loans that banks refuse to make? Why or why not? When does the risk of making loans outweigh the potential benefits?

- What factors do governments consider when they set up loan funds?

- What types of businesses in your community should receive government loans? Why?

- How do revenue-based industrial development bonds differ from general obligation bonds? Why might a local government prefer issuing industrial development bonds?

- Under what conditions are equity financing arrangements desirable for government entities? What factors should local officials consider when exploring opportunities to become involved in equity financing arrangements?

- How can a community shift tax burdens to create a more favorable business climate? Is this a viable long-term strategy for economic development? Why or why not?

- What are the risks that TIF strategies carry? When are TIF strategies especially useful?

- Would your community benefit from being more aggressive in preparing sites for industrial or commercial use? Why or why not? If so, what sources of funds could your jurisdiction look to?

- Would enterprise zones be useful in your community? What issues can you foresee in implementing the concept?

- Should your community invest in upgrading the skill levels of residents? Why or why not? What specific policies could your community enact that would enhance skill levels and earning potential of residents?

1 Robert Bland, *A Revenue Guide for Local Government* (Washington, D.C.: ICMA, 1989), 153.

2 Matz and Ledebur, "The State Role in Economic Development," 85–102; National Association of State Development Agencies, National Council for Urban Economic Development, and the Urban Institute, *Directory of Incentives for Business Investment and Development in the U.S.* (Washington, D.C.: Urban Institute Press, 1983).

3 Matz and Ledebur, "The State Role in Economic Development," 87.

4 Eisinger, *The Rise of the Entrepreneurial State,* 93.

5 Jeffrey Luke, Curtiss Ventriss, B. J. Reed, and Christine Reed, *Managing Economic Development* (San Francisco: Jossey-Bass, 1988), 187.

6 Christopher J. Walker, "Revolving Funds for Economic Development," in *Financing Economic Development,* eds. R. Bingham, E. Hill, and S. White (New York: Praeger, 1990), 177–190.

7 Matz and Ledebur, "The State Role in Economic Development," 91.

8 Roger Hamlin and Thomas Lyons, *Economy Without Walls: Managing Local Development in a Restructuring World* (Westport, Conn.: Praeger, 1996), 53.

9   Robert D. Lee Jr. and Ronald W. Johnson, *Public Budgeting Systems,* 6th ed. (Gaithersburg, Md.: Aspen, 1998), 383.

10 Preferred stock can be another attractive alternative; it also does not carry voting rights.

11 Hamlin and Lyons, *Economy Without Walls,* 62.

12 Timothy J. Bartik, "Business Location Decisions in the United States: Estimates of the Effects of Unionization, Taxes, and Other Characteristics of States," *Journal of Business and Economic Statistics* 3 (1985): 14–22; Leslie Papke, "Subnational Taxation and Capital Mobility: Estimates of Tax-Price Elasticities," *National Tax Journal* 40 (June 1987): 191–203.

13 Gerald A. Carlino and Edwin S. Mills, "The Determinants of County Growth," *Journal of Regional Science* 27, no. 1 (February 1987): 39–54; Roger Schmenner, *Making Business Location Decisions.*

14 Michael Wasylenko, "The Effect of Business Climate on Employment Growth: A Review of the Evidence," in *Financing Economic Development,* eds. R. Bingham, E. Hill, and S. White (New York: Praeger, 1990), 34–54.

15 Bland, *A Revenue Guide for Local Government,* 156.

16 Thomas R. Plaut and Joseph E. Pluta, "Business Climate, Taxes and Expenditures, and State Industrial Growth in the United States," *Southern Economic Journal* 50, no. 1 (1983): 99–119; Bartik, "Business Location Decisions in the United States"; Bland, *A Revenue Guide for Local Government,* 158.

17 Bland, *A Revenue Guide for Local Government,* 164.

18 Ibid., 163.

19 Robert Tomsho, "Public Interests: In Toledo, a Tension Between School Funds and Business Breaks-Hefty Tax Abatements Keep Firms in Town but Drain Education Coffers, Too-Moldy Walls, Aging Boilers," *Wall Street Journal,* 18 July 2001, A1.

20 Tanya Sasser Rutledge, "Developers Hit the Trail Out of San Antonio," *Wall Street Journal,* 8 November 2000, T1; Steve Strunsky, "The Cities: Is Jersey City Too Alluring?" *New York Times,* 8 October 2000, A6; Edwin McDowell, "Residential Real Estate: Mixed-Use Tower Rising Near General Post Office," *New York Times,* 4 May 2001, B9; Michael J. Ybarra, "Telecom Corridor," *Upside* (July 2001): 68–75;

Tomsho, "Public Interests: In Toledo, a Tension Between School Funds and Business Breaks."

21 Bland, *A Revenue Guide for Local Government,* 165.

22 Robert T. Greenbaum and John Engberg, "An Evaluation of State Enterprise Zone Policies," *Policy Studies Review* 2/3 (2000): 29–46.

23 Thomas E. Lambert and Paul A. Coomes, "An Evaluation of the Effectiveness of Louisville's Enterprise Zone," *Economic Development Quarterly* 15, no. 2 (May 2001): 168–180.

24 Marlon G. Boarnet and William T. Bogart, "Enterprise Zones and Employment: Evidence from New Jersey," *Journal of Urban Economics* 40, no. 2 (1996): 198–215.

25 Arthur O'Sullivan, *Urban Economics,* 4th ed. (New York: Irwin-McGraw-Hill, 2000).

26 Margaret G. Wilder and Barry M. Rubin, "Rhetoric versus Reality: A Review of Studies on State Enterprise Zone Programs," *Journal of the American Planning Association* 62 (Autumn 1996): 473–491.

27 John Mikesell, *Fiscal Administration: Analysis and Applications for the Public Sector,* 4th ed. (Belmont, Calif.: Wadsworth Publishing Company, 1995), 367.

28 Michael E. Bell and John H. Bowman, "Property Taxes," in *Local Government Finance: Concepts and Practices,* eds. J. Peterson and D. Strachota (Chicago, Ill.: Government Finance Officers Association, 1991), 95.

29 Hamlin and Lyons, *Economy Without Walls,* 73.

30 Bland, *A Revenue Guide for Local Government,* 165.

31 Ibid., 167; Eisinger, *The Rise of the Entrepreneurial State,* 184–188.

32 Hamlin and Lyons, *Economy Without Walls,* 40.

33 "Cape Cod Towns Build Fund to Control Land Development," *New York Times,* 7 March 1999, 26.

34 Blakely, *Planning Local Economic Development,* 142.

35 Trust for Public Land, San Francisco, Calif., www.tpl.org.

36 Eisinger, *The Rise of the Entrepreneurial State,* 178.

37 Warren Strugatch, "L.I. @ Work: Pulling Communications into the 21st Century," *New York Times* 11 August 2002, 6.

38 Stuart Butler, *Enterprise Zones: Greenlining the Inner City* (New York: Universe Books, 1981); Susan E. Clarke, "Enterprise Zones: Seeking the Neighborhood Nexus," *Urban Affairs Quarterly* 18, no. 1 (1982): 53–71.

39 Butler, *Enterprise Zones: Greenlining the Inner City,* 5.

40 Angela Paik, "Linking Workers to Firms in Need; County Program to Tap Baltimore's Jobless Residents," *Washington Post,* 11 November 1999, M1; Roger Barnes, "It's a 'Go' in Detroit," *Black Enterprise* (September 2001): 50; "Johnnie Cochran in Deep Water" (editorial), *New York Times,* 20 November 2001, A18.

41 "Yale's Biotech Boom Is a Bust for City of New Haven, Conn., Report Says," *Chronicle of Higher Education* (October 26, 2001): A33.

42 Barry Rubin and C. Kurt Zorn, "Sensible State and Local Economic Development," *Public Administration Review* (March/April 1985): 333–339.

43 Luke et al., *Managing Economic Development,* 212.

44 National Commission on Excellence in Education, *A Nation at Risk: The Imperative for Educational Reform, A Report to the Nation and the Secretary of Education* (Washington, D.C.: U.S. Department of Education, April 1983); Steven G. Koven, Mack C. Shelley II, and Bert E. Swanson, *American Public Policy* (Boston: Houghton Mifflin, 1998), 160–164.

45 Robert B. Reich, *The Next American Frontier* (New York: Penguin Books, 1983), 238.

46 Joan Fitzgerald, "Labor Force, Education and Work," in *Theories of Local Economic Development,* eds. R. Bingham and R. Mier (Newbury Park, Calif.: Sage Publications, 1993), 125–146.

47 Luke et al., *Managing Economic Development,* 156.

48 Diane Cardwell, "City Closer to Opening New Centers for Jobs," *New York Times,* 3 November 2001, D6; Sabrina Jones, "Fiber-Optics Training Seen as a Bright Idea: Ex-Corvis Workers Seize an Opportunity," *Washington Post,* 25 October 2001, T5; Heidi Nye, "A True Taste of (and Test for) the Trades," *Air Conditioning, Heating & Refrigeration News* 213, no. 16 (August 20, 2001): 9–10.

49 Ethan Bronner, "Qualified Applications Flood U.S. Colleges," *Louisville Courier Journal,* 12 June 1999, A5.

50 Luke et al., *Managing Economic Development,* 148.

51 Michael I. Luger and Harvey Goldstein, "What is the Role of Public Universities in Regional Economic Development," in *Dilemmas of Urban Economic Development: Issues in Theory and Practice,* eds. R. Bingham and R. Mier (Thousand Oaks, Calif.: Sage Publications, 1997), 113.

52 Ibid., 126.

53 Ibid., 127.

54 Eyal Press and Jennifer Washburn, "The Kept University," *Atlantic Monthly* (March 2000): 39.

3 Business attraction and retention

Learning objectives

You should be able to:

- Differentiate among the three waves of economic development policy
- Cite examples of the opportunities and limitations of the business attraction strategy
- Provide examples of the business retention strategy and delineate the process of business retention
- Name four current policy issues that local governments need to consider before they embark on a course of business attraction and/or retention
- Analyze various business attraction and retention strategies to determine whether they will serve a specific local jurisdiction.

Business attraction and retention

One useful way of thinking about recent economic development policy is as a changing set of strategies, sometimes referred to as waves.[1] The first wave, beginning in the 1930s, was simple business attraction: states and localities competed against each other to lure firms to their jurisdictions. This approach to economic development relied on tax incentives of all varieties, loan guarantees, direct loans, and a host of other incentives targeted to individual firms.[2] In the era of traditional manufacturing, this was called smokestack chasing. With the shift to high-tech manufacturing, this business attraction strategy became known as chip chasing.

In the second wave, which began in the early 1980s, economic development practitioners moved away from attraction toward encouraging the retention and expansion of existing firms and the creation of new ones.[3] Incentives were more indirect and involved activities such as business incubation, microenterprise development, venture capital forums and other types of capital provision, and various technical assistance efforts.[4] This type of economic development is described in more detail in Chapter 4.

More recently, economic development policy has moved into a third wave,[5] emphasizing industrial clusters and other forms of networking, public-private partnerships, human-capital building, and strategic planning.[6] The focus is on creating the environment that is most conducive to growth and development.[7]

The wave metaphor of economic development policy is useful for understanding business attraction and retention because it places attraction and retention within an evolutionary progression and clarifies the role of these two strategies relative to others. However, the wave metaphor does not mean that business attraction has been replaced by industrial retention and creation, which in turn has been usurped by an approach that emphasizes strategic human- and social-capital building. In fact, all three policy paradigms are still in use. The best state and local economic development offices use all of these approaches together, strategically and synergistically.

While still very much in use, business attraction in its traditional form has been criticized in many evaluative studies of its success versus its cost. While debate still rages about the cost-effectiveness of incentives for luring businesses, the argument of those researchers who have found that incentives amount to little more than windfall profits to individual firms and that business attraction, in general, is a zero-sum game (one can win only if another person loses)[8] has slowed state and local governments' pursuit of this strategy. Several high-visibility cases in which states have offered millions of dollars in incentives to attract large manufacturing plants to their jurisdictions have also brought this economic development strategy under public scrutiny.

Current attraction practices are more commonly in line with third-wave thinking. Economic development planners try to create and foster a local or regional environment that is strategically attractive to outside firms and that provides opportunity for networking with similar companies, high levels of relevant education, attractive quality of life, and support for research and development (R&D). This is particularly true when the community or state is trying to attract high-tech businesses.[9]

This focus on creating growth-inducing localities has spawned a still stronger emphasis on marketing the advantages offered by these communities or regions. Glossy promotional brochures have long been a staple of business attraction efforts, and recently there has been an emphasis on the strategic marketing of locales.[10] Strategic marketing targets the needs of desired businesses or industries and then promotes the capacity of the community to meet those needs. Competition among communities enhances the importance of community rating services, such as those provided by *Places Rated Almanac* and *Inc.* magazine. These ratings can serve as a marketing boon to those communities that rank high on the indicators used. They can also create a political furor in communities that do not fare as well.

Wave 1: Business attraction

Despite the shifting focus toward third-wave strategies, business attraction with the use of financial and nonfinancial incentives remains popular. Every state in the union offers recruitment incentives, as do most local communities. Conway Data's *Site Selection Handbook* each year tallies all the different varieties of industrial-location incentives and details each state and its inducements. Chapter 2 describes several of these incentives.

Arguments in favor of this approach emphasize the political realities of intercommunity and interstate competition for economic development. Although many governments rely on inadequate evaluation when deciding which incentives to use and how to use them, some governments have added a new level of sophistication to the incentive process in the form of incentive negotiation strategies. Jurisdictions willing to engage in incentive negotiation recognize that businesses want to obtain the best possible deal and that the government must protect itself from bad deals. These governments are starting to take an investment approach to the use of incentives: quantifying the costs and benefits of a given project, calculating an appropriate rate of return and investment level, and strictly maintaining that investment level unless it can be shown that a higher level of investment will pay correspondingly higher benefits.[11]

Most incentives are used either as a marketing mechanism to increase the number of firms that will consider relocating to the jurisdiction or as a tool for completing a deal once a prospect (or a few prospects) has been identified and negotiations are under way.[12] Incentives are most likely to be effective as tools of business attraction when they are targeted to the specific needs of the firms being recruited.[13]

Foreign investment

Although incentives are used in all types of business attraction deals, perhaps the most extensive use of incentives has come in those deals involving so-called reverse foreign investment or direct foreign investment. Reverse investment takes a variety of forms: foreign interests take equity positions in U.S. firms, foreign investors acquire U.S. real estate, and foreign corporations locate operations in the United States. U.S. economic developers especially seek foreign firms to locate here.

In particular, state and local governments pursue foreign manufacturing operations, especially in the automotive industry, in response to the interest European and Japanese automakers have shown in locating facilities in the United States in order to reach the large U.S. market more effectively.

Attracting foreign investment—Manassas, Virginia

Manassas, Virginia, partnered with the commonwealth of Virginia to put together a $165.7 million incentive package to induce IBM and Toshiba to build a $1.2 billion chip manufacturing plant in this suburban community near Washington, D.C. The city's share of the package was $117.5 million, including $95.8 million in local tax breaks on equipment. Virginia made a loan of $38.4 million to IBM and Toshiba, with repayment deferred until years five through ten of the plant's operation. In addition, Virginia provided a job tax credit, a reimbursement to the companies for worker training, and funding to create a new electronics manufacturing curriculum to be offered at state universities.

The new plant employed approximately 1,200 workers and an additional 2,800 jobs were projected. About 20 percent of the initial 1,200 employees were transferred into Manassas from other locations.

Source: Steven Pearlstein, "A Dream of Silicon Virginia: Hoping to be a Chip off the Block, Region Tries to Cash in on High-Tech Boom," *Washington Post,* 14 August 1995, F10.

Jurisdictions use two major approaches to attract foreign corporations: one is the project approach, involving the pursuit of a particular business; the other creates and markets a business climate that is desirable to firms looking at alternative locations. The project approach is the more traditional first-wave approach; improving the business climate reflects third-wave models. The project-oriented model tailors a package of incentives to the deal being pursued. Two well-known cases involving this approach have been Alabama's successful effort to induce Mercedes-Benz to build an automobile plant near Tuscaloosa (discussed beginning on page 81) and the deal that brought the German automobile manufacturer Bayerische Motoren Werke AG (BMW) to South Carolina. South Carolina offered a $150 million package and, in return, BMW built a $1.2 billion plant and created 3,000 jobs.[14] While most of this kind of business attraction activity takes place at the state level, local communities also get involved. An example of this is the successful effort of Manassas, Virginia, in 1995 to attract a Japanese computer chip maker.

The project-oriented approach to attracting foreign investment has been the most common model, with dozens of cases all over the United States. Many have received considerable press coverage, making them highly visible to the public. The debate in most of these cases has been over the cost-effectiveness of these deals to the public sector (Is this money well spent, or could it be more appropriately used elsewhere?).

In the business climate–oriented model, the incentives are not tailored to a given firm's needs but are designed to have broad appeal (for example, lower tax rates, streamlined government permitting processes, quality-of-life amenities, and appropriately trained workforce). One example of a jurisdiction that actively pursues this approach is the small community of Mitchell, South Dakota. Mitchell uses its strategic location near the Canadian border and the provisions of the North American Free Trade Agreement (NAFTA) to attract "foreign transplants" to its community.[15] It has been quite successful, attracting investment by such international firms as Universal Packaging Corporation of the United Kingdom and Toshiba of Japan.[16]

The debate over incentives

Public incentives have come under considerable scrutiny over the past two decades, highlighting a rift between those who question the use of incentives as an economic development tool and those who support incentives. Opponents of incentives believe that:

- Incentives create unnecessary competition among government jurisdictions and often amount to zero-sum games

- Companies should exhibit loyalty to their communities because it is the right thing to do, not because they are receiving incentives

- Once incentives are extended to private firms, those firms will continue to demand more from government

- Monies that go to businesses as incentives would be better spent on social, educational, and other programs instead of on government assistance to large corporations

- Firms are rarely held accountable for staying in the community or for generating jobs or other economic development outcomes once they have received incentives.

  Proponents believe that:

- New businesses generate additional tax revenues that are essential for providing public services; despite tax incentives, the community keeps most of the additional revenues generated

- Businesses are important members of the community; if businesses remain competitive, the community's efforts for businesses will redound to the community's benefit

- Incentives to firms amount to a community's investment in its economic future; the return on investment makes the risk worth taking.[17]

There has been substantial academic study of the merits of these arguments, and the academic literature is itself divided on the appropriateness of incentives. However, most research tends to show that these divisions are based largely on differences in theoretical perspective, the research method, and the time perspective (short term vs. long term). Studies appear to agree on three key points.[18]

- With few exceptions, incentives will not effectively influence firm location decisions

- The truly important factors in business location decisions are transportation considerations, labor quality, and markets

- The best way for governments to influence firm location is to create and sustain quality communities.

Another finding is that incentives look better when used as a short-term strategy. It is interesting that more jobs are created by expanding existing businesses in the community than by attracting new businesses from outside the community.[19] A recent study in Nebraska found that incentives have a positive impact on economic development in counties that are already economically strong but no significant impact in counties that are economically depressed. This study concluded that incentives may be exacerbating economic disparities among localities in that state.[20]

Although economic development professionals now understand that incentives cannot mask a community's long-term deficiencies, the public sector—with a short-term mind set—continues to use incentives for business attraction purposes. Local policy is still heavily influenced by politicians and other laypeople who seek the favorable publicity that comes with luring a major employer to the community.[21] Particularly in regions of the United States that feel that they must continue to play economic catch-up, these incentives are still used extensively.[22]

Wave 2: Business retention

For many years it has been clear that, in terms of job creation, business retention as a strategy is superior to business attraction.[23] If incentives are used at all, they should be made available to existing firms as well as to new prospects.[24] When prioritizing their economic development programs for funding, governments should place business retention efforts ahead of business attraction.

A business retention strategy makes sense for a variety of reasons. Any community's existing firms are important assets to its economy. They are the current employers. They also are, and have been, taxpayers. Business retention requires less speculation than firm attraction. The firm is already located in the community and, as a result, has already developed attachments and loyalties. It is often easier for a firm to stay and expand than to relocate operations. Packages designed to induce that firm to stay and expand might be viewed as rewards for that loyalty, whereas inducements designed to attract new firms may be perceived by existing firms as implicit signals that they are either taken for granted or are perceived to have less value than newcomers.

When a community elects to pursue a business retention strategy, it usually takes several steps. First, it makes a complete inventory of all existing businesses. Second, it contacts these firms to determine their current situation and their needs. The government prepares a simple and short survey, focused on learning what factors each firm thinks would make it more successful and how the government can help. The survey might include straightforward questions such as "What single action could this economic development office take that would make your business more successful?"[25] The local government will not unquestioningly provide what existing firms claim to need, but it will analyze the feedback to determine where and how best to use its business retention resources. Information derived from a survey of existing firms can be assembled into a computerized database for easy reference and analysis.[26] And, third, the community initiates an ongoing effort to meet existing firms' short-term needs, and it maintains a pro-business attitude.[27]

Business retention strategies and tactics can take a variety of forms. Financial inducements—including tax incentives, loans, and loan guarantees—constitute one retention strategy. Nonfinancial incentives, also important, can include training targeted at specific labor needs.

A local government in the position to do so could also provide subsidized R&D assistance or access to public R&D know-how and facilities, for example, at public research universities. Research assistance is particularly useful to small and medium-sized businesses that do not have enough resources to invest in R&D but must innovate to survive. Even some large firms find the costs of ongoing, in-house R&D prohibitive.[28] This particular business retention incentive has proved especially effective in helping to build high-tech industry clusters when some firms in the industry already exist in the community. Establishing these existing businesses as solid industry anchors permits the community to use these clusters to its advantage when it promotes itself to new high-tech firms. The experience of Austin, Texas (Case study 5–1), provides an example of this strategy.

Custom Training—Lancaster, California

The desert northeast of Los Angeles is home to Air Force Plant 42 and a number of defense contractors including Boeing, Northrop, Lockheed, British Aerospace, and Crissair. The cities of Palmdale and Lancaster support active business attraction and retention programs that tie in the companies' ongoing training needs with offerings of Antelope Valley College (AVC).

Part of the mission of the college, which has about 13,000 students whose average age is 29, is to respond to the requirements of regional business and industry and offer a vocational and technical education curriculum that graduates individuals who are qualified to meet the requirements of local businesses. For example, in addition to its regular academic offerings, AVC offers a certified program in airframe and powerplant technologies at Fox Field in Lancaster and other special programs geared specifically to the needs of local aerospace companies.

Since mid-2001, two college programs—the laser-tracking program and the blueprint reading program—have grown as a consequence of industry-college cooperation. Boeing had come to AVC and explained that the company needed skilled employees to do the job of laser tracking. Boeing suggested a qualified vendor to do the initial training, so the college arranged for one employee to be trained by the vendor; that trained individual then returned and trained the additional employees Boeing needed.

AVC has also modified its regular classes to offer 190-employee Crissair, a Palmdale manufacturer of precision components for both military and civilian aircraft, a class on blueprint reading for computerized machinery.

These special college programs were funded through a U.S. Department of Labor work skills shortage demonstration grant, a program that covers workers who are already employed. It does not require a minimum class size or a minimum number of hours in class. Through the grant, AVC has been able to offer both employees and employers enhanced opportunities for training.

Sources: Antelope Valley College, www.avc.edu; Steve Contreras, director of corporate and community education, Antelope Valley College, 2002.

Some retention activities, tilting toward the third wave, include providing adequate, appropriate physical infrastructure and access to sufficient energy resources. Physical infrastructure includes the building of roadways, public transit facilities, water and sewer lines, high-speed communication networks, airport facilities, and speculative industrial buildings. As part of its overall effort to retain its UPS air hub, Louisville, Kentucky, lengthened existing runways and built a new runway to accommodate the large jets used by UPS on overseas flights.

Local governments can benefit from investing in speculative industrial buildings if they plan this type of venture carefully and enlist the technical help of experienced development professionals.[29] A number of private development firms, motivated by expectations of profit, are developing speculative industrial buildings and parks. Local governments might take advantage of this trend by identifying sites for these developers and making certain that adequate infrastructure is in place to make these developments work. High-speed communication facilities such as T-1 lines and routers have become part of the essential infrastructure for many businesses.

Server farms

One interesting manifestation of the Information Age is the server farm. A server farm is a collection of data servers located in one physical place, providing certain economies of scale. An example is the server farm being constructed by U.S. Dataport in San Jose, California, which will cover 174 acres, occupy 10 air-conditioned warehouses, and cost $1.2 billion. When it is completed it will be the world's largest data center. It will continuously use 180 megawatts of electricity, almost enough energy to serve all of Honolulu's residential needs.

Despite this high level of electricity consumption, server farms are relatively energy efficient: "a server farm that has a 200-kilowatt capacity may use as little as 30 kilowatts to 40 kilowatts per square foot of energy. By contrast, the average commercial office building uses roughly 8 kilowatts per square foot, according to the Washington, D.C.–based American Council for an Energy-Efficient Economy."

Nevertheless, communities that want to attract or develop server farms must be able to generate sufficient energy.

Source: Rachel Konrad, "Server Farms on Hot Seat Amid Power Woes," C/NET News.com (May 14, 2001), http://news.com.com/2100-1017-257567.html.

Energy supplies are also important. Many firms came to their current locations because they provided access to ample water, electricity, natural gas, and geothermal or other sources of power for their operations. For some communities, retention of these firms depends only on guaranteeing that these energy sources continue to be accessible and affordable. With dramatic changes in technology, however, other communities may be challenged to meet the energy needs—adequate types of energy as well as adequate supplies—of their resident businesses.

One example of this is the situation in California's Silicon Valley. Since about 1990, electricity transmission lines in the region have been operating at nearly full capacity, and almost all of the valley's electricity is imported. As a result, the cost of power has become so high and its reliability so diminished that firms are leaving the region in search of better access to electrical power. Stability of the energy supply is also crucial because power disruptions caused by inadequate capacity, lack of system management sophistication, or other factors can drive firms away.[30]

Wave 3: Contemporary issues in business attraction and retention

Various present-day economic development issues such as quality-of-life and environmental concerns, social costs of growth, redistribution issues, and the role of government also affect business attraction and retention. Although government incentives can still be used as tools in economic development and retention efforts, these contemporary issues bear upon third-wave initiatives.

Quality-of-life and environmental concerns

One of the pressing current issues in local economic development is growth management. To recruit businesses to a community as well as retain firms

---

The quality-of-life rating game

Places Rated Almanac (by David Savageau and Ralph B. D'Agostino, Foster City, Calif.: IDG Books, 2000), first published in 1981 and now in its sixth edition, ranks 354 metropolitan areas in the United States and Canada on nine preselected indicators: cost of living, transportation, jobs, education, climate, crime, the arts, health care, and recreation. One coauthor is a professor of mathematics specializing in statistics, and the book breaks down complex data for each category and provides detailed explanations of how data in each category were weighted.

Places Rated Almanac and other quality-of-life rankings—on the Internet see http://money.cnn.com/best/bplive/bplive_form.html and www.bestplaces.net/—have come to play a significant role in defining quality of life, in general, and the quality of life of any given community, in particular. For this reason, they have become important to local business attraction and retention strategies.

Those communities that rank high on quality-of-life scales can use them in marketing themselves to firms. Those that rank low are left with a clearer picture of what they have to change in order to compete in the quality-of-life arena. Although some argue that this kind of competition is unproductive and perhaps even detrimental to achieving a community's social goals, these rankings have become a fact of life in the local economic development sphere.

---

already in residence, communities need to maintain a good quality of life and high environmental standards. It is a delicate balance. On the one hand, quality of life and environmental standards are considered amenities that can attract and retain businesses. On the other hand, they are both affected by the results of successful economic development. Quality of life and environmental quality are also closely linked.

Quality of life is an amorphous term used to connote a bundle of amenities generally recognized as positive assets in any given community. People disagree, however, about precisely which amenities should be included in the bundle. Some argue that a community's quality-of-life amenities are specific to the context and, therefore, vary from community to community. One planner of small towns and rural areas explained that "they are the things you would take Aunt Mary to see when she comes to visit."[31] Other experts have tried to identify a set of quality-of-life categories that are common to all communities. The *Places Rated Almanac*, a good example of this approach, includes cost of living, employment outlook, crime, health care, transportation, education, the arts, recreation, and climate in its list of categories.

Quality of life and business location   Quality of life was not always a major consideration in business location decisions. Early location theory focused on transportation costs and a business's need to be situated close to its sources of inputs or close to its markets, depending on the weight and bulk of the input versus the weight and bulk of the final product. A 1982 study was one of the first to put quality of life among the top industrial location factors:

> The most fearsome competitive advantage the high technology industry can wield is a happy, productive staff of engineers. Since proximity to markets or supplies is not essential in such companies, such firms can be extraordinarily free to locate in attractive places for engineers and managers to live.[32]

Quality of life continues to be an important factor in high-technology industrial location decisions. Despite predictions that high-tech firms would do everything virtually, thereby making location irrelevant, these firms still do care about location for reasons of cost, access to communications infrastructure, and quality of life.[33]

With the emergence of high-technology businesses in particular came the concept of the footloose firm—one that, because it is free to choose any location, focuses on retaining its highly educated labor force and chooses the most attractive situation based on quality-of-life considerations. Examples of such companies include biotechnology and computer software firms, among others, as well as most corporate headquarters. Because quality of life has become a major business location factor, it is both an issue and a strategy for firm attraction and retention.

Enhancing and protecting quality of life   Quality of life can be influenced by public intervention[34] and is therefore amenable to economic development strategizing. The question becomes, "How might the public sector most effectively intervene?" Researchers in the early 1990s surveyed business CEOs from a variety of industries in the Wichita, Kansas, area. The CEOs evaluated several quality-of-life factors (public education, higher education/technology, local government services, climate, city appearance, housing, entertainment, and community image/spirit) and related them to their ability to retain skilled employees. Two quality-of-life factors were cited by the CEOs as being important, no matter what their industry. These common factors were entertainment (restaurants and cultural amenities) and community image and spirit (festivals and other community events). The researchers who conducted the study noted that their finding was "important from a policy perspective since entertainment-related additions to the local environment can be achieved in the short-run, although they will likely require public-private sector cooperation."[35]

The authors of the study found, however, that the remainder of the quality-of-life factors tended to vary in value by industry type. Manufacturing firms tended to value public education more than businesses in other industries; and finance, insurance, and real estate firms identified local government services as being most valuable to them. Thus they concluded that efforts at business attraction and retention by means of specific quality-of-life improvements are best targeted to specific types of businesses.

Recent literature on business attraction and retention tends to assume that quality of life is an important factor. While other factors have waxed and waned in importance depending on the industry surveyed, quality of life has found a spot on everyone's list and is broadly defined.[36]

Because quality of life is so broadly defined and displays so many facets, the impact of economic development on quality of life will be diverse as well. Additional tax revenues generated by new and expanded businesses can enhance public schools and other services. There may be additional markets and revenues for entertainment and image-building activities. Conversely, economic growth, if not managed well, can overburden the school system and public service infrastructure, make housing unaffordable to many current residents, and create blight and aesthetically unattractive areas.

Environmental damage caused by some businesses, particularly those that engage in so-called heavy manufacturing (for example, durable goods, chemicals, and petroleum), is a quality-of-life issue. Most suburban communities seek only clean industries (R&D facilities and corporate headquarters are two examples); their concerns over maintaining property values, health, aesthetics, and safety drive these efforts. From a fiscal perspective, most suburbs can afford to be selective about the industries they recruit.

Seeking environmental justice—Covent, Louisiana

The predominantly African American community of Covent, Louisiana, is located along the Mississippi River between New Orleans and Baton Rouge, in St. James Parish. This area is known as Louisiana's "cancer alley" because it is home to 16 toxic industrial facilities. Covent has a high school dropout rate of 51 percent and an unemployment rate of 61 percent. It also has the third highest level of toxic industrial emissions in the state.

In 1996, Shintech proposed to construct a $700 million polyvinyl chloride (PVC) plant in Covent. The company stated that the plant and its construction would employ approximately 2,000 workers and could spawn an additional 6,000 indirect jobs. Only 165 of the 2,000 jobs would be permanent, however.

Despite the potential job creation benefits of the siting of the new plant, the citizens fought its construction for 18 months. With help from the Tulane University's Environmental Law Clinic as well as Greenpeace, Covent's citizens filed complaints with the U.S. Environmental Protection Agency (EPA) regarding air permits issued for the project by the Louisiana Department of Environmental Quality (LDEQ). They cited a presidential executive order that required that federally funded state agencies take into consideration the impact of pollution on minority and poor communities when making their permitting decisions. Consequently, EPA put a stop on the air permits and opened an investigation into the possibility that the LDEQ had violated the civil rights of Covent's citizens. In the fall of 1998, Shintech dropped its efforts to locate in Covent.

Sources: L. Terry, "Activism on the Bayou: Shintech Case Redefines Outreach," *Chemical Week* 161 (May 26, 1999): 59; Ziba Kashef, "Saving Our Backyard," *Essence* 30 (September 1999): 160–164.

Many inner-city and rural areas are not as fortunate. Low property values and resulting fiscal constraints may force them to be less discriminating about the types of businesses they attract and retain. Less-desirable development can further exacerbate blight, decline in property values, and health and safety problems already present in these areas. When these problems persist in inner-city minority neighborhoods and rural minority communities, environmental justice becomes an issue. Citizens may ask whether business or government officials are intentionally locating polluting industries in minority communities.

Tourism   Tourism has become the principal economic development strategy in numerous communities throughout the United States. No matter how grand or how minimal the scenic, historical, recreational, or cultural amenities of a given community, in many places tourism is viewed as a panacea for local economic woes. This is particularly true in rural areas where agriculture has declined in economic importance (or never was a factor) and where there are few other options.

Tourism, however, is a double-edged sword. Because it can bring outsiders to the community to spend their money, it is viewed as a kind of export industry and, thus, a successful business attraction strategy. Yet when visitors arrive, they often clog roadways, overtax public services, and despoil the landscape. Branson, Missouri, for example, has been very successful in attracting a thriving country music industry. The community rivals Nashville as a mecca for country music enthusiasts. The town boasts numerous clubs where country headliners perform on a regular basis. But the little town has become overwhelmed by its own success as the main thoroughfare is regularly jammed with the automobiles of visitors. The rush to capitalize on this success has sometimes been so great that it has become difficult and costly for the local government to keep up with the demand for an expanded physical infrastructure.[37]

Intensified human activity may threaten the survival of the natural and scenic amenities that tourists come to see. Yosemite National Park, for example, has had to take steps to reduce the amount of automobile traffic in order to cut back on the ecological damage caused by auto emissions. These consequences have led a number of communities to back away from more traditional tourist strategies and look at other alternatives like eco-tourism and agri-tourism, which have had substantial positive impacts on state and local economies.

Eco-tourism Eco-tourism is tourist activity that is ecologically sensitive. The focus is on human interaction with the ecosystem being visited, with an emphasis on educating people about the ecosystem's value and importance and thereby fostering appreciation for its preservation. The number of eco-tourists permitted in an area is carefully limited. Their accommodations are tailored to the natural environment, and their access is controlled (for example, no automobiles within an established distance of the ecological amenities). This approach permits the community to protect its assets and control tourist activity in a way that is in keeping with the local carrying capacity.

A 1996 Pennsylvania survey yielded some important findings about the impacts of eco-tourism. While 1.6 million Pennsylvania residents fish and hunt, 3.4 million engage in wildlife watching, and these wildlife watchers spent $858 million while doing so. In 1999, Hawk Mountain Sanctuary, a Pennsylvania wildlife preserve, hosted 83,000 visitors from 33 states and eight foreign countries. The visitors added between $2.5 and $3.7 million to the local economy and supported 65 lodging businesses, 150 eating establishments, and many gasoline stations located outside the sanctuary.[38]

The beaches of Cape May, New Jersey, serve as stopovers for migratory shorebirds traveling between the Arctic and South America. These beaches also draw thousands of tourists who come to view the shorebirds. Towns on the shore hold birding festivals in both the spring and the fall to educate visitors as well as show them a good time. The Division of Fish and Wildlife of the New Jersey Department of Environmental Protection reports that tourists who come to bird-watch tend to stay for an average of four days and three nights and generate between $7.8 and $11.8 million per year for the local economy, and an additional $700,000 to $1.1 million for the state economy.[39]

Agri-tourism Agri-tourism is a strategy used in rural areas that are home to agricultural activities that may be of interest to visitors. Rather than building large hotels, numerous eateries, and other man-made tourist amenities that disrupt the agricultural focus of the areas, these communities "sell" tourists on the experience of blending into the agricultural enterprise completely and naturally. For example, in the bluegrass region of Kentucky, some thoroughbred horse farms take in a limited number of people to actually live on the farm for a week or two and engage in farm activities. Agri-tourists can assist farmhands in feeding and exercising horses, cleaning stables, and carrying out other farm chores. To date, these agri-tourism efforts have proved quite successful in attracting visitors while preserving the integrity of the horse farm region.

Agri-tourism creates a variety of economic opportunities for rural communities. It not only promotes agriculture, but it yields opportunities for the support and creation of complementary businesses as well. In the Cowichan Valley in Canada, Cherry Point Vineyards found that the ready availability of wild blackberries in the area made sweet blackberry wine a viable product to sell to winery visitors. These sales in turn created opportunities for local residents, who began picking blackberries and selling them to Cherry Point Vineyards. Cherry Point hired a local artist to design the label for the new wine.[40] Because the Cowichan Valley is sparsely settled and inhabited by a largely aboriginal population, a single agri-tourism business—a winery—made a major difference in the economic quality of life of the region.

Sustainable development Concerns over the compatibility of economic development policies and environmental preservation are at the heart of the sustainable development movement in the United States. Advocates of sustainable development believe that economic development and environmental protection can, and should, take place in harmony. Carefully planning and managing economic development efforts to ensure their compatibility with the ecosystem in which they take place can accomplish this.

Eco-industrial parks Some local governments seeking sustainable development are building eco-industrial parks. An eco-industrial park is a parcel of land that has been designated for occupancy by a collection of businesses. These firms are recruited because they are deemed environmentally responsible[41] or because their businesses are compatible, allowing them to pool resources and exchange inputs and outputs, including residuals (waste by-products). For example, one firm in the park may produce steam as a by-product. Instead of releasing the steam into the atmosphere, it sells it to other firms in the park that use it as input.

Although the rate at which eco-industrial parks are springing up across the country is increasing, there are still relatively few fully operational examples. One of the best-known eco-industrial parks in the United States is in Londonderry, New Hampshire, a long-time dairy-farming region. Several years ago, when dairy farming declined, the people of the region were anxious to retain and revitalize the industry. One of their strategies was the development of an eco-industrial park that was sensitive to and compatible with the agricultural region and that would attract businesses that would stimulate the local dairy-farming industry. They at first attracted a manufacturer of yogurt, and then compatible businesses such as a packaging plant and a recycling facility joined the park. The Londonderry Eco-Industrial Park continues to be an effective business attraction and retention tool for the region.

A larger urban example is the Fairfield Ecological Industrial Park located in South Baltimore. It is situated in an empowerment zone and used a very explicit recruitment strategy to attract its approximately 60 businesses. It targeted a small number of large firms to generate significant employment and to give the park a high profile. It also targeted a larger number of environmental technology firms whose purpose was to build the recycling and pollution prevention linkages in the park. In addition, Fairfield strategically targeted small service firms to meet the needs of other firms in the park. Finally, Fairfield has actively sought to encourage the expansion of firms already in the park.[42]

Smart growth Yet another public policy manifestation of the relation among quality of life, environmental protection, and local development is

---

10 Principles of smart growth

1. Mix land uses.
2. Take advantage of compact building design.
3. Create a range of housing opportunities and choices.
4. Create walkable neighborhoods.
5. Foster distinctive, attractive communities with a strong sense of place.
6. Preserve open space, farmland, natural beauty, and critical environmental areas.
7. Strengthen and direct development toward existing communities.
8. Provide a variety of transportation choices.
9. Make development decisions predictable, fair, and cost-effective.
10. Encourage community and stakeholder collaboration in development decisions.

For more information, visit www.smartgrowth.org.

---

the smart growth movement. Smart growth policies are aimed at curbing the negative effects of suburban sprawl. Supporters of this approach to managing growth and development attempt to find common ground for wise management of development through a coalition of traditional adversaries: anti- or slow-growth groups (environmentalists, some current residents of the community in question), pro-growth groups (real estate developers, home builders, and some land owners), inner-city development supporters (city planners, central city officials, community-based organizations), and better-growth groups (those who support reasonable growth).[43]

These groups often disagree about what constitutes smart growth, and definitions vary from locale to locale. The Smart Growth Network, a national network sponsored by the U.S. Environmental Protection Agency, promotes 10 principles of smart growth (see the list above). Universal agreement probably exists about four general concepts:

- Protecting the natural environment and preserving open space
- Encouraging inner-city redevelopment
- Making it easier to design innovative communities that encourage compact development
- Encouraging community and regional identity.[44]

The smart growth movement has important implications for local economic development practitioners. It suggests that new development must be considered from a regional perspective. How will growth at the urban periphery affect the health of the inner city, and vice versa? What kinds of demands will a new development project place on public infrastructure? What is the relation among residential, commercial, and industrial development? What affect will development have on the natural environment and the supply of open space, and vice versa? Strategies for attracting and retaining businesses should take the answers to these questions into account because the ability of the region to continue to grow and maintain its quality of life depends on how efficiently, effectively, and equitably growth is managed. Some of these issues are addressed again in the next section on social costs.

Social costs

The issue of the social costs of growth is also germane to business attraction and retention activities. Policymakers often focus on the job and income generation aspects of economic development at the expense of other considerations. They assume that "a rising tide will lift all boats" and, in doing so, eliminate social problems. In other cases, local policymakers simply fail to proactively consider the indirect social costs of new businesses before the new businesses arrive. Sometimes these costs are hidden or unanticipated, not revealing themselves until the policy has been in effect for a while. However, careful thought in the planning phase about the unintended effects of industrial recruitment strategies can successfully mitigate these costs.

Gaming and social pathologies One of the hottest targets of business attraction strategies in the United States today is the gambling, or gaming, industry. Whether it is traditional casino gambling, riverboat casino gambling, or betting on horse or dog races, many communities are looking to this industry to help them out of their economic doldrums. The payoffs in terms of visitor traffic and spending can be dramatic, but what is the impact of this kind of economic development on social problems such as poverty, homelessness, drug abuse, and blight? The experience of Atlantic City, New Jersey, suggests that gambling is not a panacea, and communities are legitimately concerned that gambling activities increase crime and other social problems. The discussion of gambling beginning on page 85 explores the issue of social costs and suggests that localities think twice before they open what might be a Pandora's box of social problems.

Some communities, with desperate economic problems, may see the legalization of gaming as a risk worth its potential costs because the cost of doing nothing is already high. Other communities may decide it is more important to avoid the cost associated with social pathologies linked to gambling than to take this path to economic development. Communities not in dire economic straits may choose to look for alternative strategies of economic development.

Business clustering and socioeconomic segregation Social costs of business attraction and retention are sometimes tied to business location decisions. Business clustering is the colocation of firms in the same or similar industries. It permits a variety of interactions, including joint venturing, resource pooling, just-in-time inventorying, and other benefits.[45] However, in conjunction with local zoning ordinances that tend to strictly segregate land uses, business clustering has created geographic nodes of business development that contribute to socioeconomic segregation.

Many of these business nodes are located in the suburbs, where transportation and housing costs are prohibitive for lower-middle-income and lower-income individuals and households. Clustering exacerbates the jobs-housing imbalance between inner cities and suburbs, and between suburbs with many large employers and those without large employers. Many people, particularly in low-paying jobs, can't afford to live near their places of work. In high-cost communities such as the major metropolitan areas of California, even middle-income persons may find themselves commuting for hours each day between affordable housing and places of employment.

This situation leads not only to gridlock and air pollution from auto emissions but also to lost family and civic time; it can even result in underemployment and unemployment. These are the social costs of business attraction policies that are oriented solely to the market needs of firms or that fail to consider the negative impacts of poorly conceived land use regulations.

A number of communities are thinking more comprehensively about their business attraction and retention strategies. Communities are beginning to include economic development elements in their housing and transportation plans in order to cut time, distance, and cost of travel. In Kentucky, the Cornerstone 2020 comprehensive plan for Louisville and Jefferson County provides a good example of this approach. In some high-growth states, like California, communities are being more aggressive and are forcing developers of large-scale commercial and industrial projects to either provide affordable housing or contribute to a fund for developing such housing near their projects as a condition of approval for their proposed developments.

Inner-city decline   Concern also exists, particularly in metropolitan areas, about the social costs that accompany continuing growth in suburbia and exurbia. As middle- and upper-income households flee the inner city, commercial and industrial employers follow them. This has drained the tax base of the central city while it has increased the proportion of the central city population that is in need of social services. The result has been further socioeconomic and racial segregation and "doughnut" metropolitan areas, with the "dough"—the money—surrounding an economic void at the center. Part of the blame can be placed on local economic development and planning strategies that have traditionally favored the attraction of firms to suburban and exurban sites at the expense of business retention efforts in the central city. This, in turn, has contributed to the decline of the inner city to the point that it is no longer attractive to companies.

As business retention gets greater attention, some metropolitan areas are focusing on their inner cities. The Urban Industrial Initiative (UII), a pilot program of the Philadelphia Industrial Development Corporation, seeks to retain approximately 330 manufacturing companies currently located in inner-city Philadelphia. These firms employ approximately 13,000 people and have in excess of $3 billion in sales. The UII is accomplishing this mission by building social capital among the firms and between the firms and the world outside central Philadelphia. Initial results have been encouraging: firms that, despite their relative proximity, did not previously know of each other's existence have entered into beneficial collaborative engagements, and none of these companies is considering leaving their present locations.[46]

Tourism and housing costs   Tourism activities can have social costs. For example, Branson, Missouri, has a large percentage of low-income households that are finding it harder to continue to live in Branson because of rapidly rising property values and housing costs resulting from growth. Other popular tourist destinations face similar problems.

TIFs and social equity   Another social-cost issue involving business attraction activities surrounds the use of tax increment financing, introduced on page 39. There has been great concern about using TIF when it involves tax revenues earmarked for education. Officials of school districts sometimes complain that cities and towns designate areas as tax increment districts that would have been developed anyway. Because any additional revenues a tax increment district could raise (based on increased property value) will be set aside for bond payments that will pay for improvements in the tax increment district, the school district will be precluded from receiving additional tax money from that TIF district. School district officials claim that money that would normally have come to them is "captured" when agreements are struck by others. Although they eventually should recapture their ability to tax on the increased values, they are prevented from doing so for a given period of time.

In response to this perceived problem, some states have compensated school districts for revenues estimated to be lost when tax increment districts are created. An example of this can be found in Minnesota, where the state school aid formula guarantees local districts a fixed amount of money per student.[47]

Some argue that, although TIF may ultimately result in greater tax revenues for the local school district, it is unfair to penalize students currently in the system by temporarily freezing revenues from the TIF district, particularly if it is a large one. This has become such an issue that some states—Michigan before it abandoned property taxes as a source of education funding is one example—have eliminated the school share of property tax revenues from TIF formulas.

Redistribution of wealth

Public spending on the incentives offered to businesses raises questions about the distribution of wealth. Many people argue that the money spent to attract and retain businesses would be better spent on education or social programs. At the core of this debate is the fact that most local economic development is undertaken by business and political elites. These groups—growth machines, some call them—pursue economic development to further their personal and collective agendas, which do not necessarily include alleviating the plight of the lower socioeconomic classes.[48] Thus, their policies encourage development, not redistribution. Nevertheless, the business and political elites see economic development as benefiting the entire community because any improvement to the economy will ultimately trickle down to low-income individuals and households.

Advocates of redistributive policy, on the other hand, seek broader citizen participation in the policy-making process, with the hope that those with a greater stake in the redistribution of wealth will be successful in pushing for the adoption of redistributive approaches to community problems. Although most business attraction programs are not redistributive, there appears to be some recent interest in attraction strategies that do more to benefit the less-affluent segment of communities. Empowerment zone and enterprise community programs were implemented as part of the Clinton administration attempt to make low-income, inner-city neighborhoods more attractive to businesses that might not otherwise locate there. While the incentives still go to individual businesses, the goal is to bring jobs and greater wealth to residents of the inner city.

Michael E. Porter's recent work on competitive advantage in the inner city has also spawned new interest by firms in investing in the central city and greater activity by inner-city community development corporations in industrial recruitment efforts.[49] Again, the focus is on luring firms, but the intent is to link the inner city more closely to the metropolitan economy, thereby increasing development and incomes in the inner city.

Attracting outside firms to the inner city has its drawbacks, however. Corporations that locate branch plants, grocery stores, or operations other than their headquarters in the inner city often have little real commitment to the neighborhood where the facility is located. If and when economic circumstances change, they may pull out of the neighborhood as easily as they came in. This has happened, with devastating consequences, in small, rural communities throughout the United States.[50] Corporate presence in the inner city can also result in a form of colonization. For example, when a grocery chain with headquarters in the suburbs of a metropolitan area opens a store in an inner-city neighborhood, it may employ local residents at low wages. While this provides new jobs, the profits reaped by the chain from selling groceries to neighborhood residents will typically go back to the chain's headquarters. This is less desirable to the community than having money generated by a business circulate locally.

Mom-and-pop shops, in contrast, are more likely to be owned by neighborhood residents, and money generated by these establishments can be recycled back into the community. However, economies of scale may make it difficult for small enterprises to compete with local outlets of massive corporations.

Another example of a type of colonization might be a manufacturing branch plant that locates in an inner-city neighborhood but has headquarters outside that neighborhood. The plant takes advantage of the low-cost labor to create a value-added product. The product can be sold around the world, but the profits do not come back to the neighborhood. In fact, the product may even be sold back to people in the neighborhood. Thus, some argue that the corporation has benefited twice at the expense of the neighborhood: first, from profits generated by sales and, second, from being able to employ low-wage laborers.

These are reasons that some people advocate business creation strategies over business attraction approaches. Homegrown businesses are thought to be more likely to remain loyal to the community, and profits generated are more likely to return to the local economy. Business creation is believed to be a more sustainable strategy for local economic development over time. In addition, if colonizable neighborhoods are defined as those without productive capacity in terms of goods or services, a feasible strategy to end colonization would be to generate capacity where none previously existed.

Creating productive capacity in inner-city neighborhoods can be a daunting task, given the inherent advantages of large multinational corporations with corporate locations outside the community and great technological capability. Decentralization of production to less-powerful interests in society also runs counter to the dominant U.S. trend of concentration of production and massive mergers of already large companies. Case study 4–1 describing Wautoma, Wisconsin, suggests that it is possible to attain some redistribution through the development of community-based businesses. In Wautoma, proactive government behavior helped establish production and service businesses that might not have been created without public sector assistance.

Another tool for redistributing wealth in inner cities is the microloan. See Chapter 4 for a discussion of this approach.

Role of government revisited and the need for collaboration

Government in the United States has traditionally played the role of watchdog of the public interest and regulator of private sector activities. The recent antitrust suit brought against Microsoft by the federal government typifies this watchdog role. Regulation of large corporate entities has been in place in the United States for more than 100 years, beginning in 1887 with the Interstate Commerce Act that established the Interstate Commerce Commission to regulate the railroads—a newly dominant industry—and establish "just and reasonable" rates. In 1890 the Sherman Antitrust Act prohibited all monopolization or attempts to monopolize. This act directly affected trusts and other monopolistic businesses that dominated many areas of production including oil, sugar, whiskey, and meatpacking.

Despite these regulatory activities, for the most part the public sector left economic development to the private sector. Then, in the first half of the twentieth century, state governments began intervening in private markets to attract development. In the 1930s states, particularly in the southern region of the United States, began to offer financial incentives for business attraction purposes.[51]

Today the boundaries between public and private roles in economic development continue to blur. On the one hand, it has become apparent that markets are imperfect; therefore, pure market-driven development strategies are flawed and incapable of generating efficient, effective, and equitable economic development without government intervention at some level. On the other hand, since the inception of the Reagan brand of New Federalism, it is also clear that local governments do not have the resources to deliver the kinds of services their citizens would like. This has created a need for collaboration between the sectors, each bringing its own resources and expertise, to solve community problems.[52]

In the realm of business attraction and retention, this collaboration has tended to manifest itself in a variety of ways—some focused on accomplishing a single project and others on carrying out long-term development strategies. In many communities, the need for collaboration has resulted in structural changes in the way attraction and retention efforts are implemented and managed.

From the 1930s until the early 1980s, a public agency usually carried out economic development activities. The agency might have been a city or county government office assigned to deliver business attraction and retention inducements. Today, however, an increasing number of communities have created new, nonprofit entities—typically various kinds of public-private partnerships—that involve local governments, chambers of commerce, and other local players in the economic development arena:

- **Mixed partnerships,** involving formal collaboration among the public, private, and nonprofit sectors to undertake economic development programs or projects
- **Limited partnerships,** in which one or more of the partners manages the undertaking and bears most of the risk while attracting other limited-liability investors
- **Mixed condominiums,** wherein individual partners divide ownership of the given development project in order to spread the costs
- **Government authorities,** which can include downtown development authorities, local economic development authorities, state development authorities, and port authorities
- **Private corporations with a public purpose,** which may be either for-profit or nonprofit.[53]

While public-private partnerships make a great deal of sense in today's development environment, they are not always successful. Critics argue that they are not partnerships at all, but rather co-optation of the public sector by the private—a claim that has often been true because the public sector has typically lacked the business and negotiation savvy of the private sector and cannot always compete as an equal partner. Focused private sector interests also may be able to greatly influence elected leaders who are interested in protecting and expanding their tax base. Over time both partners have gained experience in creating and maintaining collaborative relationships by making use of several key factors:

- Clearly identified mutual goals and benefits
- Tailored structures and roles to fit these goals

- Clearly delineated roles for the partners
- Strong leadership.[54]

A growing phenomenon is regional collaboration—in some areas, local governments, private sector interests, and nonprofit organizations work together at a regional level to implement economic development strategies. In the southeastern United States, the number of regional partnerships for economic development more than tripled over a 10-year period, from 5 in 1987 to 18 in 1997, while a recent study identified a total of 191 regional partnerships for economic development in U.S. metropolitan areas. An overwhelming majority of these partnerships target their efforts to specific industries.[55]

The role of government in business attraction and retention efforts has clearly changed over time. With the emergence of public-private partnerships and regional cooperation comes a new set of challenges. And, as the lines between public and private efforts in this arena become less distinct, new ethical questions arise. Continuing due diligence must be performed if attraction and retention are to benefit the entire community.

Case studies and research case

Two case studies and one research case are offered below for a glimpse at the variety of business attraction and retention strategies at work throughout the United States. The first case, an effort to retain the international air hub of United Parcel Service in Louisville, Kentucky, explores a unique approach to business retention—a partnership created to help UPS solve a labor availability problem.

The second case examines Alabama's success at attracting Mercedes-Benz to locate an assembly plant near Tuscaloosa. It provides insight into what it takes to be successful at the business attraction game. The research case study examines gambling as an economic development strategy.

Case study 3–1 | ## United Parcel Service and Metropolitan College: Retaining jobs in Louisville, Kentucky

The employment environment of the late 1990s required innovative thinking by employers wishing to attract and retain workers as well as governments hoping to protect their economic base. In contrast to slack economic times when employers could advertise a handful of jobs and receive hundreds of applications, the low-unemployment period of the 1990s was marked by aggressive employer initiatives to find and retain capable workers.

United Parcel Service

In 2000, United Parcel Service (UPS) was the largest single employer in the Louisville metropolitan area. Founded in 1907 in Seattle, Washington, UPS grew to become the largest package distribution company in the world. The company served more than 200 countries and territories and employed more than 330,000 people worldwide. In 1998, UPS's revenues exceeded $24.8 billion on a volume of 3.14 billion packages and documents. UPS has been recognized as *Fortune* magazine's most-admired transportation company. In 2000, after the events described in this case study, its Metropolitan College program was named the top workforce training program in the country by *Business Facilities* magazine.[56]

In 1997, UPS threatened to relocate its Louisville air hub if it could not be guaranteed an adequate supply of package sorters for its next-day air operations. Although UPS received approximately $120 to $140 million in the usual tax breaks, it also needed 6,000 additional employees, in particular, workers to staff the hardest-to-fill, part-time, package-handling night shift.[57] Turnover in the $8.50/hour jobs is a constant headache for UPS, which invests $1,400 per hire in training costs.

The threat to relocate immediately caught the attention of state and local leaders who not only wanted to retain the company but wanted to make sure that UPS would go ahead with a planned $1.1 billion expansion. To secure this expansion, public officials devised a plan that would ease the company's anxiety over its ability to find adequate numbers of part-time package handlers. A result of this plan was the creation of the Metropolitan College program, an innovative partnership between public and private leaders dedicated to solving common problems.

Metropolitan College program

In the fall of 1998, in what was pronounced as the first program of its kind, UPS, the University of Louisville, Jefferson Community College, Jefferson Technical College, and the commonwealth of Kentucky joined forces to expedite free tuition at any of the three local colleges for about 1,000 part-time, night shift UPS employees. The agreement among UPS, the commonwealth of Kentucky, and colleges in the Louisville metropolitan area created a win-win situation: it promised to bolster the public tax base, increase student enrollment at local colleges, and assure an ample supply of workers for UPS.

Each of the three colleges has separate strengths and capacities. Jefferson Technical College offers more than 35 degree and certificate programs and provides education and training for those already in the workforce, retraining for those who want to change occupations, and lifelong learning for anyone in the community. Jefferson Community College focuses on small classes and features programs in culinary arts, early childhood education, nursing, occupational therapy, and physical therapy. The University of Louisville, an up-and-coming research university, offers more than 170 programs in a wide variety of subjects. Each college controls its own admissions.

The collaborative program (officially labeled Metropolitan College) provides tuition waivers and employee benefits. UPS assumes responsibility for payment of half the tuition cost at the end of each semester for students who are employed at the UPS next-day air operation if those students take classes at Jefferson Technical College, Jefferson Community College, or the University of Louisville; sign an employment contract each semester; and receive a grade of D or better in their classes. Students who withdraw or receive a failing grade pay for the classes on their own.

As part of Metropolitan College, participating students apply to their educational institution for financial aid each year. Because the UPS/Metropolitan College program pays full tuition only for Kentucky residents and residents of some Indiana counties, applicants from other areas must pay the difference between in-state and out-of-state tuition. The commonwealth of Kentucky assumes responsibility for half the tuition (the other half is paid by UPS) if tuition is not paid by federal grants or college scholarships. Classes for the Metropolitan College program (colloquially termed UPSU) are set up for late afternoons and early evenings to accommodate the late-night schedules of package handlers. Some classes in the fall semester end by Thanksgiving so that students can work extra hours at UPS during the peak shipping season. Special bus routes run each night from the three college campuses to the company's sorting center.[58]

Students attending at least half time (6 credits) each semester (fall, spring, and summer) or 18 hours for fall and spring become eligible for a housing allowance. Students are required to work at UPS 12 months each year. Those who decide to take off from work beyond their allotted vacation time might not be able to return to the program.[59]

Recruitment for UPS next-day air operators

The Metropolitan College program represents just one component of an aggressive campaign by UPS to attract and retain part-time package sorters. The full strategy to expand the number of available workers includes job matching (pairing two part-time jobs—one at UPS, the other at a local company), recruiting workers from economically depressed areas in the state, attracting workers from parts of the metropolitan area that have high unemployment rates, and finding ways to make the package-handling jobs more attractive to college students.

One problem with the job-matching approach is that workers who were interested in this option were already able to exercise it in the tight job market. A problem with recruiting workers from economically depressed areas of the state is the reluctance of rural and small-town Kentuckians to move to the "big city" of Louisville. UPS also found that when it recruited workers from pockets of high unemployment within the city of Louisville, it also had to address issues such as child care, providing mentors for workers, and the need to teach English to job prospects. By 1999, it was evident that the fourth approach—attracting college students—was the most promising.[60] That year it was reported that more than 930 students were enrolled in Metropolitan College and another 500 were on a waiting list.

To attract workers, UPS created advertisements that emphasized the advantages of physical fitness and how work as a package handler could lead to looking good, having more energy, increasing body toning, and enhancing flexibility. Advertised financial benefits included 100 percent paid tuition, up to $65 per class for books, and $1,240 per year for designated housing. In addition to these benefits, students can qualify for health benefits, paid vacations and holidays, 401(k) savings plans, and stock ownership.[61] Total annual benefits to students (including wages, loans, housing benefits, book stipend, and tuition) were estimated to be $15,560.[62] By the fall of 2000, students had access to 224 apartments in a new four-story building adjoining the University of Louisville campus. The apartments can house 493 students, and they offer amenities such as a courtyard, a swimming pool, a volleyball court, and 24-hour security.[63]

Perceptions of Metropolitan College

In an interview in early 2000, the executive director of Metropolitan College noted that the program benefits from a great deal of political backing, especially from the governor of Kentucky, Paul Patton. The executive director felt that the initial nervousness on the part of all parties involved in the creation of the program already had eased. UPS is pleased because students stay on the job for longer periods of time than other part-time package handlers and are likely to view their work as a several-year opportunity to better themselves instead of as just a low-paying, dead-end, part-time job. Educators' initial concerns that the company would meddle in university affairs have proved unfounded. The executive director responded to critics who charge that the program's basic trade-off—free classes for undesirable work hours—exploits the lower- and middle-income people who are most likely to sign up; he noted that the proper comparison is with the opportunity for education if the program did not exist.[64]

UPS had an eight-year goal of hiring 2,200 students through the Metropolitan College program, but by February of 2000 (after fewer than two years of operation) the program had 1,800 students. In 2000, when

90 percent of the participants were from the local Louisville area, Metropolitan College officials began recruiting more aggressively statewide. Open houses were held in the economically depressed eastern Kentucky cities of Ashland, Prestonburg, and Hazard in an effort to attract participants to the Metropolitan College program.[65] Participation from eastern Kentucky is still lower than desired, however. Many rural residents express discomfort with the idea of living in a large city. Housing students in a neighboring rural county and busing them into UPS is one of a number of ideas for improving the recruitment of workers from outside the city of Louisville.

By 2001, UPS already exceeded its 2005 objective of hiring 2,100 part-time package handlers. A total of 2,100 had been hired; 1,100 were attending Jefferson Community College, 960 were attending the University of Louisville, and 70 were attending Jefferson Technical College.[66]

Metropolitan College:
A model for future private-public partnerships?

The associate provost of the University of Louisville, the president of Greater Louisville, Inc. (GLI), and the executive director of Metropolitan College believed that Metropolitan College was working well, could be replicated, and could serve as a model for communities. They believed, however, that a convergence of essential factors had transpired in Louisville. First, the program had the necessary political support. The governor of Kentucky, Paul Patton, brought all essential parties together. Second, political pressure came about in an environment of crisis: the immediate prospect of the relocation of UPS outside Kentucky. Third, the private sector firm (UPS) was willing to contribute a portion of the funding for the program. Finally, the institutions of higher learning agreed to participate in the program, a choice no doubt influenced by the fact that all these institutions depend on the state for funding and an uncooperative attitude could have been detrimental to their futures.

The associate provost at the University of Louisville contended that the model could probably be implemented in areas with a shortage of workers. He believed that the program could help students (particularly students from eastern Kentucky), the University of Louisville (through funding for additional faculty as well as money targeted to advances in the University of Louisville's information technology programs), and the private company (by expanding the available labor supply and reducing turnover). He noted that money for new faculty hires had already been provided to the three institutions of higher learning and that existing faculty would not have to teach additional courses. The University of Louisville hired new faculty to teach in the program and tried to avoid reliance on temporary or adjunct faculty. In addition, with money from the Metropolitan College program, the University of Louisville set up a library laboratory specifically designated for the program's students.

The president of GLI, the economic development arm of the Louisville Chamber of Commerce and the city of Louisville, was also generous in his praise of the Metropolitan College program. He noted that consultants had told UPS that relocating to Rickenbacker International Airport in Columbus, Ohio, would be in the best interest of the company. With such a move, UPS would better satisfy its hiring needs (given the flat trend lines for growth in the city of Louisville and the presence of approximately 50,000 students at Ohio State University). The president of GLI concluded that the Metropolitan College program was instrumental in preserving an important part of the economic base of the Louisville area and helped students to reach their educational goals.

Gains seem to have accrued to all of the parties involved. The three universities acquired additional students, tuition money, and goodwill from powerful political leaders such as Governor Patton. Public leaders and economic development officials took credit for keeping jobs in the state. UPS enjoyed improved retention of its part-time package handlers. On the night shift, the average turnover among workers who were not students was roughly 100 percent in 1999, but only 20 percent of Metropolitan College students have quit UPS.[67]

Community leaders involved with Metropolitan College found a solution to UPS's problem of retaining low-wage, night-shift workers when both private and public leaders came together. Their solution is consistent with the general idea of cooperative public-private approaches to economic development that marked the 1990s.[68] The Louisville program differs from others, however, in that it uses the considerable resources of the state to alter one of the factors of production—labor supply—that confronts a large, private sector employer. In supply-and-demand terms, the Metropolitan College program expands the supply of a special group of workers—the physically fit, dependable, relatively low-wage workers who are willing and able to work part-time on night shifts. Metropolitan College provides the reward of education to increase the number of such workers, and the disincentive of having to pay for their own tuition deters students from leaving their jobs at UPS.

UPS has expanded its education initiatives. In August 1999, it launched the Earn & Learn program, in which students can earn a starting salary of $8.50 an hour, get $3,000 in tuition assistance per calendar year, and qualify for loans from UPS of $2,000 per year. The company absorbs a portion of the loans depending upon how long students stay on their jobs. By the fall of 2000, approximately 8,000 students were participating in the Earn & Learn program at 40 of the largest UPS locations around the country.[69] This program (similar but not identical to the Metropolitan College program) was actually initiated in the city of Louisville.

The Louisville example suggests that universities can be mobilized to expand a community's pool of hard-to-find workers; this is especially valuable in tight labor markets such as those of the late 1990s. In addition to helping businesses meet their immediate labor needs, universities find that by instituting innovative programs such as Metropolitan College they can also assist in expanding opportunities for average citizens. In the tight labor markets of the future, universities might increase their assistance to businesses that need to fill vital jobs.

Case study 3-2   Luring Mercedes to Alabama

In September of 1993 a management team from world-renowned Mercedes-Benz AG, a unit of Daimler Benz AG (now DaimlerChrysler) decided to build its first automobile plant outside of Germany—in the state of Alabama. This case study describes the development of the plan that lured Mercedes to Alabama, relates various assessments of the costs and benefits of the plan, and offers conclusions about what the Mercedes project means for future job attraction strategies.

The Alabama plan

The decision of Mercedes to locate its plant in Vance, a tiny hamlet in the red clay hills of Alabama—12 miles east of the university town of Tuscaloosa and 32 miles west of Birmingham, the state's largest city—was not entirely expected.[70] North Carolina or South Carolina—states where many German companies had already located operations—seemed the more likely choice. In contrast, Alabama had a struggling education system, the fifth-highest poverty rate in the country, a history of racial problems, and a largely unskilled labor force. Mercedes nevertheless seemed to be attracted by a $253 million package of tax incentives, site acquisition and preparation, highway improvements, utilities, training payments, and other personalized incentives such as the special Saturday School run by the University of Alabama to help German students keep up with the math and science standards of students in Germany.

Although some analysts stated that Alabama foolishly "gave the farm away," others claimed that the package was typical of the job retention strategies that marked the early 1990s. Alabama did not want to lose out in what may described as bidding wars for economic development. Alabama had seen its neighbor Tennessee acquire a $1.9 billion Saturn plant in Spring Hill, Tennessee. The Saturn plant was built in Tennessee after the state and General Motors negotiated a package in which the state provided funding for industrial training, highway access, other public works, and property tax reductions—although among contenders for the plant, Tennessee did not offer the lowest taxes. Of the 15 states that were seriously considered for the Saturn plant, Tennessee was sixth lowest in taxes. Other factors such as Tennessee's central location, work ethic, right-to-work law, low wages, and proximity to the state's Nissan plant outweighed the financial and tax considerations."[71]

In 1992, South Carolina had lured a BMW plant with a package of at least $130 million in incentives. Such incentive packages were not unusual for the time. In 1992, Northwest Airlines acquired $270 million in loans from the state of Minnesota, and New York City awarded $30 million to both the Morgan Stanley Group and the Kidder, Peabody Group when these prosperous brokerage companies threatened to move their operations to the New Jersey or Connecticut suburbs if they did not receive tax breaks.[72]

What Alabama officials did to land the Mercedes plant tells the story of job attraction economic development competition of the time. When Alabama officials started to court Mercedes seriously, North Carolina was considered the front-runner for the plant, and Mercedes had so little interest in locating in Alabama that Andreas Renschler, head of the Mercedes site selection team, stated that he did not even plan to visit.

In 1993, Renschler was a 38-year-old, fast-rising Mercedes executive with a taste for rock and roll and an assignment to recruit a management team to conceive, design, and build from scratch a manufacturing facility to construct and market globally a sport-utility vehicle (SUV) costing in excess of $35,000. This vehicle was to uphold the Mercedes-Benz image of high quality and was to contain an unusual three-valve-per-cylinder V-6 engine with a five-speed automatic transmission, rack-and-pinion steering, an electronically controlled four-wheel drive, and dual front and side air bags. Within a month, the project was formally incorporated into a new company, Mercedes-Benz United States International, Inc. The new company had a mandate to produce and deliver 60,000 to 70,000 new SUVs annually by fall 1997.[73]

While Mercedes was seriously considering North Carolina, where the Mercedes parent company Daimler-Benz AG had already built Freightliner trucks, Alabama officials sprang into action. The new governor of Alabama, Jim Folsom, was eager to make history. He appointed Billy Joe Camp, former secretary of state under two governors, as head of the Alabama Development Office. Camp and Folsom aggressively courted Mercedes. They agreed to meet all of Mercedes's requests, even a request for the state to assume responsibility for the salaries of Mercedes's 1,500 workers during

Table 3–1

Alabama's package of incentives

Incentive	Cost to Alabama (in millions of dollars)
Acquire land for plant site in Vance, Alabama	17.4
Train employees of Mercedes plant	60.0
Pay for part of plant construction	42.6
Build a visitor center	30.0
Improve roads	58.0
Extend utilities	19.5
Abate sales taxes	8.1
Miscellaneous	17.7
Total cost	253.3

the first year. North Carolina's governor and secretary of state had unequivocally rejected the notion of paying wages for Mercedes. The German company had argued that in the first year the workers would really be in training, not yet producing any automobiles.

The Alabama full-court press was impressive. When Renschler decided not to visit the state, Alabama officials invited others on the selection team to meet with Japanese and British managers of foreign-owned companies that were located in Alabama. The head of Alabama's state pension fund offered to put money into the project. A group of businesses led by Alabama Power agreed to provide an $11 million subsidy. Businesses promised to buy Mercedes vehicles, and local government agencies offered low-interest loans. Members of the site selection team were excited enough to convince Renschler to postpone his return to Germany and visit Alabama.

Renschler's trip would prove to be fruitful for Mercedes. In an effort to satisfy Mercedes's demands, Governor Folsom hurried legislative approval of special tax concessions (dubbed Alabama's Mercedes Law). Alabama officials even agreed to place Mercedes's distinctive emblem (free of charge) atop the scoreboard for a nationally televised football game. To satisfy the company's land request, Tuscaloosa County officials went door-to-door negotiating to buy people's homes. The land was then offered to Mercedes for $100. A topographical map that normally would take four months to prepare was completed in four weeks and sent to Mercedes-Benz consultants by chartered jet to avoid missing a deadline. In August of 1993, when Mercedes needed more information, Governor Folsom canceled his appointments and flew to Daimler-Benz headquarters in Stuttgart, Germany, on three-days' notice.

To allay worries about Alabama's racial history, the governor conveyed the message that Alabama was no more the state it had been in the 1950s and 1960s than Germany was the country it had been under the Nazis. Alabama's promised education spending (including paying salaries during training) was double any other state's promise. Alabama was the clear choice. Billy Joe Camp stated that the project was simply worth more to Alabama that it was to any other state.[74] Details of Alabama's $253.3 million incentive package are in Table 3–1 on this page.[75]

The $253.3 million package was controversial. Critics who denounced the agreement as overly generous claimed that the costs of attracting the

Mercedes plant could never be justified and that the package represented corporate welfare that would hurt the state in the long run. Others, however, supported the venture, and by 2001 the supporters were winning converts. The diversity of opinion surrounding the Alabama incentive plan reflected disagreement among citizens about the value of job attraction strategies.

Criticism and support for the Alabama incentive package

When Alabama landed the Mercedes plant in 1993, officials of competitor states claimed the state had given up too much in the name of economic development. An economic development official in North Carolina stated that the Alabama legislature had gone too far in its bid for Mercedes. He contended that the Mercedes plant could not jump-start an economy as moribund as Alabama's and the state would have been better off saving the money for education. Other state recruiters screamed that the deal for Mercedes was a dangerous escalation of giveaways to corporations. J. Mac Holladay of the Governor's Development Council of Georgia blamed Alabama for escalating "absurd" demands for incentives by relocating companies.[76]

When the deal was finalized, the *New York Times* wrote that Alabama was spending far beyond its means. A Georgia newspaper said that Alabama was dreaming up ways to sock it to the poor. The *Wall Street Journal* observed that Alabama would pay dearly. Anger over the incentives helped to defeat Governor James Folsom in 1994. Former labor secretary Robert Reich stated that Alabama's tax base would erode. Educators in Alabama contended that tax incentives would reduce the amount of income tax revenue to pay for schools and teachers.

As SUV production started in 1997, some of the early skepticism over the plant began to dissipate. A senior economist at the Federal Reserve Bank of Atlanta stated that the general feeling was that the deal may not turn out to be crazy. Auto parts suppliers began moving into the area. In 1999 *Forbes* speculated that Alabama might have made a smart investment.[77] In 1998, Mercedes built an $80 million expansion and employed 1,800 people, 300 more than the company originally planned to employ by 2000. A study by an economist at Auburn University at Montgomery estimated that Daimler-Chrysler was spending $1.1 million in Alabama every year for supplies, electricity, and other resources. It was also estimated that Alabama was getting back $15 million a year in increased income, sales, and property taxes. Much of the $15 million was spent for schools, roads, and police. Bringing Mercedes to Alabama may have also helped to bring in other foreign companies. In May 1999 the Japanese auto company Honda chose Lincoln, Alabama, for a $400 million engine and auto assembly plant that promised to employ 1,500 workers in 2002.

By 2001, it had become evident that the worst fears of the critics had not been realized. DaimlerChrysler had been so successful selling its M-Class SUV that the waiting list was five months long. Mercedes planned a $600 million capital investment to increase the plant's output capacity to 160,000 vehicles a year. The expansion would create an additional 2,000 jobs at the plant.[78]

Conclusions

The offering of large tax incentives to lure Mercedes to Alabama was a gamble that is still difficult to assess. It appears, however, that some benefits have already been acquired. Perhaps the biggest long-term payoff to Alabama will be in terms of image. Companies and economically productive citizens may be more willing to locate in Alabama if its reputation for ignorance, lynchings, and racism begins to fade. The *Financial Post* of Toronto reported in 1993 that the decision by Mercedes was an immense psychological boost for Alabama, a state that still suffered from a redneck image and had lagged behind neighboring states in attracting high-profile investment. In the *Washington Post* on February 21, 1994, Auburn University professor Wayne Flynt predicted, "A lot of people are going to have to rethink their image of rednecks and good old boys. Or at least change it to rednecks and good old boys who make darned good cars."[79]

Evidence from the Mercedes plant in Alabama may force analysts to rethink their criticism about "giving away the store" to large corporations. It is relatively easy to calculate costs in terms of lost taxes, training, infrastructure, plant construction, and other expenditures. It is more difficult to definitively assess indirect benefits and the costs of inaction. Alabama had not aggressively pursued high-quality jobs for many years, and the state's image suffered. The Mercedes case therefore is as much about intangibles (such as image change) as it is about job creation. An image change such as Alabama may be experiencing can attract other businesses that previously were scared off by a stereotypical perception of the state. The multiplier effect of an image change for Alabama is tangible but difficult to quantify. It is a fact, however, that Alabama's economic growth lagged behind growth of other states when Alabama was burdened by its old image.

In economies where growth is sluggish, state and local governments are pressured to offer more and more concessions to large corporations. These concessions can gain acclaim for politicians who need to demonstrate tangible accomplishments during an election cycle. It is too early to say whether the heavily criticized pattern of chasing big companies will prevail in the future. What may change, however, is that rather than "stealing" factories from other states, state governments may try to attract global companies that promise to make major investments in the area. These investments are clearly worth a great deal to communities, which are likely to be in competition with other communities that also offer incentive packages. Large multinational corporations have a vested interest in trying to negotiate what they believe is the best deal they can get from communities. Although these companies may assist local development, their primary interest is in maximizing profit for their stockholder. When they offer benefits to large companies, communities take a calculated risk that the costs of corporate incentives will eventually be outweighed by future benefits.

Research case 3–1 Attracting jobs: Is gambling a good economic development bet?

Gambling no longer is an activity that is routinely condemned by government officials who wish to impose ethical standards on their communities. In some parts of the country gambling has been embraced and promoted as a legitimate strategy of economic development. In theory, lotteries, racetracks, casinos, and electronic games can fill government coffers with funds to support worthy government programs. Supporters say gambling can provide jobs with good benefits to people who are either unemployed or underemployed. To become legitimized, however, it has been necessary to transform perceptions of gambling from a problematic social issue to an ethically neutral form of entertainment. Government has helped in this transformation by openly hawking various forms of state gambling such as lotteries and numbers games.

Growth, but emerging resistance

Some critics of gambling (the industry prefers to call it gaming) warn of its potential impact on personal behavior and on the mores of society. Nevertheless, the industry continues to grow. In 1999, 37 states plus the District of Columbia had lotteries, 21 states sanctioned casinos, and 45 states supported bingo. All but two states (Hawaii and Utah) allowed some form of gaming. Revenue from legal gambling was estimated to have risen from $10.4 billion a year in 1992 to $50.9 billion a year in 1997. By the end of the 1990s gambling revenues had increased every year for more than two decades.[80]

Much of the increase in gambling revenue was linked to the growth of casinos. Before 1978, when casinos were legalized in the state of New Jersey, Nevada was the only state to permit casino gambling. Since the late 1980s, land-based casinos have operated in South Dakota and Colorado. In 1991, the first river-based casinos began operating in Iowa and Illinois. Riverboat casinos opened later in Mississippi (1992), Louisiana (1993), Missouri (1994), and Indiana (1995). Casinos became a source of cash for state and local officials who suddenly discovered the value of legalized gaming. These officials, in general, express a great deal of satisfaction with the gambling venues that they sanctioned.[81]

Critics of casinos note, however, that in places such as Atlantic City, local casinos have generated revenue for stockholders or for the state of New Jersey but have provided little direct benefit to Atlantic City itself. Studies indicated that by many measures Atlantic City was negatively affected by the casinos. A well-respected 1983 report concluded that from the standpoint of the poor in Atlantic City, the casinos had little impact because most of the money went to companies outside the city. Furthermore, because casino food and alcohol were subsidized or given away free, existing restaurants and bars found themselves at a competitive disadvantage and were forced to close.

In a decade, Atlantic City lost 40 percent of its independent restaurants. Four years after the introduction of casinos, about one-third of the city's retail businesses had closed and the anticipated boon to employment had not materialized. The year before casinos were introduced, the unemployment rate in Atlantic City was 30 percent higher than the state average. Ten years later, the unemployment rate for the city was 50 percent higher than the state average. Since the introduction of casinos into Atlantic City, the city has lost more than 25 percent of its population. Three years following the opening of its first casino, there was an approximate tripling of crime. Sternlieb and Hughes remarked that prostitution was so widespread that the city's chief of police recommended that it be legalized.[82]

While the Atlantic City experience raised questions, it did not stop other cities from taking their own chances. In 1999, Detroit became the largest U.S. city to sponsor casino gambling. The $220 million MGM Grand Detroit represented the first of three planned casinos for the city. Mayor Dennis Archer hoped that the casinos would give the city's ailing economy a "shot in the arm" and predicted that $250 million in casino taxes could be generated over four years. The three casinos were expected to add 7,000 to 8,000 jobs in Detroit, a jurisdiction in desperate need of economic activity. Unemployment in the city was more than double the unemployment rate in the Detroit suburbs.[83]

Smaller cities have also jumped aboard the gambling bandwagon. In 2000, Mohegan Indian tribal leaders unveiled a planned $800 million expansion of their Mohegan Sun casino, to be located in Montville, Connecticut, 128 miles from New York City. The expansion was expected to double the 20,000 daily visitors and add 4,000 jobs to the 5,500 workers already

Electronic gaming

Robert Hunter, a clinical psychologist in Las Vegas who specializes in problem and pathological gambling, called electronic gambling devices "the distilled essence of gambling" and claims that video poker's hold on people is produced by the game's rapid pace, people's opportunity to play for long periods of time, and the mesmerizing effect of music and rapidly flashing lights. Hunter notes that users of electronic gambling devices escape into the machine and make the world go away. He calls these electronic devices the "crack cocaine of gambling," suggesting that this new, low-cost gaming product could quickly addict users to engage in self-destructive behavior.

Source: *Gambling Impact and Behavior Study: Report to the National Gambling Impact Study Commission* (National Opinion Research Center at the University of Chicago, April 1, 1999), 2–6, www.norc.uchicago.edu/new/pdf/gamble.pdf.

employed. Tribal leaders expected that their new expansion (expected to be completed in 2002) would increase gross gambling revenues to more than $1 billion annually; up from approximately $750 million. The new complex would include a 40-story hotel and a 10,000-seat sports arena.

Mohegan leaders hoped their entertainment complex would capture business from the Foxwoods Resort Casino, located 10 miles away in Ledyard and run by the Pequot Indian tribe. The Foxwoods casino opened in 1992 and by 2000 was grossing over $1 billion a year. The Pequot and Mohegan tribes were the only two Native American tribes in Connecticut recognized by the federal government, a necessary prerequisite to opening casinos.[84]

Detroit and Connecticut were not alone in endorsing gambling as a strategy of economic development. The state of Illinois legalized riverboat gambling, hoping to capture the lucrative Chicago market. In addition to Illinois, the states of Alabama, North Carolina, South Carolina, Tennessee, West Virginia, Massachusetts, and Kentucky all considered legalizing either casinos or lotteries. Some states enjoyed multiple gambling venues. For example, in 1999 the state of Florida allowed wagering at 17 dog tracks and 4 horse tracks, and California allowed wagering at 13 horse tracks.[85]

In a few instances, however, gaming interests have failed to win approval. In 1999 the South Carolina Supreme Court ruled that the state's electronic gaming devices had to be unplugged within a year. Gambling opponents were energized by the court ruling. Church groups had been campaigning against the video gaming devices. The legal victory in South Carolina combined with Alabama's October 1999 rejection of a lottery encouraged church groups in their efforts to limit gambling in the South.

Economic benefits of gambling

Confusion surrounds the question of how many new jobs and how much revenue casinos and other forms of gambling have created. According to the accounting firm Arthur Andersen, in 1995 the casino industry recorded $22 to $25 billion in total revenues, paid a total of $2.9 billion in direct taxes, directly employed 300,000 people, disbursed $7.3 billion in wages, paid an average wage countrywide of approximately $26,000, created 13 direct jobs for every $1 million in revenues, supported 400,000 indirect jobs, and spent a large majority of its revenues within the United States.[86]

Some analysts, however, claimed that these figures grossly overestimate the economic benefit of gambling. They argue that the regional benefits from gambling can come about only if visitors from outside the area leave their money at the casinos and go home. Unless an area has the prospect of attracting a major flow of national or international visitors, the only justification for licensing a casino is for the enjoyment value to local citizens.[87]

The National Gambling Impact Study Commission in 1999 noted that gambling could produce significant economic benefits. This commission observed that legalized gambling has had positive economic benefits in some communities where workers are able to secure unionized jobs with benefits and better pay than they had previously received.[88]

Native Americans noted that the expansion of gambling on tribal property provides jobs and generates money for worthwhile public services. Mayors from Mississippi, Illinois, New Jersey, and Iowa also testified that revenues for their cities had grown as a consequence of legalizing gambling. These officials cite studies that document positive impacts in terms of employment, income, tax revenues, tourism, recreational opportunities, and local property values. Their favorable view was not universally accepted, however. A telephone survey by the National Opinion Research Council of a sample of nationally representative households found mixed perceptions about the value of casinos. A majority of the respondents surveyed complained that casinos provide low-paying and/or part-time jobs with few or no benefits.[89]

Critics of gambling claim that economic development studies do not adequately measure social costs that are linked to gambling. The National Gambling Impact Study Commission maintains that analysis of the economic effects of gambling is "poorly developed and quite incomplete." The commission notes that the social costs of expanding gambling must be considered in any assessment of gambling's net benefit. Such an assessment is problematic because, according to the commission, the social costs of gambling are too ill defined for firm conclusions to be reached.[90]

Social costs of gambling

A number of studies have identified social costs linked to gambling. A 1997 Harvard University study estimated that there were 5.3 million adult problem gamblers, 2.2 million pathological gamblers, and 7.9 million adolescent problem or pathological gamblers in the United States. Studies in Mississippi and Louisiana estimated that approximately 7 percent of adults in these states were problem or pathological gamblers. Surveys in 17 other states estimated that the proportion of problem or pathological gamblers ranged from 1.7 percent of state populations to 7.3 percent.[91]

Negative life choices were linked to problem or pathological gambling. Behavior associated with this type of gambling includes suicide, divorce, homelessness, and family abuse or neglect. Behavior associated with adolescent problem or pathological gambling includes alcohol and drug use, truancy, low grades, and illegal activities to finance gambling. Surveys of nearly 400 Gamblers Anonymous members revealed that two-thirds of the respondents had contemplated suicide and 77 percent stated that they wanted to die. University of California, San Diego, sociologist David Phillips found that Las Vegas displayed the highest levels of suicide in the nation, for both residents and visitors. Nevada regularly reports the highest rate of suicide among the 50 states. In 1995, the suicide rate in Nevada was more than twice the national average. In Atlantic City, Phillips also found abnormally high suicide levels for residents and visitors.[92]

Other negative outcomes are linked to gambling. The National Gambling Impact Study Commission heard a great deal of testimony about the links between compulsive gambling and heightened levels of stress and tension in marriages. A spouse's gambling was identified as a significant factor in divorce. A study by the National Opinion Research Council reported that 53.5 percent of identified pathological gamblers were divorced compared with 18.2 percent of nongamblers and 29.8 percent of low-risk gamblers. In addition, spouses of compulsive gamblers suffered a greater incidence of a variety of emotional and physical problems.

Various studies link gambling to domestic violence. One such study contends that between one-quarter and one-half of spouses of compulsive gamblers are abused. A domestic violence counselor from Mississippi reported a 300 percent increase in the number of requests for domestic abuse intervention following the arrival of casinos in that state. The attorney general of Rhode Island noted a significant increase in domestic assaults after the opening of the nearby Foxwoods casino.

Individuals with gambling problems also constituted a relatively high percentage of the homeless population. A survey in Chicago found that 33 percent of homeless individuals cited gambling as a contributor to their condition. The Atlantic City rescue mission reported that 22 percent of its homeless clients linked their condition to gambling. In a survey of 1,100 clients at dozens of rescue missions across the nation, 18 percent of the homeless clients contended that gambling was a cause of their homelessness.[93]

Studies indicate that as many as 1.1 million adolescents between the ages of 12 and 18 could be classified as pathological gamblers. This represented a higher percentage of pathological gamblers than present in the adult population. Proximity to legalized gambling was cited as a major factor in encouraging adolescent gambling.[94]

Social costs of gambling can be considered from both individual and societal perspectives. Individual financial problems related to problem or pathological gambling include crime, loss of employment, and bankruptcy. Relatives and friends are often the source of money for gamblers. Employers experience losses in the form of lowered productivity, embezzlement, and time missed from work.

The National Gambling Impact Study Commission noted that social pathologies and addictions disable individuals and force others to pay for their dysfunctional behavior. The commission stated that in certain areas, the arrival of casino gambling produced benefits to the communities in the form of new and better jobs, increased purchasing power, and social support facilities such as schools and hospitals. The commission recognized, however, that it is not appropriate to speak of those benefits without acknowledging the unknown and presently unmeasured negative effects that arise from citizens who became problem or pathological gamblers. The central question therefore becomes whether the net increases in income and well-being from gambling are worth the acknowledged social costs.[95]

Gambling also is a regressive tax that falls disproportionately on those with less income. Riverboat casinos that draw many customers from depressed local areas transfer money from lower-income gamblers to upper-income casino owners who in all likelihood live outside the local community. Data indicate that riverboats are often located in poorer neighborhoods and that local residents gamble. A high proportion of casino winnings are awarded to residents of communities where casinos choose to locate,[96] which suggests that local residents assume a large share of the gambling tax burden. It also suggests that, to a great extent, social pathologies linked to gambling will not be exported to other areas but will manifest themselves at home.

The National Gambling Impact Study Commission

On June 18, 1999, the National Gambling Impact Study Commission delivered its final report to the president, Congress, governors, and tribal leaders.

Commission members were drawn from the gaming industry, labor, government, private industry, and the nonprofit sector; and many offered clear statements representing their various philosophies and self-interest.

One Native American representative to the commission stated that gaming furthered Indian self-determination and provided economic benefit to the surrounding communities. A former chair of the California Commission for Economic Development focused on such redeeming qualities of gaming as helping Native Americans achieve a better quality of life, providing Americans with better jobs, and helping some economically depressed communities. A labor representative asserted that those who called for analyzing the social costs of gambling had an obligation to consider costs of preventing low-wage workers from moving up to better-paying casino jobs. A casino industry executive expressed regrets that more of the positive impacts of gaming were not strongly identified in the commission report.

Negative perceptions of gaming were expressed by representatives of nonprofit organizations, who contended that on balance the American people were net losers in a society of pervasive gambling.

Perhaps the most incendiary antigambling rhetoric was expressed by psychologist and family advocate James Dobson. Dobson stated that gambling was a destroyer that ruined lives and wrecked families. He noted links between gambling and divorce, child abuse, domestic violence, bankruptcy, crime, and suicide. Dobson observed that when other activities, such as smoking, have been shown to be harmful, the hue and cry for regulations to warn and protect the public has been loud and long. He asserted that the silence of most American leaders about the risks of gambling was "deafening."

Source: *Gambling Impact and Behavior Study: Report to the National Gambling Impact Study Commission.*

State lotteries are also considered to be highly regressive because of the characteristics of lottery customers. Studies indicate that people with incomes under $10,000 contribute approximately 25 percent of state lottery losses, greatly exceeding their 11 percent proportion of total household income.[97]

Lotteries are also beset by ethical questions, specifically the question of whether government should promote activities of questionable value. William Safire, summarizing the objection to state-supported gambling, has contended that the state "belongs in the business of protecting and educating the public, not in the profitable dodge of bilking the public."[98]

Conclusions

Miles Law—Where you stand depends upon where you sit—predicts correctly that those who stand to gain economically from gambling will support it. On the issue of gambling, numerous interests support or oppose each other depending on their immediate self-interest. Elected government leaders often see gambling as a means of solidifying the city's economic base by bringing suburbanites to a moribund downtown area. Bureaucrats in agencies that are promised gaming revenues often support gambling to pay for agency activities. Owners of large casinos tend to support gambling when they will benefit from the operation but oppose it if they view it as competition.[99] In 1992, for example, Nevada casino owners joined forces with California's anti-casino factions to attack a proposed expansion of casinos into California. The Nevada owners—although they do not criticize gambling when it is in their own casinos—portrayed casinos as financial losers likely to lead to "increased crime, prostitution, laundering of money" and "a regressive form of entertainment" that would be "most damaging to minority populations."[100]

Gambling can be viewed as an individual social pathology, a societal menace, a viable tool for growth, a growing source of governmental revenue, and as a specific means of assisting deprived groups. Each perspective possesses some credibility. Whether the gaming industry can operate as a legitimate tool of economic development will depend largely on a resolution of these conflicting perspectives.

Summary

Economic development policy in local jurisdictions is often thought of as a series of related waves: from simple business attraction that makes use of financial and nonfinancial incentives, to retention and expansion of firms already in place, and then a flow into industrial clusters and networking, public-private partnerships, human-capital building, and strategic planning. Although research shows that location decisions by businesses are usually not determined by specific incentives—this leads to ongoing debate about the usefulness of attraction efforts—financial and nonfinancial retention strategies are seen as appropriate and welcome rewards for community loyalty.

Business attraction and retention incentives raise several policy issues. Offering an excellent quality of life is important for attracting desirable companies, and many communities are enhancing their tourist attractions and sustainable development efforts. Social costs of growth—an increase in dysfunction because of legalized gambling; the trend toward business clustering and the resulting gridlock, pollution problems, and decreased family time; and unevenly distributed benefits—can be serious issues. Large corporations often have little loyalty to where they locate, and economic conditions or better opportunities can cause them to relocate. Homegrown businesses are more likely to have enduring attachments to their communities. The nature of the government–private sector relationship is a topic of debate, as is the proper balance between the public and the private.

The two case studies and the research case provide practical examples for the issues presented here.

Study questions

- Under what circumstances might a business attraction strategy be the best economic development option for a local community?

- Compare a recent business attraction effort and a business retention effort undertaken by your state or local government. What were the benefits derived in each case? What were the costs of each? Which was more cost effective?

- How would you define quality of life? If you were a local economic development official, how would you go about taking into account quality-of-life considerations in your professional practice?

- What are the pros and cons of gambling as an economic development approach in depressed communities? Do the economic benefits outweigh the social costs? Why or why not?

- What type of public-private partnership is the Metropolitan College program? Who are the public and private participants in this partnership? What benefit(s) does each partner derive from its participation?

- If you were a local economic development official, what specific kinds of questions would you ask existing companies in order to determine how to proceed with your business retention efforts?

- Although geographic business clustering has potential social costs, what might be some of the economic development advantages of encouraging business clusters? How might a community go about encouraging business clusters while avoiding the jobs-housing imbalances discussed in this chapter.

- Can you think of other potential social costs of tax increment financing as a business attraction strategy (funding for education was noted in this chapter)? How might such costs be mitigated?

- Could the UPS case be accurately described as a third-wave economic development strategy? If so, list its specific third-wave characteristics. If not, why not?

1 Kevin T. Leicht and J. Craig Jenkins, "Three Strategies of State Economic Development: Entrepreneurial, Industrial Recruitment and Deregulation Policies in the American States," *Economic Development Quarterly* 8, no. 3 (1994): 256–269.

2 Blakely, *Planning Local Economic Development;* and Thomas S. Lyons and Roger E. Hamlin, *Creating an Economic Development Action Plan: A Guide for Development Professionals* (New York: Praeger, 1991).

3 Ted K. Bradshaw and Edward J. Blakely, "What Are 'Third-Wave' State Economic Development Efforts? From Incentives to Industrial Policy," *Economic Development Quarterly* 13, no. 3 (1999): 229–244.

4 Susan E. Clarke and Gary L. Gaile, "Local Politics in a Global Era: Thinking Locally, Acting Globally," *Annals of the American Academy of Political and Social Science* (1997): 28–43; and Doug Ross and Robert E. Friedman, "The Emerging Third Wave: New Economic Development Strategies in the '90s," *Entrepreneurial Economy Review* 9 (1990): 3–10.

5 Ross and Friedman, "The Emerging Third Wave."

6 Bradshaw and Blakely, "What Are 'Third-Wave' State Economic Development Efforts?"

7 R. Scott Fosler, "State Economic Policy: The Emerging Paradigm," *Economic Development Quarterly* 6, no. 1 (1992): 3–13.

8 Bennett Harrison and Sandra Kanter, "The Political Economy of State Job-Creation Business Incentives," *Journal of the American Institute of Planners* 44, no. 4 (1978): 424–435; Donald D. Steines, "Business Climate, Tax Incentives, and Regional Economic Development," *Growth and Change* 15, no. 2 (1984): 38–47; Brian Dabson et al., "Business Climate and the Role of Development Incentives," *The Region* (Federal Reserve Bank of Minneapolis) (1996): 47–49; and J. Krohe Jr., "Do You Really Need a Mission Statement?" *Across the Board* 32, no. 7 (1995): 16–21.

9 E. J. Blakely, B. H. Roberts, and P. Manidis, "Inducing High Tech: Principles of Designing Support Systems for the Formation and Attraction of Advanced Technology Firms," *International Journal of Technology Management* 2, nos. 3–4 (1987): 337–357; and E. J. Blakely, "A New Role for Education in Economic Development," *Education and Urban Society* 29, no. 4 (1997): 509–523.

10 Philip Kotler, Donald H. Haider, and Irving Rein, *Marketing Places: Attracting Investment, Industry, and Tourism to Cities, States, and Nations* (New York: Free Press, 1993).

11 K. McEnroe, "Incentives as a Public Business Investment," *Economic Development Review* 12, no. 4 (1994).

12 Ibid.

13 Thomas S. Lyons and Roger E. Hamlin, *Creating an Economic Development Action Plan: A Guide for Development Professionals,* rev. ed. (Westport, Conn.: Praeger, 2001) and McEnroe, "Incentives as a Public Business Investment."

14 J. Brauer, "Letters to the Editor: Auto Town Blues," *Wall Street Journal,* 27 September 2000, S4; K. E. Thuermer, "The Southeast Picks Up the Pace," *World Trade* 11, no. 9 (1998): 58–63.

15 Benno Wymar, "Foreign Investments and South Dakota," *South Dakota Business Review* 55, no. 3 (1997): 1, 4, www.usd.edu/brbinfo/businessreviews/1997/march97.htm#top.

16 Ibid.

17 McEnroe, "Incentives as a Public Business Investment."

18 Henry W. Herzog Jr. and Alan M. Schlottmann, "Industrial Location in the United States: Some New Evidence of Public Policy Efficacy," *Survey of Business* 29, no. 1 (1993): 9–16.

19 Ibid.

20 Ernest P. Goss and Joseph M. Phillips, "Do Business Tax Incentives Contribute to a Divergence in Economic Growth?" *Economic Development Quarterly* 13, no. 3 (1999): 217–228.

21 Edward J. Jepson Jr., "Grappling with the Complexity of Economic Development," *Economic Development Review* 12, no. 3 (1994).

22 Michael M. Phillips, "More States Reassess Business Incentives—Pullback Comes Amid Growing Skepticism about Cost," *Wall Street Journal,* 20 March 1997, A2.

23 Raymond C. Lenzi, "Business Retention and Expansion Programs: A Panoramic View," *Economic Development Review* 9, no. 1 (1991): 7–12.

24 Herzog and Schlottmann, "Industrial Location in the United States."

25 Lyons and Hamlin, *Creating an Economic Development Action Plan,* rev. ed., 36–37.

26 Lenzi, "Business Retention and Expansion Programs."

27 Ibid.

28 Lyons and Hamlin, *Creating an Economic Development Action Plan,* rev. ed.

29 J. Halverson, "Planning and Developing a Speculative Industrial Building," *Economic Development Review* 9, no. 4 (1991): 31–35.

30 Alan Goldstein, "A California Crisis Symbol: The Plant Not Built," *Dallas Morning News,* 24 June 2001.

31 J. A. Segedy, "Preserving Community Character" (presentation to the American Planning Association Conference, New York, N.Y., April 18, 2000).

32 Schmenner, *Making Business Location Decisions,* 38.

33 Laurie Joan Aron, "Clicks and Bricks Meet Head On in the Software/IT Location Revolution," *Site Selection* 45, no. 3 (2000): 582, www.siteselection.com/features/2000/may/software/index.htm; and Ginny Deal, "Tech Traffic Travels to Bargain Spots," *Site Selection* 46, no. 1 (2001): 93–96, www.siteselection.com/features/2001/jan/pacific/.

34 Mark Glaser and John Bardo, "The Impact of Quality of Life on Recruitment and Retention of Key Personnel," *American Review of Public Administration* 21, no. 1 (1991): 57–71.

35 Ibid., 64–65.

36 Deal, "Tech Traffic Travels to Bargain Spots"; Jerry D. Johnson and Raymond Rasker, "The Role of Economic and Quality of Life Values in Rural Business Location," *Journal of Rural Studies* 11, no. 4 (1995): 405; and Lisa L. Love and John L. Crompton, "Role of Quality of Life in Business (Re)Location Decisions," *Journal of Business Research* 44, no. 3 (1999): 211–222.

37 B. Becker and S. Bradbury, "On the Road to Branson, Missouri," *Planning* 59, no. 5 (1993): 23–26; and S. Ilium, "Branson, Missouri: Marketing Boom or Bust," *Parks & Recreation* 29, no. 9 (1994): 82–90.

38 Audubon Pennsylvania, "Eco-Tourism: A Quiet Revolution," http://pa.audubon.org/Eco_Tourism.htm, 2002.

39 "Study Reveals Shorebird Viewing Delivers Huge Economic Benefit," New Jersey Division of Fish and Wildlife, New Jersey Department of Environmental Protection, August 16, 2000, www.state.nj.us/dep/fgw/news/2000/brdecobn.htm.

40 Royal Bank of Canada, "Open the farm gate to opportunity," www.royalbank.com/agriculture/reference/enterprises/ente_may_2002_001.html.

41 Larisa Salamacha and Michael J. Palumbo, "Fairfield Ecological Industrial Park, Baltimore, Maryland" (presentation at White House Community Empowerment Conference, Washington, D.C., April 14–16, 1997), www.smartgrowth.org/casestudies/ecoin_fairfield.html.

42 Ibid.

43 A. Downs, "What Does 'Smart Growth' Really Mean?" *Planning* 67, no. 4 (2001): 20–25, www.anthonydowns.com/smartgrowthmean.htm.

44 Ibid.

45 Porter, *Competitive Advantage*.

46 G. A. Lichtenstein, *Building Social Capital: A New Strategy for Retaining and Revitalizing Inner City Manufacturers* (Philadelphia, Pa.: Philadelphia Industrial Development Corporation, 1999).

47 Robert Bland, *A Revenue Guide for Local Government*, 166.

48 John Logan and Harvey L. Molotch, *Urban Fortunes: The Political Economy of Place* (Berkeley: University of California Press, 1987).

49 Michael E. Porter, "New Strategies for Inner-City Economic Development," *Economic Development Quarterly* 11, no. 1 (1997): 11–27.

50 Barry Bluestone and Bennett Harrison, *The Deindustrialization of America: Plant Closings, Community Abandonment, and the Dismantling of Basic Industry* (New York: Basic Books, 1982).

51 Donald R. Gilmore, *Developing the "Little" Economies,* supplementary paper no. 10 (New York: Committee for Economic Development, 1960).

52 Hamlin and Lyons, *Economy Without Walls,* 7–9.

53 Ibid., 29–37.

54 Ibid., 172–173.

55 Julie Cencula Olberding, "Diving into the 'Third Waves' of Regional Governance and Economic Development Strategies: A Study of Regional Partnerships for Economic Development in U.S. Metropolitan Areas," *Economic Development Quarterly* 16, no. 3 (August 2002): 251–272.

56 "UPS's College-Based Recruiting Initiative Named Best in the Country," United Parcel Service press release, January 11, 2000, www.pressroom.ups.com/pressreleases/archives/archive/0,1363,3538,00.html.

57 G. Jaffe and D. Blackmon, "Just in Time: When UPS Demanded Workers, Louisville Did the Delivering," *Wall Street Journal,* 24 April 1998, A1.

58 Steven A. Holmes, "College Schedules for Night Workers: Louisville Program Saves U.P.S. Jobs and Promotes Education," *New York Times,* 9 December 1998, A26.

59 Metropolitan College, FAQs, www.jctc.kctcs.net/mc, or http://216.69.32.126/FAQs/FAQs.stm.

60 David McGinty, "UPS Recruitment Results Mixed," *Louisville Courier Journal,* 7 March 1999, E1.

61 Metropolitan College, FAQs, www.jctc.kctcs.net/mc, or http://216.69.32.126/FAQs/FAQs.stm.

62 Steven J. Koven and Stuart Strother, "Saving Jobs in Louisville, Kentucky," *Economic Development Journal* (Winter 2002): 21.

63 J. Jones, "UPS Recruits Workers in Eastern Kentucky," *Louisville Courier Journal,* 22 January 2000, B1.

64 Ben Gose, "Working Nights for $8.50 an Hour and a Free College Education,"

Chronicle of Higher Education (July 23, 1999): A68.

65 Jones, "UPS Recruits Workers in Eastern Kentucky."

66 Koven and Strother, "Saving Jobs in Louisville," 21.

67 Ibid.

68 S. Clarke, "Economic Development Roles in American Cities: A Contextual Analysis of Shifting Partnership Arrangements," in *Public-Private Partnerships for Local Economic Development*, eds. N. Walzer and B. Jacobs (Westport, Conn.: Praeger, 1998), 19–45.

69 P. Sherrid, "It's a Paradise for Student Workers: Part-Time Employment Trends," *Business Week* (September 18, 2000): 80–81.

70 Larry Reynolds, "Mercedes: Alabama Experiment," *Europe* (February 1997): 26–30.

71 R. Scott Fosler, ed., *The New Economic Role of American States* (New York: Oxford University Press, 1988), 188–190.

72 E. S. Browning and H. Cooper, "Ante Up: States' Bidding War Over Mercedes Plant Made for Costly Chase—Alabama Won the Business but Some Wonder If It Also Gave Away the Farm—Will Image Now Improve?" *Wall Street Journal*, 24 November 1993, A1.

73 Reynolds, "Mercedes: Alabama Experiment," 26.

74 Browning and Cooper, "Ante Up."

75 L. Chappell, "Incentives Draw Flack," *Automotive News* 71, no. 5735 (1997): 32M.

76 K. Gepfert, "Reassessing Mercedes: Is It Paying Out?" *Wall Street Journal*, 29 January 1999, S1.

77 M. Murphy, "Touchdown," *Forbes* 164, no. 3 (1999): 54.

78 M. Bird-Meyer, "If Growth Is What You're After, Then Alabama Is the Place," *Expansion Management* 16, no. 3 (2001): 88–91.

79 "The Buzz: Both Yeas and Nays," *Automotive News* 71, no. 5735 (October 13, 1997): 32M.

80 Warren Cohen, "Don't Bet on Gambling Reform Anytime Soon," *U.S. News & World Report* (June 14, 1999): 26; and *Gambling Impact and Behavior Study: Report to the National Gambling Impact Study Commission* (National Opinion Research Center at the University of Chicago, April 1, 1999), www.norc.uchicago.edu/new/pdf/gamble.pdf.

81 R. Parvin and S. Koven, "Limits on Economic Development Policy: State Supported Gambling in Iowa," *Policy Studies Review* 14, no. 3–4 (1996): 432.

82 Robert Goodman, *The Luck Business: The Devastating Consequences and Broken Promises of America's Gambling Explosion* (New York: Free Press, 1995), 22.

83 Robyn Meredith, "Detroit, Still Blighted, Puts Hopes in Casinos," *New York Times*, 30 July 1999, A12.

84 Paul Zielbauer, "Mohegans to Build $800 Million Casino Expansion," *New York Times*, 16 February 2000, A27.

85 Cohen, "Don't Bet on Gambling Reform Anytime Soon," 26; and Kentucky Center for Public Issues, "Gambling in America," *Kentucky Journal* (April/May 1999): 9.

86 Kentucky Center for Public Issues, "Gambling in America," 6–7; and D. Phares, C. Leven, and C. Louishomme, "Gaming in the United States: Taxation, Revenues, and Economic Impact," in *Handbook on Taxation*, eds. W. Bartley Hildreth and James A. Richardson (New York: Marcel Dekker, 1999), 275.

87 William Eadington, "Economic Development and the Introduction of Casinos: Myths and Realities," *Economic Development Review* 13, no. 4 (Fall 1995): 51–54.

88 *Gambling Impact and Behavior Study.*

89 Ibid.

90 Ibid.

91 Ibid.

92 Ibid.

93 Ibid.

94 Ibid.

95 Ibid.

96 Ibid.

97 Vicki Abt, James F. Smith, and Eugene Martin Christiansen, *The Business of Risk: Commercial Gambling in Mainstream America* (Lawrence, Kans.: University Press of Kansas, 1985), 65.

98 William Safire, "Lotteries: How States Bilk Their Citizens," *Louisville Courier Journal*, 22 June 1999, A11; Safire, "Just Not You," *New York Times*, 21 June 1999.

99 Goodman, *The Luck Business*, 77.

100 Ibid., 78.

4 Business creation

Learning objectives

You should be able to:

- Define "entrepreneur" and "enterprise development"

- Describe two main types of financial assistance available for small-business entrepreneurs

- Name at least three services a full-service incubator provides its tenants

- Describe how a microenterprise program works

- Cite three current political and societal issues that often come up during business creation

- Name five services/advantages the CAPsell Center (a successful incubator) provided its tenants.

Business creation

One tenet of the demand-side theory of growth is that growth is promoted through the creation of new businesses. Proponents of demand-side theory believe that local business creation is advantageous because new local firms:

- Tend to remain in the community where they originated
- Will be exporters of goods and services and importers of income to the local economy
- Tend to use local resources as inputs to their production processes.

Because small firms account for the majority of all new jobs created in the United States, local jurisdictions in recent years have looked to business creation, also called enterprise development, to expand employment opportunities for local residents. Although some people question the data on new jobs,[1] the push by local, state, and federal policymakers to support entrepreneurship continues. This demand-side economic development strategy is widely viewed as a viable approach to dealing with such pressing problems as layoffs of manufacturing workers, welfare-to-work requirements, and the time it takes to get new technologies to market. This strategy began as a second-wave strategy of economic development, but, as this chapter demonstrates, it has adapted itself well to the third wave described in Chapter 3.

Before we examine the literature of enterprise development as an economic development strategy, explore major policy issues, and look at a case study, we should define "entrepreneurship" and "enterprise development."

The target of an economic development strategy that features business creation is the entrepreneur, a person who is "a production innovator who perceives the opportunity to provide a new product or implement a new production method, and then organizes the needed production inputs and assumes financial risk."[2] In other words, the entrepreneur capitalizes on a business opportunity through innovation—the creation of a new product or service.[3] The vehicle for providing this new product or service is a business that the entrepreneur, singly or as part of a group, has founded. Public policymakers hope that the entrepreneur will make a success of the business, hire employees, and generate wealth that will be shared among members of the immediate community.

It is well documented, however, that from 50 percent to 90 percent of new enterprises fail within their first three to five years of operation. They fail for a host of reasons: undercapitalization, poor management, and relatively high overhead costs of operation, among others.[4] Many local and state governments, and the federal government as well, have decided it is in the public interest to attempt to reduce this dramatic failure rate, and they have therefore created a wide variety of public and nonprofit entities—small-business incubators, microenterprise programs, entrepreneurship forums, venture capital clubs and alliances, small-business loan and loan guarantee programs, and manufacturing networks, among many others. All these programs engage in enterprise development, which can be defined as assistance to entrepreneurs in support of the creation, growth, and survival of their businesses.[5]

Very little has been written on enterprise development strategy as a whole—most writings are chapters in readers or primers on economic development.[6] The focus has been on types of enterprise development service providers. Thus there is a small literature on business incubators and an emerging literature on microlending and microenterprise programs. The paucity of literature has exacerbated policymakers' propensity to approach enterprise development in a nonsystemic, piecemeal fashion.

Some literature is available on the development in the high-tech sector of the economy of entrepreneurial communities such as Silicon Valley in California and the Golden Horseshoe in the Boston area.[7] Chapter 5 presents the case of Austin, Texas, a university-community partnership to encourage economic development via business creation in the high-tech arena. Other works have focused on technology and regional development.[8] Still others examine technology business creation through the lens of economic sector analysis.[9] These studies assess the performance of communities in terms of expected performance of entire sectors, for example, the banking sector or the entertainment sector.

Enterprise development tools

Because so much of the enterprise development literature is tool specific, we have selected a few major tools, which fall into two categories: tools aimed at providing financing and tools that offer business development assistance to entrepreneurs. At least two tools—business incubators and microenterprise programs—offer both these types of assistance.

Financing assistance

Financing assistance to new enterprises can be provided in the form of either debt capital or equity capital (see the Chapter 2 section on financial incentives). Several types of capital are useful to growing enterprises, depending on their stage of development. Nascent enterprises are typically in need of start-up capital to help them acquire the space, equipment, supplies, and other inputs needed to launch any business. Businesses also need working capital for meeting day-to-day operating needs. Mezzanine capital, as the name implies, helps the entrepreneur bridge the gap in capital resources from one stage of business development to another.

Small Business Administration loan programs   Other than commercial banks, perhaps the best known provider of debt capital to small businesses is the U.S. Small Business Administration (SBA). Since 1953, the SBA has been supporting entrepreneurship in a variety of ways. While it does play the role of referral agency for certain kinds of business development assistance, the SBA's principal focus is its lending programs, especially the 7(a) Loan Guaranty Program, the 7(m) Microloan Program, 504 Certified Development Companies, and the Certified and Preferred Lenders Program.

7(a) Loan Guaranty Program   As its name suggests, the 7(a) Loan Guaranty Program backs loans made to small businesses by private lenders by reducing the private lender's risk in the event of default. The SBA guarantees up to 80 percent of loans of $100,000 or less as well as 75 percent of loans over $100,000, up to a maximum guarantee of $750,000. Except for very small loans, the SBA caps interest rates at 2.75 percent above the prime lending rate. The 7(a) program has several subsidiary programs aimed at specific needs:

- The Low Documentation (LowDoc) program streamlines application red tape by reducing SBA's application form to one page for loans of $100,000 or less

- The Women's Prequalification Loan Program is a pilot program that allows the SBA to prequalify a woman entrepreneur for a loan guaranty before she goes to a private lender

- The Minority Prequalification Loan Program is aimed at qualified minority-owned businesses

- CAPLines provides loans for working capital

- FA$TRAK works with selected lenders to provide loans of up to $100,000 to small businesses; participating banks use their own paperwork and procedures, and the SBA guarantees up to 50 percent of each loan

- The Export Working Capital Program (EWCP) provides short-term loans (12 to 18 months) for export activities

- The International Trade Loan (ITL) program guarantees short- and long-term loans for export-related activity and also assists businesses that have been hurt by import competition

- The Defense Loan and Technical Assistance (DELTA) program assists small defense contractors that have been adversely impacted by defense cuts to make the transition into commercial markets.

7(m) Microloan Program   This program uses nonprofit microenterprise programs (see page 112) as conduits for making loans of less than $100 to $25,000 to very small enterprises. These loans may not be used to pay existing debts but can be used for working capital, inventory, and supplies.

504 Certified Development Companies   This program uses nonprofit entities, which may be publicly or privately sponsored, to provide long-term, fixed-asset financing to small businesses. Through the 504 programs, the SBA can guarantee debentures that may cover as much as 40 percent of a given project, not to exceed $1 million.

Certified and Preferred Lenders Program   This program supports and encourages highly active and expert lenders by giving them preferential lending authority. The difference between a certified lender and a preferred lender lies in the amount of lending authority delegated by the SBA: certified lenders receive partial authority, while preferred lenders receive full authority for lending. The goal is to make more capital available for private enterprises.

Venture and angel capital   Once a young business has a business plan and a reasonably well-defined product or service, it may have reached a point where it requires a fairly substantial infusion of capital in order to take that product or service to the next level, opening up larger markets. This capital infusion is typically not available through commercial banks or other traditional lending sources. In fact, it may not be debt capital at all. It may be equity capital.

There are two principal sources of equity capital: angel capitalists and venture capitalists. Both are typically very wealthy individuals who made their money as successful entrepreneurs. They tend to provide relatively large amounts of financial capital: from several hundred thousand dollars up to several million, depending on the project. They prefer to take equity positions (share of profits) in the companies to which they supply capital, and they expect to be permitted a certain degree of oversight in the management decisions of those companies. Once they commit, these capitalists take major financial risks on untested companies and ideas and therefore expect a high return on their investments and a hand in guiding the destiny of each business.

Angel capitalists generally make smaller capital injections than venture capitalists and are also less concerned with substantial participation in the management of the businesses in which they invest. Angel capitalists also usually demand a smaller equity share of each business than venture capitalists.

Entrepreneurs who seek angel or venture capital should proceed with both realism and caution and clarify their expectations for their businesses and their willingness to give up substantial control. Because angel and venture capitalists are always seeking to invest in companies that have the ability to capture large national and international markets, many small businesses will never get their assistance. This is particularly true of businesses located in inner-city communities that may have an important role to play in their local economies but, because of their lack of profit potential, are unlikely to capture the attention of venture capitalists.

Community development venture capital   In response to the lack of venture capital for low-income, inner-city businesses, a relatively new form of capital—community development venture capital (CDVC)—has been created by local communities to aid entrepreneurs.

The ultimate objective of CDVC is often job creation through the successful generation and growth of new enterprises. CDVC funds are typically operated by, or as, nonprofit entities although for-profit CDVC providers exist. The money for establishing the funds comes most often from private foundations, private companies, and government sources.

CDVC providers generally are less stringent in their requirements of businesses than are traditional venture capitalists. However, because they face performance pressures from their investors, they may find themselves skimming the best prospects off the top of the pool of inner-city companies in order to increase their success rate. Although this is a rational investment approach, it also limits the ability of CDVC providers to truly transform the economies of low-income communities because the group of entrepreneurs receiving investment remains small.[10]

Entrepreneurship forums   An increasingly popular approach to bringing entrepreneurs and venture capitalists together is the locally based entrepreneurship forum. The purpose of such forums is to overcome the "visibility obstacle" to obtaining capital by making venture capitalists and owners of small businesses aware of each other.[11] An example of this is found in the Venture Club of Louisville, Inc. (VCL).

Much of the literature on angel and venture capital is descriptive, comprising discussions of the venture-capital industry,[12] guides for entrepreneurs about locating venture capital,[13] and bibliographies and descriptions of the way venture financing works.[14] More recently, the emerging literature on entrepreneurship has offered an analytical look at venture capitalists, their criteria for selecting businesses in which to invest, and their impact on those businesses.[15]

Venture Club of Louisville

The Venture Club of Louisville, Inc. (VCL) is a nonprofit venture capital forum created in 1995 by a group of concerned venture capitalists, bankers, businesspeople, educators, and government economic development officials, under the auspices of what was called at the time the Greater Louisville (Kentucky) Chamber of Commerce. VCL established monthly general meetings to which all interested venture capitalists and entrepreneurs were invited.

To make either a five-minute presentation or a one-minute announcement to explain the nature of his or her business, each entrepreneur is required to formally apply for permission. The VCL then determines the appropriate format for each case.

After all attending entrepreneurs make their presentations, the meeting takes on a less formal tone, and business owners and potential investors are encouraged to mingle with the entrepreneurs. It is during this part of the meeting that deals are made. VCL's meetings have attracted hundreds of entrepreneurs since its inception and numerous deals have been finalized. The club publishes a monthly newsletter that recounts highlights of the presentations from the previous month's meeting and offers brief articles on topics of interest to entrepreneurs.

Business development assistance

The federal government, especially the Small Business Administration, also offers nonfinancial assistance to entrepreneurs.

Small-business development centers   Small-business development centers (SBDCs) are essentially one-stop-shopping facilities for all types of business development (management and technical) information and assistance. They are funded and administered by the SBA. Because the SBA is unable to provide all of this information and assistance itself, it establishes a cooperative network of providers—including state and local governments, colleges and universities, and private businesses—in any community where an SBDC is located. Most SBDCs are located on the campuses of community colleges or universities, but they can be found in a variety of environments, recently including small-business incubators (see page 104).

The SBA in 2001 put the total number of SBDCs at 58, with almost 1,000 service locations in all 50 states.[16] In addition to making a wide variety of management assistance more readily available to small businesses, SBDCs also make management assistance more affordable, thereby reducing overhead costs to small businesses and helping enhance their chances for survival. SBDCs also help small businesses prepare applications for SBA loans.

Business information centers   Business information centers (BICs) are also supported by the SBA. They are essentially sources of business-related information made available through access to the latest computer equipment and software as well as the counseling services of volunteers from the Service Corps of Retired Executives (SCORE). SCORE, an SBA operation, comprises approximately 12,400 former businesspeople nationwide who volunteer their expertise across the range of business management specializations including finance, budgeting, human resources, organization development, and marketing. They offer essential business information many small companies cannot afford on the open market.

Supporting entrepreneurs

Beginning in 1989, Littleton, Colorado, gave up on trying to recruit companies with the use of tax breaks and other incentives. With its New Economy Project, Littleton's business and industry affairs department instead dedicated itself to promoting entrepreneurial growth and business retention and expansion from within the community. The project's primary tool has been technology applications, and its primary target has been entrepreneurial companies that are capable of rapid growth. Department staff subscribe to many commercial computer databases and specialty business databases, maintain a GIS, and educate themselves about advanced business practices. Staff use these resources to develop marketing lists, do competitor analysis, chart industry trends, research business problems, and provide other technical assistance and information to entrepreneurs in the city.

Source: www.littletongov.org/bia/NewEcon.

Comprehensive assistance

The following tools offer both financial and nonfinancial assistance to entrepreneurs.

Business incubation   There was no incubation activity of any real consequence in the United States until the late 1970s. Today, the National Business Incubation Association (NBIA) estimates that there are over 700 incubators in operation throughout North America.

Traditional business incubators are buildings that house several new businesses under one roof, an arrangement that takes advantage of economies of scale and other synergies to assist firms through their perilous start-up periods. Typical incubators provide their clients flexible space and affordable rents, shared business services, business development training and coaching, financial assistance, and the opportunity to network with peers.[17]

This type of incubator is called a residential incubator because its client businesses are in residence in the incubator facility. Incubators at first were a community development strategy—not merely an economic development tool—because they were typically housed in abandoned factories or warehouses retrofitted for the needs of an incubation program and its clients. The buildings became a viable part of the community again. Recently so-called purpose-built incubators—new facilities designed specifically for business incubation—have become popular. Sometimes this approach is less expensive and faster than retrofitting an aging building. It also permits the incubation program developer to design the facility to fit precisely the program's mission.

Some enterprising real estate developers have attempted to capitalize on the cachet of business incubation by calling their office or business condominium developments incubators although the facilities provide nothing in the way of financial or business development assistance to their tenants. Traditional incubator programs provide their clients with a common package of services; such programs are called full-service incubators.[18]

Full-service incubators   Full-service incubators offer tenants flexible and affordable space, a collection of business services, business development assistance, and financial assistance.

The first service in a full-service incubator package is flexible and affordable space, space that can be adjusted to fit the changing needs of each business. Typically, the space allocated to a given tenant can be expanded with the growth of that business, up to a point. To enable the incubator to continue to serve several clients at a time, most incubators have a policy about the maximum square footage allocated to any one tenant. In some cases where an incubator tenant has been permitted to expand to occupy the entire building, the incubator program sold the building to the tenant business and used the proceeds to purchase another building for its activities.[19]

The price of incubator space has changed over time. Originally below-market rents were standard practice in all incubation programs. The goal was to lower overhead costs to the fledgling companies being served. As time went on, however, business incubator operators came to realize that the other services they offered to their clients (such as financial and business development help) were of such value that they could charge market or even slightly above-market rents and still attract clients. Program sponsors began to clamor for financial self-sufficiency on the part of the incubators they supported, and charging at least market rates for rent was an important development.

One of the most popular services of a full-service incubator is its collection of business services, known in business incubation circles as shared services. Shared services represent the kind of resource pooling that makes incubators a unique and effective business creation tool. Most incubators provide a set of relatively standard shared services, which include reception and telephone answering; access to a copy machine, a fax machine, and a kitchen area; facilities for conferences and meetings; security; janitorial service; and parking. Clients using incubator services who want to lower overhead costs typically pay on a fee-for-service basis and, because these resources are shared, their cost is often less than what it would be outside the incubator. Some shared-service programs are innovative: one high-technology incubator in Madison, Wisconsin, offers a checkbook balancing service.

Business development assistance—sometimes many varieties—is another service in the package offered by full-service incubators. Seminars and workshops are often provided to incubator tenants at low, or no, cost. Topics can include training in a host of skills or core competencies necessary for successful entrepreneurship: bookkeeping, marketing, strategy, legal considerations, and human resources management. Sometimes incubator staff provide this training. Sometimes it is delivered by outside consultants. SCORE, sponsored by the SBA, provides this service at no charge. Some incubator programs have also built alliances with business development professionals in their communities who provide training to incubator clients at no charge in exchange for the opportunity to develop long-term relationships with the entrepreneurs and their businesses.

Business development assistance is also provided via mentoring and coaching. One of the most important aspects of any incubation program manager's job is to act as a mentor and coach to client entrepreneurs. Some programs also ask members of their boards of directors to play this role.[20]

A full-service incubator helps with financial assistance in a variety of ways. Most simply, the credibility afforded by being part of the incubator program helps the client approach traditional lending institutions. An incubation program also helps new businesses develop a business plan attractive to traditional lenders and coaches them on how to present that plan.

Because these approaches might not be enough to help some new enterprises, many incubators have set up revolving loan funds to provide access to scarce start-up or working capital for their client businesses. Incubators make small loans to client companies at below-market interest rates and with more relaxed collateral requirements. As clients pay off their loans, the money is recycled for use by other clients.

Some incubators, particularly those that work with high-technology start-ups, have linked up with angel and venture capitalists. A few incubators even have venture capitalists with offices on site. Others have needed to be more creative. For example, an incubation program in the small town of McAlester, Oklahoma, without a venture-capital community was having difficulty helping its clients find traditional sources of financing. As a result, entrepreneurs were leaving McAlester for larger cities where they could get financial support, and their businesses were flourishing in these other locations. The incubation program reached out to a group of wealthy retirees living in the community and convinced them to start investing in local start-ups. These newfound angel capitalists were hesitant to take risks individually, however, so they organized themselves into an angel capital network and pooled their risk by investing as a group. This angel capital network now provides both debt and equity capital to companies in the incubator.[21]

The final service offered by a full-service incubator is, perhaps, a natural outcome of the incubator setup: the opportunity for networking that occurs when several companies are brought together under the same roof. Some businesses in the incubator actually purchase goods and services from each other. Still others participate in joint ventures or establish other forms of partnership. Perhaps the simplest and most beneficial form of networking is the exchange of neighborly advice and the sharing of information and knowledge among incubator tenants.[22]

All incubator programs also have to set up internal management procedures, including admitting new clients to the program, determining how long a client can stay in the program, establishing reliable financing, and deciding whether to specialize in certain types of businesses.

Because incubators need to manage the tenure of their clients, the first issue is how new clients are admitted to the program. When business incubation was still a brand-new concept, no one paid much attention to a protocol for admitting clients. In fact, early incubators were so anxious to fill their facilities that they would take almost anyone. Most programs have come to realize that this is not a viable strategy in the long run. Expending incubator resources on entrepreneurs with weak business concepts or a lack of commitment to starting and growing a business is not productive.

Most incubators now have relatively clear entrance requirements. Most require each prospective tenant to submit a business plan for review by the incubator manager. Until the manager approves the business plan the entrepreneur is not admitted to the program. Some programs now lay out expectations for their tenant companies as part of the lease agreement. At the Louisville Enterprise Group, an incubator in Louisville, Kentucky, management asks that clients agree to listen to and work with incubator staff, something that entrepreneurs do not always do well. This incubator also formally assesses the client's situation upon its entrance to the incubator and uses this information to track the client through the program in the most efficient and effective way possible.

A second issue—how long clients should be permitted to stay in residence in the incubator—has evolved with time and with increased understanding of the incubation process. Incubator operators and policymakers at first established a preset maximum incubation period. Because most incubators were then publicly sponsored, it was in the best interests of the public to incubate as many new businesses as possible and provide access to incubators for the greatest possible number of entrepreneurs. This led to the establishment of arbitrary maximum incubation periods, such as the limit of

18 months that the Michigan legislature wrote into that state's original business incubation enabling legislation. When later research revealed that the average incubation time for a new business is 30 to 36 months,[23] it became clear that forcing a business out of the incubator too soon was self-defeating. When a fledgling company failed for lack of support, resources already invested by the program were lost.

But incubator tenants cannot be permitted to linger indefinitely. Many incubators now collaborate with their tenants on goals for tenants' growth, and the incubator monitors the tenants. When the business achieves its self-sufficiency goal, it leaves the incubator—in other words, it graduates.

Incubator developers and operators also need to consider financing. The majority of incubators draw their financial support from a variety of sources, mostly local. Municipal governments, private corporations, and nonprofit organizations such as community development corporations and chambers of commerce have all supplied start-up and operating capital to incubators. State government initiatives, such as Ohio's Edison Program, also provide substantial support. Federal agencies—especially the U.S. Department of Commerce through its Economic Development Administration—have been active in financing the physical aspects of incubator development.

Sponsors that want to make incubator programs financially self-sufficient have developed a number of innovative financing strategies. Many incubation programs have begun to take equity positions in their client firms. This can be quite lucrative, particularly for high-technology-focused incubation programs. The Arizona Technology Incubator in Scottsdale, for example, succeeded with this strategy.[24] But this practice is not a solution for all incubators; in particular, programs that work with small service businesses will find it difficult to make the practice pay. In fact, insisting on an equity position could damage some businesses and discourage entrepreneurs from availing themselves of the services of these incubators.[25]

Traditional business incubators are often structured similarly, but they nevertheless display notable variety. In the early days of business incubation in the United States, the great majority of incubators were publicly sponsored, most often by city or county governments. Some local government–sponsored incubation programs can still be found. In Virginia, the Nottoway County Incubator is a 7,000-square-foot facility that houses seven young businesses. It is supported by grants from the U.S. Department of Agriculture (USDA) and the commonwealth of Virginia. It opened in October 2000 and recently received funding to construct a 10,000-square-foot addition to the existing facility.[26] The West Piedmont Business Development Center, also in Virginia, serves the city of Martinsville and Franklin, Henry, and Patrick counties. Its focus is on assisting entrepreneurs whose businesses are engaged in light manufacturing. It has 23,500 square feet of incubator space that can accommodate between 10 and 20 businesses. Its financial support comes from grants from Martinsville, the USDA, the EDA, and the Virginia Department of Business Assistance.[27]

A few state governments (Michigan's, for example) sponsored individual incubators as well.[28] Today, however, fewer incubators are sponsored solely by the public sector; more are backed by mixed groups of sponsors, often public-private partnerships involving local government, the area chamber of commerce, and postsecondary educational institutions.

The number of private sponsors of incubation is growing rapidly. Some incubators are owned by real estate development firms and some are part of corporate efforts to encourage the spin-off of new businesses by their employees.

Some incubators specialize in certain types of clients. Some programs work exclusively with light-manufacturing businesses. These incubators tend to be large; they offer services such as access to loading docks and a forklift, and they are equipped to deal with the residuals, noise, and other problems created by manufacturing processes. Other incubators cater solely to service businesses; they function physically much like office buildings and are sensitive to the image that young businesses in the service sector want to present. Historically, there have been only a few retail incubators located around the country; these have proved very difficult to sustain. Finding affordable locations that permit sufficient foot traffic or other access is not easy.

One of the most common types of incubators over the years has been the mixed-use program that houses clients from more than one economic sector. Most common is a mix of service and light-manufacturing firms. The advantage to the incubator is that it can cast its net more widely for client businesses. But mixing business types can create unforeseen conflicts. In one mixed-use incubator in the Midwest, airborne particulates from a particleboard manufacturer found their way into the product of a salsa maker, requiring the latter to stop operations until a filtering system could be installed.

Recent years have seen the rise of incubators designed to support the development of a microindustry. They bring together companies that are in the same business but are not necessarily competitors. Some examples are incubators that exclusively serve entrepreneurs in the import-export business, in food processing, or in the manufacture of ceramics. Bringing together businesses with common needs permits greater efficiency in providing assistance. For example, food-processing incubators typically have a common kitchen that either can be used by several small businesses simultaneously or can be scheduled in a manner that serves all incubator clients. Industry-focused incubators also enhance opportunities for networking by linking companies that are more likely to complement each other.

The most recent trend in industry-focused business incubation is in research and development. Large research universities operate incubators intended to encourage the transfer of technology from the research laboratory to market. Many of these incubators focus on biotechnology or biomedicine, but other fields are represented as well. The University of Louisville's Ideas-to-Action Incubator, for example, focuses on information technology.

The incubation concept has expanded to include affiliates programs that extend the incubator's services beyond its walls to other small firms in the community on a fee-for-service basis.[29] Although the impetus for affiliates programs was the pressure for financial self-sufficiency brought by incubator sponsors and the subsequent scramble for additional revenues, affiliation represents an advance in thinking about business incubation and its potential.

Virtual incubation programs Increasingly popular are virtual incubation programs, that is, incubators without walls that offer no rental space but instead coordinate the activities of community service providers that assist local entrepreneurs. Virtual incubators are especially popular and efficient in rural areas, where suitable buildings are either nonexistent or in short supply and resources are limited and spatially dispersed. Furthermore, virtual incubation can avoid the distractions of real estate management that have preoccupied residential incubators at the expense of their business development function.[30] The concept of virtual incubation has evolved very slowly, however, possibly because most federal and state programs that support business incubation are still focused on the bricks-and-mortar aspects that tend to encourage residential incubators.

Nevertheless, interest in virtual incubation is growing, particularly for community or regional incubation systems. Regional incubator systems consisting of networks of individual residential incubation programs operating

---

The Entrepreneurial Development System

Gregg A. Lichtenstein and Thomas S. Lyons developed a conceptual model—which they call the Entrepreneurial Development System (EDS)—for a community-wide business incubation system that organizes both entrepreneurs and business development service providers. The EDS operates on the premise that successful entrepreneurship requires relevant skill building and that in order to transform their businesses from start-ups to thriving companies the skill levels of entrepreneurs must be transformed as well.

To help accomplish this transformation, the EDS provides entrepreneurs a clear ladder for skill building and helps entrepreneurs rank themselves by skill much as professional baseball organizes its players into leagues (rookie, single A, double A, triple A, and the major leagues). Enterprise development assistance can then be matched with the need.

The EDS also helps the community or region organize its enterprise development system by identifying existing service providers (for example, business incubators, microenterprise programs, and small-business development centers), documenting gaps in service delivery, noting overlap, and determining at which entrepreneurial skill level each service provider works most effectively. The EDS then helps to link service providers into a coherent network that complements the ladder of entrepreneurial skills. The EDS can help create a systemic and strategic community or regional business incubation program.

Source: Gregg A. Lichtenstein and Thomas S. Lyons, "The Entrepreneurial Development System: Transforming Business Talent and Community Economies," *Economic Development Quarterly* 15, no. 1 (2001): 3–20.

---

in local communities in a defined geographic region are becoming more popular in rural areas with limited resources and markets. Two such systems can be found in rural northeast Mississippi and rural northeast Alabama. The Appalachian Center for Economic Networks (ACEnet) has taken virtual incubation into cyberspace with its Virtual Business Incubation program (VBI) designed to help small businesses expand markets and enhance customer service by getting them involved in the World Wide Web. Each client business of VBI is provided one year of assistance in designing, building, and maintaining a Web page and in customer service via the Internet.[31]

Focusing on clients Early literature on incubators was descriptive; it focused on their structure and their benefits to the economy.[32] Then the focus shifted to evaluative studies of business incubators' efficacy. This branch of the literature, which continues to thrive, has yielded some useful published reports and articles documenting the abilities of incubators to spawn new businesses, create jobs, and generate wealth.[33] Most recently, the incubation literature has turned its attention to principles and practices. As the tool has matured, so has the analysis of its processes and structures.[34]

Most incubator programs have been developed on a programmatic basis, with an emphasis on the ideal structure, or form, to be used. Incubators often preselect a program of services and then expect local entrepreneurs to flock to take advantage of them. If this does not happen, the programs assume the supply of entrepreneurs is too limited.[35] Actually this cookie-cutter approach is not as responsive to the specific needs of entrepreneurs in a given context as it might be.

Figure 4–1
Diagnosing
entrepreneurial needs

Required resources	Obstacles								
	1 Availability	2 Visibility	3 Affordability	4 Transaction barriers	5 Self-awareness	6 Accountability	7 Emotions	8 Capability	9 Creativity
1 Business concept: Idea for product or service									
2 Physical resources: Supplies/raw materials, space, equipment/ plant, money/capital									
3 Core competencies/skills: Managerial, technical/operational, financial, legal, administrative									
4 Market: Product or service, customers, distribution channels, transportation									

Source: Adapted from Gregg A. Lichtenstein and Thomas S. Lyons, *Incubating New Enterprises: A Guide to Successful Practice* (Washington, D.C.: Aspen Institute, 1996).

Responsiveness might be improved by getting away from the programmatic approach to incubation and, instead, taking a practices-based approach.[36] To do this, incubators must be more client focused, that is, they should determine the needs of prospective clients in the area they serve and then adopt practices (activities, policies, and programs) that fulfill those needs. Incubator staff can learn these needs (the obstacles to obtaining resources crucial to success in starting, growing, and sustaining a business) by performing a diagnosis of the situations of prospective clients.

One tool for this purpose is an entrepreneurial-needs diagnostic matrix (Figure 4–1 on page 110) that assists enterprise developers in considering the relation between the resources essential for entrepreneurial success and the obstacles that interfere with access to or use of the necessary resources.

Four major categories of resources are essential to entrepreneurial success:

- **Business concept**—an idea for a product or service that is innovative and can be sold. Most people view such a concept as a prerequisite to entrepreneurship; however, this is not always the case. Some entrepreneurs start with weak business concepts that need substantial refining. Others have no initial business concept at all, but when they are introduced to a concept, they can turn it into a successful business.

- **Physical resources**—plant, equipment, inventory, human capital, and financial capital.

- **Core competencies/skills**—a wide-ranging resource category that includes technical/operational, managerial, marketing and sales, financial, and administrative skills.

- **Market**—all those things necessary for accessing and retaining markets, including customers, distribution channels, and the like.[37]

All these resources are essential to entrepreneurial success; however, obstacles may deny access to these resources or cause their use to be difficult. By strategically identifying obstacles to local success, incubator programs can strategically adopt practices to overcome them:[38]

- The required resource may not be **available** in the context in which the entrepreneur is operating

- The resource may be available but not **visible** to the entrepreneur; that is, the entrepreneur may be unaware of where to find it

- The resource may not be **affordable** to the entrepreneur

- The entrepreneur may face **transaction barriers**—problems with the exchange—in acquiring the resource; transaction barriers may include required government permits or licenses, racism, gender bias, inability to speak/write in English

- The entrepreneur may lack **self-awareness** and not know what resource(s) are actually needed

- The entrepreneur may lack **accountability,** in other words, the willingness or the know-how to take responsibility at the level required of a business owner

- The entrepreneur may face **emotional** obstacles to success, for example, false pride, analysis paralysis, misplaced anger

- The entrepreneur may not have developed the **capability** to use the resource after it is acquired; for example, many entrepreneurs with access to financial capital squander it through mismanagement

- The entrepreneur may lack **creativity** in recognizing opportunities and seizing them and in developing innovative solutions to emerging problems.[39]

How to use the diagnostic matrix

One of the uses of the diagnostic matrix provided in Figure 4–1 on page 110 is to determine whether a small-business entrepreneur qualifies for a loan.

Suppose the manager of an incubation program has a revolving loan fund established to provide small loans to women and minority entrepreneurs who need financial capital and are unable to qualify for commercial bank loans. This fund lends at reduced interest rates and has collateral requirements lower than what local banks require. An entrepreneur comes in for a loan: she is the owner of a dry-cleaning business who has been successful at attracting customers. But although her operation is busy six days per week, she still is not making a profit. She believes that if she could get money to buy additional equipment, she could handle a higher customer volume and finally achieve her elusive profit. She has already approached several banks in the community and has been turned down. In some cases, she was unable to meet the banks' interest or collateral requirements; in others, she was viewed as too great a risk because she was a woman entrepreneur operating a marginal business. On the Figure 4–1 diagnostic matrix, she faces affordability obstacles and transaction barriers to accessing a physical resource—financial capital.

The manager of the incubation program is inclined to make the loan, especially because the owner of the dry cleaning business is a woman entrepreneur who cannot get bank financing for reasons the revolving loan fund was designed to address. She is apparently the ideal client. All the manager has so far, however, is this entrepreneur's self-diagnosis of her situation. The program manager must dig deeper and review the financial records of the business in order to provide the most useful assistance. After a review of the financials, it is apparent that the reason the business is not making a profit has nothing to do with access to capital. Instead, the entrepreneur has priced her service to cover costs but has failed to build in a profit.

Now the required resource has become a core competency—how to properly price the good or service—not physical resources. The obstacles this entrepreneur actually faces are a lack of self-awareness (she does not really know what she needs) and capability (she has all the physical resources she needs, including money, but she does not know how to use them properly). It becomes clear that she needs help to price her services more appropriately and handle the customer relations fallout from raising her prices.

If the manager of the incubator had acted on the original, superficial diagnosis (lack of financial capital), this entrepreneur would still not be making a profit and would probably default on her loan, thereby reducing the pool in the revolving fund of the incubator. The manager of the incubator must dig for the facts and tailor the response to fit the actual needs of the client entrepreneur.

There has been much talk in business incubation circles in recent years about best practices in incubation. The danger in this is that these practices may be identified and then applied in cookie-cutter fashion. In fact, best practices may be those that are specially designed to fulfill the unique needs of the entrepreneurs in the context within which the incubator is operating, be it inner-city Cleveland, rural Louisiana, or the campus of a major research university.

Microenterprise programs   U.S. microenterprise programs (or MEPs as they are now being called) have their roots in the Grameen Bank concept (*grameen* means village) of making very small loans to entrepreneurs in a local community to finance the start-up of the entrepreneurs' businesses.[40] These loans are made from a revolving loan fund managed by a peer group consisting of the target microentrepreneurs themselves. Through a combination of peer pressure and support, the entrepreneurs ensure that loans are properly used and repaid in a timely manner. This approach to assisting low-income entrepreneurs has enjoyed considerable success in Bangladesh, where it originated, as well as in India, Indonesia, and numerous other developing countries throughout the world.

In the United States, the Grameen model was first used in so-called microloan programs, which stuck fairly closely to the prototype. Microloan programs evolved into microenterprise programs that added a new dimension: in addition to start-up loans, microenterprise programs required a minimum level of technical training in functions associated with any business—accounting and bookkeeping, marketing, industry research, human resources management, and business operations. Some microenterprise programs still use the peer lending system; others have abandoned it for a variety of other structures.

Microenterprise programs differ from other business lending institutions in that they focus on being lenders of last resort, that is, they lend only to entrepreneurs who cannot get capital anywhere else because of poor credit, a lack of collateral, or an enterprise that may not promise much in the way of profits in the future. Microenterprise development is an urban and rural community development approach that considers social welfare as well as economic development as it attempts to help the poor help themselves by starting their own businesses on a very small scale. It brings to entrepreneurship people who might not otherwise be entrepreneurs; it hopes they become self-sufficient, at least, and build wealth, at best.[41]

Today's microenterprise program is usually operated as a nonprofit organization. It draws its resources from various sponsors, including local governments, the SBA, local banks, community-based organizations, and private foundations. Many microenterprise programs are run by community development corporations. Although the federal government was budgeting more than $100 million yearly for microenterprise development activities during the 1990s, in 2001 the federal budget for microenterprise development was $75 million, coming from several sources. In 2002 it dipped further to $68 million, all of which came from the Community Development Financial Institutions fund.[42]

Growth of microenterprise programs as part of a local business creation strategy for economic development has been impressive. In 1987, the United States had fewer than 10 such programs, but by 1996, the number had increased to more than 300.[43] In 1994, microenterprise programs were credited with helping in the creation of more than 50,000 small companies in the United States.[44]

The target of microenterprise development efforts is, of course, the microentrepreneur. Although microenterprise programs aim to assist low-income individuals, the typical microentrepreneurs in the United States who benefit from these programs cannot be stereotyped.[45] Some common characteristics, however, are identifiable. Microentrepreneurs are usually members of minority groups (66 percent) and women (75 percent) and they also are reasonably well educated, with the vast majority possessing high school diplomas and one-third possessing post-secondary degrees. About half the microentrepreneurs in the United States own their own homes.[46] Incomes of microenterprise program clients vary widely: in the mid-1990s, approximately 20 percent had incomes of less than $6,000 per year, but 15 percent made more than $30,000 per year.[47] This may imply that skilled, educated people are not being well served by traditional financial institutions.[48]

Microentrepreneurs are often people who have been forced to become entrepreneurial when they have found themselves unemployed as a result of global economic shifts and resultant corporate downsizing in the United States.[49] Microentrepreneurship is also increasingly viewed as an option for people in welfare-to-work programs.

The literature on microenterprise focuses largely on descriptions of existing programs, evaluations of selected programs, and the benefits of microenterprise as a tool for achieving economic development that is aimed at low-income and minority individuals and groups.[50] Evaluations thus far indicate that MEPs are potentially useful economic development tools for people at the low-income end of the economic ladder, but studies to date have been limited in number.

A recent study found that MEPs can increase the rate of movement from welfare to self-employment although the absolute number of people who make the move is small.[51] One major drawback is that most people on welfare, even with MEP assistance, are not appropriately equipped for successfully operating a business. A study of the Unemployment Insurance Self-Employment Demonstration program found that only a tiny percentage of the unemployed actually elect to use MEPs.[52] In fact, support other than providing capital and technical training classes might be more important for increasing employment among the unemployed.

A study of three inner-city MEPs in San Francisco, New York City, and Boston found these programs are more helpful to those who exist at the margins of the mainstream economy than those who are completely cut off from the economic mainstream.[53] Conclusions of this study are optimistic because MEPs are shown putting their clients on the right track by giving them hope and helping them be strategic about the goals of their businesses and their lives. MEPs do not maintain the poor; instead MEPs invest in the poor. Other MEPs in the United States are adding further value by building social capital among service providers in their communities and between their clients and these service providers.[54] (Chapter 1 provides a discussion of the concept of social capital in economic development.)

What are the limits of microenterprise programs to grow businesses?[55] At what level in the evolution of a business and the skills of the entrepreneur does a microenterprise program no longer have the capacity to help that business? Preliminary analysis of a MEP in Louisville, Kentucky, indicates that MEPs are quite effective in assisting during the start-up phase, but once a business gets to approximately its third year of development, it faces a new set of challenges. It is here that the MEP is unable to help, and budding entrepreneurs find that the only place to turn for this level of assistance is the private business development community. Most MEP clients cannot afford to pay for this level of assistance. One possible solution is a community-level, low-cost or no-cost business development assistance bridge loan (funding to pay for development) that can get MEP clients from start-up to a level of operation at which the client can afford private consultation.

Contemporary issues in business creation

Like all other economic development strategies, business creation strategies have both supporters and critics. The following is a discussion of some of the contemporary issues surrounding small businesses and business creation.

Quality-of-life and environmental concerns

One of the hottest issues in economic development today is economic and environmental sustainability. Although sustainability remains a vague concept, with many competing definitions, most interested people can agree that it has to do with the current generation's use of resources in a way that ensures that future generations will also be able to use those resources. This definition of sustainability is relevant for new business creation.

Advocates of sustainable development often maintain that a truly sustainable local economy must have at its base an appropriate critical mass of small, home-grown businesses. Such companies tend to be more loyal to their communities than businesses headquartered elsewhere. They are more likely to purchase inputs locally. In keeping with economic base theory, when they export to other regions, they bring outside income to their locales. Because these companies are small, they usually tax local resources and the environment less than larger firms. Because they are local, they are apt to share local values regarding sustainable behaviors.

Some communities have encouraged environmentally sustainable microindustries or a sustainable, compatible industrial mix. An eco-industrial park may look like other industrial parks—an industrial subdivision, publicly owned, that may offer low land prices, speculative buildings, and quality public infrastructure to firms setting up branch facilities. However, the eco-industrial park is designed to encourage its resident businesses to interact in ways that reuse waste streams, recycle inputs, and use other mechanisms to create an industrial ecosystem. Many firms in eco-industrial parks are companies attracted from elsewhere, but some parks also incorporate small-business incubators to nurture start-ups compatible with the industrial ecosystem of the park. After these new companies outgrow the incubator, they can spin off to other sites in the park.

Another approach to sustainable development is the smart growth movement described in Chapter 3. Smart growth implies that decisions about the locations of the newly created firms should be strategic. Local governments need to weigh opportunities for enterprise development that revitalize inner-city economies against other opportunities that foster growth at the urban fringe. Smart growth principles may also suggest the types of new businesses to be supported. Young firms whose activities do not contribute to local and regional environmental degradation may take priority in enterprise development plans.

On the other hand, small businesses are likely to remain small and will employ relatively few persons. Large corporations still drive growth and employment and, in the long run, sustain many local economies;[56] and when a large corporation is involved, its advocates tend to ignore the issue of environmental sustainability or relegate it to a secondary position behind job creation.

Social costs

Small-business creation as an economic development strategy is usually perceived as an innocuous activity with few social costs. The American ideal of rugged individualism lends itself well to entrepreneurship, and the public usually supports efforts to foster it. Growing an economy via new enterprise development tends to take place on such a small scale that the public barely sees it and rarely scrutinizes it.

Despite public complacency, societal interests are at stake. As large corporations continue to downsize, finding jobs for displaced workers in other large organizations becomes increasingly difficult. Placing former welfare recipients in large firms is a growing challenge. The United States may be increasing its reliance on entrepreneurship and small-business development to keep its economy afloat. Policymakers encourage displaced workers to become either entrepreneurs or self-employed, but because entrepreneurship and self-employment are two very different activities (see the box on page 116), policies for encouraging these activities should be very different.

Entrepreneurship vs. self-employment

The distinction between entrepreneurship and self-employment revolves around the existence of an innovative business concept or idea. Entrepreneurs are attempting to develop something new. People who are self-employed, by contrast, typically engage in selling their labor to perform a specific set of tasks that are to some extent routine, but that might differ in quality depending on who does them. (Of course, there are self-employed entrepreneurs, but they are usually exceptions.)

Source: Gregg A. Lichtenstein and Thomas S. Lyons, *Incubating New Enterprises: A Guide to Successful Practice* (Washington, D.C.: Aspen Institute, 1996), 22.

When policymakers do not differentiate, the policy that emerges is either too broad or too specific to bring about the desired behavior.

Can entrepreneurship and self-employment take up the employment slack left by corporate downsizing? What percentage of the population can and should be expected to succeed in individual businesses? How many self-employment opportunities exist in the economy? Will large corporations try at some point to put small entrepreneurs out of business? What alternatives will there be in the future for those who are not able or choose not to operate their own businesses? Is the current enterprise development assistance infrastructure capable of coping with the increased demand for creating new businesses and, if not, what will happen to the large percentage of small-business owners who continue to fail in their first three to five years of operation?

Redistribution of wealth

Perhaps more than any other economic development strategy, business creation efforts have attempted to address issues of unequal distribution of wealth and resources. Successful redistribution has not always been achieved, but a number of enterprise development assistance vehicles are structured and targeted so that they can and do have an impact on distribution.

The concept of business incubation emphasizes the pooling of resources (both human and physical) that can then be shared by a collection of entrepreneurs in need. It is a collaborative or communal approach to business bootstrapping (picking oneself up by one's bootstraps) that uses the advantages of networking over a lone-wolf, go-it-alone approach to entrepreneurship. Incubation distributes resources, thereby presenting the opportunity for generating wealth more widely and making it possible for more entrepreneurs to succeed.

Since the early 1990s, business incubation has become more focused in its attempts to assist low-income and/or minority entrepreneurs, in particular. Empowerment incubators are programs intentionally located in minority or economically disadvantaged communities to help entrepreneurs who are also located there overcome context-specific obstacles to success. Because of these specific goals, empowerment incubation programs go beyond standard practice and, with highly creative efforts, tailor themselves to the specific needs of the clients they serve.[57]

For example, a Midwestern business incubator, whose mission is to assist minority and women business owners, found that its clients were having an inordinately difficult time establishing supplier relationships with larger companies in the region. The incubator further discovered that the reason for this was that some larger majority-owned and -operated firms did not take minority and woman business owners seriously as businesspeople and doubted that they could deliver quality products or services. The incubator's response was to develop a roundtable in which its clients came together with representatives of the larger firms to discuss potential business relationships. This gave the minority entrepreneurs an opportunity to demonstrate their competence. The result was that barriers to supplier contracts fell.

Because microloan and microenterprise programs are in most cases created to assist the low-income self-employed, with a particular focus on woman-owned businesses, they rather successfully walk the fine line between being a social service and a business development aid.[58] Perhaps their greatest challenge is meeting their clients' substantial needs without collapsing under the weight of those needs. Many owners of minority and low-income start-ups begin their business journey with few resources and few business development skills. A full complement of such clients can drain the microenterprise program's financial and staff resources.

The answer to this problem may lie in focusing the program's efforts on those entrepreneurs most likely to succeed.[59] Although it seems realistic, this suggestion appears to fly in the face of the redistributional mission of the microenterprise program. Also, although some argue that assisting those most likely to succeed does help everyone because the survivors will eventually supply employment to those whose businesses do not survive, this rarely happens and cannot be predicted. The idea that it will benefit the whole society if the well-to-do receive certain concessions has become politically popular among some in the United States since the 1980s, but it has yet to be proved.

One alternative might be to consider microenterprise programs part of a larger community-wide enterprise development system such as the EDS described on page 109. This would permit the pooling of community resources for assisting all entrepreneurs, as opposed to picking winners.

Minority business development centers (MBDCs) are variants of the small-business development centers described earlier in this chapter. Both are one-stop facilities for information about small-business development and can be found in communities across the United States. MBDCs are distinguished from SBDCs by their focus on minority-owned small businesses. The national association of MBDCs is the Minority Business Development Agency, part of the U.S. Department of Commerce.

Role of government

Enterprise development is based largely on the concept that economic markets are imperfect and that government can intervene to correct imperfections. Not all enterprise development assistance is undertaken by the public sector, but much of it does involve government in an important role.

Government involvement takes place at all levels. The SBA provides federal loans and business development information to small businesses of varying sizes, including microenterprises. The EDA provides funding for the physical development of business incubators. HUD also provides assistance to local programs aimed at minority-owned small businesses in inner-city neighborhoods.

Many state governments support small-business creation. A 1994 study identified 27 states that had programs that supported business incubation. The state programs were of three types: those that deal exclusively with incubator development, those that build business incubators into larger economic development efforts, and those that permit incubation programs to participate in receiving funding and assistance from general economic development funds.[60]

Local governments also get involved in business creation interventions. Some operate their own business incubation and/or microenterprise programs; others are collaborators in private-public partnerships that run such programs. Local governments may be active participants in the creation of venture capital forums or community development venture capital alliances. They may support entrepreneurship-training courses that are available for a nominal fee to entrepreneurs from throughout the community. They may also play a major role in the creation of community development banks that provide nontraditional financing to small businesses operating in economically distressed urban or rural areas.

Some enterprise development practitioners, especially incubator developers and operators, think government financial participation is too limited. State and federal governments, in particular, focus their financial support on the physical aspects of business incubation—the acquisition of land, purchase or retrofit of buildings, and purchase of equipment. Although this type of assistance is valuable, the far greater costs of incubation in the long run are those surrounding the delivery of business development assistance. Government's tendency to supply bricks and mortar may stem from their tangibility; taxpayers can see them and touch them. The real work of incubators is creating and growing businesses, however, not managing real estate. If a greater share of government allocations were directed to the soft costs of enterprise development, success in business creation would likely be greatly enhanced.

Is active government participation in business creation activities appropriate? Some argue that the private sector is capable of providing needed assistance to new businesses or that the new businesses worthy of survival will do so without intervention. These are minority points of view, however, as government assistance to emerging companies appears to be an idea in good currency nowadays.

Case study

Although most empowerment incubation programs are found in inner-city communities, some have developed in low-income rural areas. Following is a description of one rural empowerment incubation program.

Case study 4–1   ## Business creation in rural America: The CAPsell Center business incubator

This case provides an example of business creation in the rural Midwest of the United States. It combines several key concepts of economic development: public-private partnerships, business incubation, empowerment of citizens, assistance to small businesses, and the role of government in the marketplace. The case describes a second-wave approach to economic development—presented in Chapter 3—as it bears on government's role in the development of new enterprises. Its approach to development is redistributional because it strives to assist low-income individuals to generate wealth through the creation of their own businesses.[61]

The CAPsell Center

The CAPsell Center—a 27,000-square-foot building in downtown Wautoma, Wisconsin—provided the physical space for a successful business incubation program in the 1980s and early 1990s. The building had been vacant between 1975 and 1981, when it was donated to CAP Services, a nonprofit corporation. CAP Services was the descendant of the community action programs of the Lyndon B. Johnson administration in the mid-1960s, and its mission was "... to bring about a permanent increase in the ability of low-income individuals to be economically and emotionally self-sufficient." The business incubator represented just another of CAP's many services to the rural region.

CAP Services, headquartered in Stevens Point, Wisconsin, with offices in several regions of the state, consulted residents, public officials, and businesspeople to carry out a triennial needs assessment in its various service areas. After the assessment, CAP Services concluded that the most pressing need of the Wautoma area was for full-time, year-round jobs paying above the minimum wage. This ultimately led to the creation of the CAPsell Center incubator and concerted attempts to help local residents start their own businesses. The business that vacated the building occupied by the CAPsell Center was, at that time, the county's largest employer. The county government provided advice to the incubator but was unable to lend financial support.[62]

When CAP Services acquired the building, it was in poor condition. CAP built a new building within the existing walls, refurbished the roof, and upgraded the electrical and heating systems. Thus, although CAP acquired the building at no cost, it spent considerable time and money to retrofit the structure to make it habitable and meet the nonprofit corporation's needs.

Tenants for the residential incubator represented a mixture of service, retail, and light-manufacturing businesses. The idea of incubating mixed uses came from a set of recommendations by the East Central Wisconsin Regional Planning Commission. In addition, the director of CAP Services maintained that a mixed-use incubator would be the only financially feasible alternative for the rural area of Wautoma. To make the incubator financially viable, CAP Services believed it needed an anchor tenant to provide a steady income stream that would underwrite other activities of the facility. The regional office of CAP Services became that anchor (in other words, CAP became its own anchor tenant), and the center housed various public-oriented CAP programs: Head Start, a summer youth employment program, the Family Resource Center, the Low-Income Weatherization Program, the Family Crisis Center, the Self-Employment Program, and housing and economic development programs.

Because a number of entrepreneurs whose businesses were not suitable for location in the incubator facility approached CAP Services for assistance, CAP created an affiliates program (discussed later in this case study) to provide business development services for businesses that were not tenants of the incubator facility. The CAPsell Center brought together a diverse group of these affiliates; they included a restaurant, an automobile service station, an aquatic-plant landscaping firm, and a health food products manufacturer. Incubator tenants made up approximately one-third of the CAPsell incubation program's client base, and affiliates or nontenants made up about two-thirds. Thus, the CAPsell Center operated as both a traditional business incubator and an incubator-without-walls.

Initial funding for start-up of the incubation program came in 1987 in the form of a grant of $25,000 from the Wisconsin Federation for Community Development; this money was used to hire the program's first manager. CAP also received two rural economic development grants from the Office of Community Services (OCS, part of the U.S. Department of Health and Human Services) to help subsidize and expand the operation. The incubation program also received financial support from Wisconsin's Community-Based Economic Development Program to cover the cost of a manager and an assistant manager for two years. Subcommittees of CAP Services' 12-member advisory board reviewed loans, prepared and reviewed leases, and provided advice on marketing.

The rural region

The service area of the CAPsell Center included all of Waushara County and a portion of neighboring Marquette County to the south. The center itself was located in Wautoma, Wisconsin, a rural community with a population of approximately 1,800. In this area of central Wisconsin, flat land is devoted to agriculture and hilly areas are left as woods. The city of Oshkosh is about 35 miles to the east and Stevens Point is 40 miles to the north. Five major state highways pass through Waushara County; three run through Wautoma, linking it with all the metropolitan areas of Wisconsin and with Chicago, Illinois.

Wautoma is the seat of government and largest community in Waushara County, a sparsely populated rural county with 19,500 residents in 1990 (it grew to 23,000 by 2000). Waushara County in the early 1990s was one of Wisconsin's poorest counties. Its 1993 unemployment rate was 7.2 percent, which was substantially higher than the state rate (4.7 percent) and higher than the national rate (6.8 percent) at the time. More than two-fifths (40 to 45 percent) of the population qualified as low income, and 13.8 percent were below the nationally designated poverty level. Nearly 6 percent of the population was on public assistance. These percentages suggest that a substantial number of the county's residents could be termed "working poor." One local stakeholder suggested that it was really an economy of haves and have-nots, and very few households could be described as middle class. The CAPsell Center's manager pointed out that the rural poor in the county were more independent than their urban counterparts who earned the same income. Many of the rural poor were landowners and subsistence farmers who hunted and fished in the area and took odd jobs, such as selling firewood and repairing homes, throughout the year.

The economies of Wautoma and Waushara County were somewhat diverse and becoming more so. Nonagricultural employment in the county in 1990 comprised retail and wholesale trade (35 percent); government (21.8 percent); services (15.5 percent); manufacturing (8.6 percent); transportation and public utilities (4.9 percent); finance, insurance, and real estate (4.2 percent); and construction (3 percent).[63] The largest employer in the county was an automobile parts manufacturing firm that employed 118 people.[64] Other major employers included nursing homes, a hospital, an auto parts dealer, a large retailer, and a couple of tourist resorts.

Agriculture was relatively strong in the county, as was recreation and tourism. Many residents (no specific figures are available) were self-employed; a large percentage worked in the local tourism industry from late spring to early autumn. During the remainder of the year, they supported themselves by doing odd jobs in the community. Thus many area residents had several occupations; for example, one CAPsell Center client was a tax accountant, a logger, a Christmas tree shearer, and a maintenance man for the local school. Although the region had a culture of entrepreneurship—in the broadest sense of that term—the area's entrepreneurs were not particularly sophisticated; they were instead "opportunistic entrepreneurs," driven largely by pure economic need. Most went from one self-employment situation to the next without improving their earning power.

Barriers to entrepreneurship

A number of constraints—probably representative of constraints in other rural areas of the nation—appear to have restricted entrepreneurial opportunities in Wautoma, Wisconsin.

Lack of financial capital Lack of financial capital was widely regarded as the chief obstacle to entrepreneurship in Wautoma and Waushara County. Area banks were conservative and were often more interested in making personal loans than commercial loans. When banks did make business loans, it was normally in very small amounts. Banks in Wisconsin had a limited supply of capital for lending because a very large percentage of their investments were in government securities. In addition, banks demanded that borrowers have a substantial amount of collateral, usually far more than local residents were able to supply. The problem of insufficient collateral was particularly acute in Waushara County, with its large number of low-income residents. The fact that there were only three banks in the area limited competition for loans and acted as a disincentive to risk taking. Furthermore, the existing banks were locally controlled, which tended to make them more parochial and less willing to embark on different types of projects.

A state program—the Housing and Economic Development Fund—that was once an alternative source of capital was depleted, with the exception of monies for agricultural business loans. State loan programs demanded more collateral than most rural entrepreneurs were capable of providing. The microloan program sponsored by the SBA was supposed to be making loans of as little as $15,000; however, the agency did not usually make loans of less than $50,000. Most entrepreneurs in the region were unable to qualify for loans of this size. The SBA also wanted substantial collateral before providing access to capital.

As a result, many local entrepreneurs had to tap informal sources of financial capital. Female entrepreneurs, especially, had to look to the personal savings of friends and relatives, credit cards, and second mortgages on homes—sources that carried with them substantial burdens and risks.

Lack of industry and markets Incubation program managers, advisory board members, program clients, and local government officials all noted a scarcity of local industry and markets as a major constraint. The lack of large firms in the area meant that there was little demand for products or services that small local entrepreneurs might provide. Community businesses were forced to pursue strategies that depended on export of goods and services to other parts of the state and the country.

Because there was little existing business in the area, there were a limited number of quality providers of business services. The United Parcel Service (UPS) did not deliver to the Wautoma area. An entrepreneur had to travel to Oshkosh to send or receive material via UPS. The absence of business-to-business services handicapped local companies; and limited transportation services hindered business attraction, retention, and creation efforts as well.

The area population was too small to be a viable market for most new businesses, especially in the manufacturing sector but also for many service and retail firms. Again, local entrepreneurs needed to develop markets outside the region; in fact, several of the CAPsell Center's clients had mail-order businesses.

The new retail firms found that local residents tended to prefer urban goods and services. People living in Wautoma and in Waushara County often traveled 35 miles to Oshkosh to purchase items that were available locally, often at lower prices. One affiliate of the CAPsell Center who operated a greenhouse and made natural health food products confirmed that many residents bypassed his business to buy plants elsewhere despite his lower prices and his belief that he provided a higher-quality product than distant competitors. This situation, in part, drove the small-business owner to focus efforts on developing markets outside the local region. Another affiliate, a retailer dealing in hardware and craft items, cited the same problem. She undertook a campaign to educate local residents about the relative advantages of shopping at her establishment: time saved, reduced expenditures on gasoline and automobile depreciation, and easy access for service or replacement. She reported that this strategy had been effective.

Lack of training and education   Most budding entrepreneurs in the region lacked the education and specialized skills to start the kinds of high-technology businesses that could be competitive in the global economy. Technical assistance was also limited because of the absence of specialized skills in the local area. Most local individuals who started businesses began low-tech, home-based firms in fields where they had knowledge and expertise (for example, engine repair and janitorial services). Despite the fact that Fox Valley Technical College was nearby, the lack of high-tech skills persisted because the people of the region did not recognize the need for more training and education. Most did not enroll in the classes at Fox Valley Tech, nor did they seek training elsewhere.

Rural areas of Wisconsin also lacked a formal youth entrepreneurship program. Youth were leaving the Wautoma region, and other rural areas, in large numbers because no work was available for them. Although schools could have sponsored this type of effort, there was no public mandate to do so.

Lack of information   The only existing sources of feasibility studies and marketing information for current and aspiring area entrepreneurs were a very small public library system, the county agricultural extension agent, and the nonprofit CAP organization. The nearest university libraries and SBDCs were approximately 40 miles away. The state of Wisconsin had several excellent databases, but they were not accessible to the community. But, again, the people of the area failed to see the need to improve local business information resources. Many times when local would-be entrepreneurs approached the incubation program manager with an idea for a business, they expressed surprise when asked whether they had undertaken a market study for their proposed product or service. They replied, "What do I need a market study for? I asked my friends, and they said they'd buy it."

Lack of transportation   Although the community benefited from the three major state highways that passed through Wautoma, no transportation options other than automobile and truck transport existed for commerce. There was no rail service to Waushara County. The nearest airport was 35 miles away in Oshkosh. The community was not served by bus, either local or intercity; nor was taxi service available. Local businesses could truck their goods to outside markets and truck in needed inputs, but the lack of a local transportation system was a hardship for the small businesses' employees and patrons, many of whom had low incomes or were senior citizens without reliable transportation. The limited transportation restricted the options of local entrepreneurs and made it harder for them to find employees and attract local customers.

Poor health   In the Wautoma area, many entrepreneurs were in poor health. Some of these individuals were Waushara County natives, but others had come to Waushara County from urban areas for the healthier environment and lower cost of living. Health problems kept most of these individuals from holding down jobs and obtaining credit; thus they were entrepreneurs by necessity rather than entrepreneurs by choice. These people found it practically impossible to obtain financial capital for start-ups from traditional sources. They also wished to limit their incomes so that they could still qualify for state and/or federal support. Some who opened businesses were forced into bankruptcy as a consequence of their health problems.

The business incubation program of CAP Services helped by providing small seed-capital loans and by representing entrepreneurs in their dealings with local lending institutions. It helped entrepreneurs maintain the balancing act that permitted them to make some money from their businesses while retaining government aid. The program informed clients of options such as incorporating their businesses to permit write-offs that, in turn, kept incomes down to levels that allowed the owners to continue to qualify for government aid.

Community resistance to business development   The demographic makeup of the local population did not encourage the creation and growth of new local businesses. The elderly population, which was large, was not enthusiastic about having additional working people in the community. They saw new business activity as a threat to the quiet, small-town lifestyle they enjoyed. Newcomer retirees who had purchased property viewed new business development negatively because businesses required more public services and, hence, higher taxes. Existing business owners, particularly those on Main Street, were not eager to see new development because they thought increased competition might force them to pay higher wages. Nevertheless, younger residents were progrowth, and most observers believed that the progrowth people were slowly wresting power from the antigrowth faction.

Some local entrepreneurs complained that the general community was slow to accommodate business interests. Some thought that the local chamber of commerce and the hometown newspaper were not aggressive in their efforts to assist employers. The local governments, city and county, were widely faulted for lacking vision; they were not viewed as obstructionist, but they received low grades for not taking the initiative to improve the local business climate. While the city worked with the state to attract industry and had begun to develop a public water system, it did not offer business retention or expansion programs, nor was it involved in new-business creation efforts. The city reacted to private sector proposals on a case-by-case basis and often followed the lead of local bankers. This sometimes led to haphazard and low-quality local development.

Barriers to business incubation

This rural area of Wisconsin also had to confront the following constraints on business incubation:

Independent nature of rural residents   The residents of Waushara County were a more independent lot than their urban counterparts. They were accustomed to doing things for themselves to subsist and did not have the extensive societal or governmental safety net available in urban areas. Rural dwellers were antagonistic to requests for documentation. Fearing others would steal their ideas, some were not willing to explore the feasibility of those ideas with a third party or to document them in a business plan.

Many local entrepreneurs viewed everything outside their sphere of experience as big business, and they were, frankly, overwhelmed by it.

The independent nature of rural entrepreneurs showed itself during interviews with incubation program clients. A surprisingly large number of these entrepreneurs indicated that the incubation program had been of little or no benefit to their businesses. Several acted as though the CAPsell Center had done absolutely nothing for them. Yet in virtually every case the incubation program had lent them seed money, helped them write their business plans, and provided other management assistance. The incubation program manager, in fact, had suggested some of the very management practices the entrepreneurs were proudly claiming as their own. Perhaps it is not important that incubation clients credit the program for its assistance as long as the clients' businesses achieve success. Over the long run, however, the clients' attitude could jeopardize the ability of the incubation program to justify its existence to its sponsors.

Opposition from local realtors and landlords   Particularly in the CAPsell Center's early days, local realtors and landlords viewed the incubator as unfair competition for two reasons: the government subsidized space at below-market prices, and it was "unworthy" competition because it amounted to a "handout" to the poor. This opposition was not out in the open but instead took the form of individuals "talking the incubator down" among residents around town. Several Wautoma residents suggested that this behavior is more typical of small, rural communities than of urban areas and that, because one's reputation for trustworthiness is vital in small communities, such talk can be damaging.

Opposition to the incubator declined over time. The incubation program credited a better-informed public and the decision to implement an affiliates program for the diminished opposition. Over time the CAPsell Center was viewed more widely as a catalyst for change in the community. As people began to see that something could be done about the community's problems, it stimulated a new level of interest in Wautoma, and most of the original complaints about competition changed to pleas for the organization's further involvement in community improvement efforts.

Lack of viable start-ups needing incubation program assistance   The CAPsell Center had difficulty finding viable new businesses to serve. The problem was not a lack of interest or a dearth of entrepreneurs with business ideas. The center received, on average, 10 to 20 inquiries per month. The chief difficulty was that few local entrepreneurs were willing to go through the process of ensuring that their ideas could be translated into a successful business. CAPsell's program entrance requirements specified that the prospective client must develop a business plan with at least three years of financial records and must take these before the incubation program's advisory board for that body's review and approval. Most of the entrepreneurs were unwilling to put this level of effort into a business idea despite the fact that the program manager worked with these individuals every step of the way and, in some cases, even wrote the business plan for them.

Inability to charge for true value of program services   Because of the socioeconomic status of its target population and CAP Services' mission of serving low-income groups, the CAPsell Center was unable to charge anything approaching market prices for most of its services. The incubation program could never become self-supporting. Instead, the CAPsell Center was forced to rely on subsidies to survive. Grant writing was a major activity for the center. CAP Services as the anchor tenant at the incubator guaranteed a steady stream of rent payments. In addition, CAP became more involved in revenue-producing enterprises such as housing development and management. Also, the incubation program itself explored taking equity positions in viable client firms and becoming involved in franchise operations to increase its revenue.

Stigma attached to incubator because of association with CAP Services

The fact that CAP Services was the CAPsell Center's sponsor had numerous important advantages: The incubation program represented just one component of a community-based, comprehensive strategy for economic and community development. CAP Services, as the incubator's anchor tenant, provided a steady stream of rent payments and guaranteed a certain level of activity at all times. Because it was a private, nonprofit corporation, CAP Services garnered revenues from enterprises such as housing development and management—CAP Services acquired a trailer park at the edge of the Wautoma city limits, for example—that would be much more difficult for a public or for-profit operation to obtain.

Despite these advantages, many in the community tagged the center as a low-income, welfare-oriented entity. Incubator tenants who attempted to operate retail activities from the facility experienced difficulty because many potential customers—perceiving the incubator facility as unsafe and unwelcoming—refused to come to the center. Some people close to the incubator felt that the CAP offices were not an appropriate anchor tenant for the facility and wanted the offices moved out to another part of town. Others thought that retail businesses were not appropriate to the incubator and that more suitable firms should locate at the CAP site. Still others believed that the community needed to be further educated about what CAP Services did for the overall quality of local life.

Unrealistic expectations of clients

On one hand, many potential clients came to the incubation program expecting to be molded into businesspeople, but they lacked the personal traits to operate their own enterprises successfully. One member of the incubation program's advisory board said, "Some people make very good farmers, but that doesn't mean they are necessarily capable of running their own accounting firms." Sometimes the best thing the incubation program did for these would-be entrepreneurs was advise them against it.

On the other hand, many clients who appeared to be capable of successful entrepreneurship came into the program with inflated expectations about its ability to help them. Because state and federal funds subsidized CAP Services, many clients expected to receive more loan money or lower rent than the center could provide. Too often, they terminated the relationship with bitter feelings. Instead of being ambassadors for the program, they became detractors who failed to acknowledge the good things the incubation program had provided their businesses.

Business incubation program practices of the CAPsell Center

The following is a catalog of the practices of the CAPsell Center's business incubation program. The catalog is representative of normal business incubation initiatives, which usually include direct services to client firms and internal incubator management focused on directing the performance of the entire incubator, including development activities and program oversight.

Direct services to client firms

In the case of the CAPsell Center, client firms included both incubator facility tenants and program affiliates. Affiliates were housed outside of the incubator but were able to use the services it provided.

Management assistance   The first contact between the CAPsell Center's manager and a prospective client was when the client applied for entrance to the incubation program. The manager usually checked the applicant's financial resources first, to determine eligibility and also to ascertain the level of assistance the prospective client would need. Because the mission of CAP Services was to serve low- and moderate-income individuals, most successful applicants fell into this category. However, the center's manager asserted that he would enroll a millionaire if the individual's plan would benefit low- and moderate-income people.

The determination of business feasibility was the first management assistance offered. The level of assistance depended on the entrepreneur's knowledge and experience. Most assistance centered on the development of a viable business plan for the proposed firm. The manager also assessed whether the individual possessed the skills necessary to run a business and determined the kind of help needed. For example, one of the incubator's tenants, the owner of a day care center, came to the CAPsell Center with excellent child care skills but without knowledge of business skills such as bookkeeping. The manager felt this entrepreneur, if she received bookkeeping assistance, was a good candidate for taking over the existing day care operation (owned by CAP Services) in the incubator. With this in mind, the manager helped arrange the sale of the business to her and immediately linked her to a local accountant.

Most business incubators provide a training program for their incoming clients. The CAPsell Center did not provide training but instead directed some clients to the Fox Valley Technical College in Wautoma or to the University of Wisconsin in Oshkosh. CAPsell, with assistance from a state job training and placement program, did organize workshops on business management topics for local entrepreneurs. CAPsell's manager worked hard to convince prospective tenants of the value of preparing a business plan and helped them to develop their own. Help ranged from providing the client with sample business plans to use as a template for their own plan to practically putting together a plan for them.

Management assistance was the most frequently acknowledged form of help the incubation program provided its clients. Even clients who were dissatisfied with other aspects of the program's assistance spoke highly of the management guidance that CAPsell's manager provided. A big part of this positive response was attributed to the fact that the incubation program manager maintained a close relationship, as both a business adviser and a friend, with each tenant and affiliate. He visited tenants almost daily and affiliates about once each week. Most clients felt they could call on him at any time for advice.

The manager was not convinced that this was enough and felt that better links must be developed between clients and community members who could share their management expertise. He maintained that expertise was available in the community and it must be better networked with those in need of assistance. The program manager believed that a local version of SCORE could be developed from among the numerous urban retirees living in the area.

Financial assistance   Financial assistance under the CAPsell Center's business incubation program comprised business plan development assistance (identifying needs and alternative sources of financing) and direct loans to client firms. Almost all the program's clients needed substantial financial assistance to get their businesses started. Many needed between $20,000 and $30,000, amounts that were not realistic. The incubation program manager helped clients determine their minimum financial need and then discussed alternative sources of funding—including approaching relatives, finding a business partner, or using credit cards—that could help leverage bank loans.

If no other avenues were available, the program could provide a small amount of money to the client from its revolving loan fund, established with Office of Community Services (OCS—a part of the U.S. Department of Health and Human Services) Job Opportunities for Low Income Individuals grants made to CAP Services. The maximum loan was for $10,000; however, most loans were for $5,000 or less. If the loan was for more than $1,000, it had to be matched by a bank loan. If it was for $1,000 or less, no such match was required. The interest rate on loans from the revolving fund was 5 percent. CAP maintained less stringent collateral requirements than the banks did. The program applied only moderate pressure on those who fell into arrears on payments and never repossessed property.

Dissatisfied with the amounts of money made available through the program (they described loans made by the incubator as "just enough to help us go broke"), a group of clients banded together to form their own business association to establish, among other goals, a pool of seed money that could be drawn on by their members. This newly formed incubator client group focused on the need to market their activities both at home and externally.

The CAPsell Center also did some creative financing for incubator tenants. For example, a cleaning service housed in the incubator received a $7,000 loan from the center, but in return for the tenant's timely repayment of the loan and for improving unfinished space, CAP forgave a portion of the cleaning service's rent each month. For the day care center tenant in the incubator, the CAPsell Center deducted $2,000 from loan payments for every year she kept her business in the incubator.

General counseling and referral on all aspects of business   The incubation program manager offered general advice on all aspects of business practice. If more detailed counsel was required, he referred the client to the appropriate source. Tenants often needed the general advice on marketing (for example, help in identifying potential customers for a product or service) that the incubator offered; but for more explicit marketing questions and needs, the incubator referred tenants to professional marketing consultants. Almost all incubator clients used this direct service.

Shared services   An incubator makes convenient the basic business support services that every firm requires on a regular basis, brings them together in one place (usually in the incubator facility), and reduces their cost by making them available on shared grounds. Within the facility, the CAPsell Center offered a limited number of services including fax, photocopying, typing, a postage meter, and large and small conference rooms. With the exception of the postage meter, CAPsell's shared services were available to both tenants and affiliates. Tenants were billed monthly, but affiliates paid for each service when they used it.

Space   The CAPsell Center provided its tenants with flexible and affordable space. It was flexible because the incubator was amenable to expanding each tenant's area as far as reasonable. For example, a tenant that manufactured and sold ceramic products expanded its operations to occupy approximately 2,000 square feet, a substantial percentage of the incubator's leasable floor space, but it was not allowed to expand farther.

The incubator's rental fees were determined on a sliding scale and were based on total square footage occupied as well as the number of new full-time jobs the tenant had created. Tenants were required to hire at least one new employee per year; if they did not do this, their rent increased.

Because business incubation is an ongoing process, the incubator helped its graduates find suitable facilities in the community. CAP Services bought local buildings and leased them back to graduates on favorable terms. Over its lifetime, the CAPsell Center had no difficulty in keeping its graduates at home in the county. It credits this success to an aggressive policy of assisting graduates and building bonds of friendship with its clients as well as the fact that most clients had been living in the area for some time and wanted to stay.

Networking Tenants bought and sold services among themselves. For example, the day care center used the accounting agency to do its book-keeping. The incubator's management initiated monthly meetings—voluntary and informal—for all the clients (both tenants and affiliates); the meetings were very successful. The client group created a business association and a loan fund. Retailers in the group developed a theme for Wautoma that was designed to attract more tourists to the community.

Development activities The CAPsell Center usually approached program development—practices that improve the incubation program—by responding to needs as they arose and following up on suggestions received. The center made a number of changes as a result of CAP advisory board recommendations. The board either identified a need to be addressed, leaving it to incubation management to generate a solution, or it suggested an answer to a previously expressed need.

Other changes came from meetings of a public awareness committee, which consisted of interested stakeholders from throughout the region, and still others were identified through individual conversations between tenants or affiliates and the incubation program manager. Tenants and the public suggested some solutions; in addition, the CAPsell Center's management looked to the National Business Incubation Association (NBIA) and the Wisconsin Business Incubation Association (WBIA) for development ideas.

Program oversight

CAPsell Center management kept a close watch on all program activities and reported regularly to CAP Services headquarters in Stevens Point, Wisconsin. The center filed a monthly report on the status of all space in the center; the report included square footage occupied by tenants, the vacancy rate, and the monthly rent paid by each tenant. Also the center reported weekly on incubation program operations. Based on information in the reports, CAP headquarters sometimes offered suggestions for improvement. The CAPsell Center manager also kept an up-to-date accounting of all outstanding loans under the revolving loan program. In addition, the manager made it a point to meet regularly with all clients.

Outcomes of CAPsell Center's practices

The CAPsell Center's manager believed the business incubation program had been successful in fulfilling its mission. First, most clients not only met but also exceeded their financial forecasts. Second, jobs as well as personal and community wealth were created. Third, the program attracted increasing numbers of requests for assistance. The CAPsell Center's success stories were apparently reaching audiences in other parts of the state because calls were received from entrepreneurs outside of the program's service area. The program's graduates and affiliates could be found throughout the county, from Wautoma's central business district to outlying areas. In 1992, the CAPsell Center won an award from the Social Entrepreneur Institute.

Table 4–1

Impact of CAPsell Center, October 1, 1990– September 30, 1993

Total number of clients served (including affiliates)	40
Businesses started	20
Business failures	6
Gender of clients served	
Female	15
Male	25
Highest education level achieved by clients served	
Less than seventh grade	1
Less than high school	3
High school diploma	23
Some college	6
College degree	4
Average years of work experience of clients served	12
Training status of clients served as of September 30, 1993	
Currently in training	9
Dropped out before completing	7
Training completed	24
Clients who have received loans from CAP	16
Average amount of loans from CAP	$5,000
Clients who have received loans from banks	8
Average amount of bank loans	$14,000
Average length of time it took for clients to obtain a loan	4 mo.
Number of existing businesses expanded through program	6

Table 4.1 provides a snapshot of the CAPsell Center's incubation program. The center can point to several modest success stories among its client businesses: a cleaning service that is growing steadily, a sawmill operation that grossed $60,000 in the first quarter of 1993, a restaurant that has been written up in *Cafe Wisconsin: A Guide to Wisconsin's Down-Home Cafés*,[65] a blacksmith shop that has more business than it can handle, a health food business that is developing an international market, and a ceramic figurine manufacturing company that does a strong seasonal business.

Perhaps the incubation program's most dramatic success was a business that harvests aquatic plants and sells them nationwide. This young firm grossed $140,000 in its first year of operation. Its combined orders for 1993 and 1994 amounted to more than $200,000. These are impressive accomplishments for entrepreneurs who were low-income persons operating in a rural environment characterized by a high poverty level.

The CAPsell Center's clients for the most part supported this picture of general success of the incubation program. Most clients rated the quality of the program's help to them at a 9 or 10 (on a scale of 0 to 10), a reflection in large part of their close relationship with the program's manager. Almost all the clients interviewed had received financial assistance, often in the form of small loans, management assistance, and usually business plan preparation. Incubator tenants also talked about the importance of low-cost space in the facility and the value of being able to network with fellow tenants.

Clients mentioned a variety of other ways in which the center had helped them. One affiliate described the advisory board as "like family," asking the difficult questions and promoting awareness of what was really needed to succeed. Almost all clients interviewed spoke positively about their relationships with the incubation program manager, citing his regular visits as a much-appreciated part of his service. One incubator tenant described the manager as her "silent partner." Even clients who were less inclined to specifically credit the incubator for direct assistance acknowledged its value to their businesses.

Criticisms and recommendations for improving the incubation program included:

- The program should do a better job of marketing itself

- Financial assistance should be in greater amounts

- The program should provide more help for clients vis-à-vis government agencies

- The incubator needed to undertake some physical improvements

- The incubator should consider revising its space-leasing policies so that tenants could expand as much as the growth of their operations and space availability warranted.

The CAPsell Center today

Since the mid-1990s, when the CAPsell Center was studied, a number of things have changed in Wautoma and at the center. Wautoma now has service from both UPS and FedEx, which has made doing business easier. The center (the building and its maintenance) has become operationally self-supporting, a good indication of its stability.

The incubator has adopted an in-house gap-financing program that enables it to provide borrowers who qualify for bank loans at 25¢ on the dollar with an additional 25¢ per dollar; in other words, this program helps entrepreneurs double the amount they can borrow. CAPsell also has obtained an Intermediary Re-lending Program loan with a 1 percent interest rate from the Rural Development Agency, part of the U.S. Department of Agriculture. This permitted the center to lend the money to clients at an 8 percent rate of interest for a period of 1 to 3 years. After that time, the loan goes into reamortization for 27 years. This provides CAPsell with additional access to below-market interest rates.[66]

CAPsell now also provides in-house microenterprise training. In 1999, Fox Valley Technical College moved into the incubator, a merging of services that has greatly increased the training and services that CAPsell can offer its clients.[67]

Perhaps the most impressive development took place in May 2000 when CAP received $298,614 from OCS to purchase and renovate as a business incubator the old Wautoma Hospital. Building renovations were completed in May 2001, and the new facility contains 20,000 square feet of easily convertible space. As of February 2002, 60 percent of the space had been leased to a computer company and a catering business.[68]

The CAPsell Center has thrived. Although no data exist regarding its impact on keeping younger residents in the community, it appears that it has successfully expanded economic opportunity for people of the region. In fact, the unemployment rate in Waushara County in 2001 was only 0.4 percent higher than the average for the state of Wisconsin and more than 1 percent lower than the average for the United States.

CAPsell Center—Conclusions and Challenges

The business development obstacles that the CAPsell Center faced were typical of rural incubation programs throughout the United States. Barriers such as a lack of financial capital resources, limited regional markets, local community resistance, and a lack of viable start-ups are on most rural incubation program managers' lists.[69] Nevertheless, the CAPsell Center framed the issues creatively and gave a fresh perspective on entrepreneurship in a low-income, rural environment.

The CAPsell Center's ability to succeed in its difficult environment can be attributed, in part, to the program's connection to a viable community action program. This arrangement made the incubator an important component of a comprehensive community development effort. Entrepreneurship represented just one of various sources of aid to residents. The CAP Services director liked to emphasize that successful rural economic development must be community based; it must come from within. For these reasons, community action programs and community development corporations provide an excellent vehicle for business incubators in rural areas.

The CAPsell Center was successful as a rural business incubation program because it:

- Took a community-based approach to economic and business development
- Focused on the particular needs of entrepreneurs in the region
- Emphasized its mentor role by building on its clients' self-reliance and tailoring interventions to the specific needs of each entrepreneur
- Structured the incubation program as both a traditional incubator and an incubator-without-walls
- Retained flexibility and creativity in developing and refining its practices.

The CAPsell Center initiative also raises broader questions about public-private collaborations. The public sector here sought to promote entrepreneurship among citizens in Wautoma, a rural region of Wisconsin. Access to capital, managerial advice, mentoring, below-market cost for space, networking, and other activities assisted people who wanted to start their own businesses. Because some people say that if enough public sector assistance is provided some successful enterprises can be formed anywhere, policymakers must also consider the broader questions:

- How much assistance should the public sector provide for developing entrepreneurship?
- Do long-term benefits of such assistance outweigh the costs?
- How should recipients of such assistance be chosen?
- Can such programs serve as a viable rural strategy?
- Are such programs efficient from the perspective of the entire economy, or do they represent suboptimal use of resources?

The mix of public versus private incentives is a continuing political issue. Strong advocates of market economies are skeptical of the long-term benefits of intrusion into the marketplace; they contend that government interference will benefit some at the expense of others. Those who benefit are likely to gain advantage through political factors rather than their ability to respond to market demands. Others contend that the public sector is already deeply involved in the marketplace and that the development of small enterprises is clearly preferable to a low-income population that depends upon government assistance. These individuals believe that, given appropriate assistance, many individuals can become more successful and more productive citizens. These productive citizens can bolster the economy, ensuring enhanced competition and future prosperity for the community.

Summary

Business creation strategies, introduced in the second wave of economic development and refined in the third wave, are aimed at entrepreneurs and make use of various tools for providing both financial and business development assistance. At the local level, financial help is provided mainly through federal programs and community development programs and individuals. Business development assistance is available through the SBA and various business information centers. Some assistance to entrepreneurs—business incubation (both full service and virtual) and microenterprise programs—encompasses both financing and development assistance.

Disagreement exists about the economic impact of business creation programs, but it seems clear that business creation assistance that targets the specific needs of local entrepreneurs is most successful. Business creation strategies often serve social as well as economic needs, providing assistance to those on the economic fringe and enabling them to become self-sufficient.

Study questions

- Is government intervention in the creation of new enterprises an appropriate use of public resources? If not, why not? If so, under what circumstances is it most appropriate?

- Why do communities encourage the creation of new businesses? On a larger scale, are there additional reasons for creating new businesses? What role have entrepreneurs played in the development of the U.S. economy?

- What are the advantages and disadvantages of debt capital and equity capital for entrepreneurs? When is one more useful than the other?

- What are advantages and disadvantages of privately owned and operated business incubation programs? Are private business incubators an approach that government economic developers should encourage and support?

- Why is it important that business incubators, microenterprise programs, and other enterprise development efforts be tailored to the specific environment in which they operate? What are the efficiency and effectiveness trade-offs when incubators are tailored to the environment?

- Is self-employment a viable strategy for transitioning individuals from welfare to work? What are its strengths and its limitations?

- Do you think entrepreneurs are made or born? What implications does the answer to this question have for economic development efforts that seek to assist entrepreneurs?

- Of the barriers to entrepreneurship listed and discussed in the case study, which are unique to rural communities and which might be found elsewhere (for example, in inner cities and in the suburbs) and why?

- How does the CAPsell Center case study exemplify the major issues—quality of life, quality of the environment, social costs, redistribution, and the role of government—discussed earlier in the chapter?

1 Bennett Harrison, *Lean and Mean: The Changing Landscape of Corporate Power in the Age of Flexibility* (New York: Basic Books, 1994).

2 J. V. Terry, *Dictionary for Business and Finance*, 3d ed. (Fayetteville: University of Arkansas Press, 1995), 102.

3 Gregg A. Lichtenstein and Thomas S. Lyons, *Incubating New Enterprises: A Guide to Successful Practice* (Washington, D.C.: Aspen Institute, 1996).

4 Thomas S. Lyons, *Birthing Economic Development: How Effective Are Michigan's Business Incubators?* (Athens, Ohio: National Business Incubation Association, 1990).

5 Lichtenstein and Lyons, *Incubating New Enterprises*.

6 Richard D. Bingham and Robert Mier, eds., *Theories of Local Economic Development: Perspectives from Across the Disciplines* (Newbury Park, Calif.: Sage, 1993); John P. Blair, *Local Economic Development: Analysis and Practice* (Thousand Oaks, Calif.: Sage, 1995); and Lyons and Hamlin, *Creating an Economic Development Action Plan*.

7 AnnaLee Saxenian, *Regional Advantage: Culture and Competition in Silicon Valley and Route 128* (Cambridge: Harvard University Press, 1996); and Ward Winslow, ed., *The Making of Silicon Valley: A One Hundred Year Renaissance* (Palo Alto, Calif.: Santa Clara Valley Historical Association, 1995).

8 Edward J. Malecki, *Technology and Economic Development: The Dynamics of Local,*

Regional, and National Competitiveness, 2d
ed. (Essex, England: Longman, 1997).

9 Amy Glasmeier, "Factors Governing the
Development of High-Tech Industry
Agglomerations: A Tale of Three Cities,"
Regional Studies 22 (1988): 287–301; Ann
Roell Markusen, *Profit Cycles, Oligopoly, and
Regional Development* (Cambridge: MIT
Press 1985).

10 Gregg A. Lichtenstein and Thomas S.
Lyons, "The Entrepreneurial Development
System: Transforming Business Talent and
Community Economies," *Economic
Development Quarterly* 15, no. 1 (2001):
3–20, www.newamericancommunities.org/
resources/Lichtenstein_-_EDS.pdf.

11 Lichtenstein and Lyons, *Incubating New
Enterprises*, 27.

12 W. Keith Schilit, *Dream Makers and Deal
Breakers: Inside the Venture Capital Industry*
(Englewood Cliffs, N.J.: Prentice Hall,
1991).

13 Robert J. Gaston, *Finding Private Venture
Capital for Your Firm: A Complete Guide*
(New York: Wiley, 1989); James W. Hender-
son, *Obtaining Venture Financing: Principles
and Practices* (Lexington, Mass.: Lexington
Books, 1988); and David Gladstone, *Venture
Capital Handbook* (Englewood Cliffs, N.J.:
Prentice Hall, 1988).

14 Chris Thompson and Kristin Bayer, *Venture
Capital: A Select Bibliography for Professional
Planners, Policy Makers, and the Interested
Lay Person* (Chicago: Council of Planning
Librarians, 1990); and Robert D. Hisrich,
ed., *Entrepreneurship, Intrapreneurship, and
Venture Capital: The Foundation of Economic
Renaissance* (Lexington, Mass.: Lexington
Books, 1986).

15 Dean A. Shepherd, "Venture Capitalists'
Assessment of New Venture Survival,
Management Science 45 (1999): 621–632,
www.dushkin.com/text-data/articles/24945/
body.pdf; and Dean A. Shepherd and
Andrew Zacharakis, "Venture Capitalists'
Expertise: A Call for Research into Decision
Aids and Cognitive Feedback," *Journal of
Business Venturing* 17 (2001): 1–20.

16 "Mission and Overview," Small Business
Development Center Program, U.S. Small
Business Administration, www.sba.gov/
sbdc/mission.html.

17 Lyons, *Birthing Economic Development*.

18 Ibid.

19 Lichtenstein and Lyons, *Incubating New
Enterprises*.

20 Ibid.

21 Ibid.

22 Lyons, *Birthing Economic Development*.

23 Ibid.

24 Roger E. Hamlin and Thomas S. Lyons,
*Economy Without Walls: Managing Local
Development in a Restructuring World*
(Westport, Conn.: Praeger, 1996).

25 Lyons and Hamlin, *Creating an Economic
Development Action Plan*, rev. ed.

26 www.sv.cc.va.us/sbi.

27 Ibid.

28 Lyons, *Birthing Economic Development*.

29 Lichtenstein and Lyons, *Incubating New
Enterprises*.

30 Ibid.

31 Appalachian Center for Economic
Networks (ACEnet), www.acenetworks.org.

32 M. Curran and D. McDonald, "Small
Business Incubators: A Tool for Local
Economic Development," *Entrepreneurial
Economy* (July 1983): 9–10; Mihailo Temali
and Candace Campbell, *Business Incubator
Profiles: A National Survey* (Minneapolis:
Hubert H. Humphrey Institute of Public
Affairs, University of Minnesota, 1984).

33 David N. Allen and Mary Ann Dougherty,
The Business Incubator Industry in 1987
(Athens, Ohio: National Business
Incubation Association, 1987); C. Campbell,
*Change Agents in the New Economy: Business
Incubators and Economic Development*
(Minneapolis: Hubert H. Humphrey
Institute of Public Affairs, University of
Minnesota, 1988); Lyons, *Birthing Economic
Development; The State of the Business
Incubation Industry* (Athens, Ohio: National
Business Incubation Association, 1990).

34 Lichtenstein and Lyons, *Incubating New
Enterprises*; Mark P. Rice and Jana B.
Matthews, *Growing New Ventures, Creating
New Jobs: Principles and Practices of
Successful Business Incubation* (Westport,
Conn.: Quorom, 1995); and Louis G.
Tornatzky et al., *The Art and Craft of
Technology Business Incubation: Best Practices,
Strategies, and Tools from 50 Programs*
(Athens, Ohio: National Business
Incubation Association, 1996).

35 Lichtenstein and Lyons, "The
Entrepreneurial Development System."

36 Lichtenstein and Lyons, *Incubating New
Enterprises*.

37 Ibid.

38 Ibid.

39 Ibid.

40 Marlese Durr, Thomas S. Lyons, and Katherine K. Cornwell, "Social Cost and Enterprise Development within African American Communities," *National Journal of Sociology* 12, no. 1 (2000): 57–77.

41 Lisa J. Servon, "Microenterprise Programs in U.S. Inner Cities: Economic Development or Social Welfare?" *Economic Development Quarterly* 11, no. 2 (1997): 166–180.

42 Mark Schreiner, "Lessons for Microenterprise Programs from a Fresh Look at the Unemployment Insurance Self-Employment Demonstration," *Evaluation Review* 23, no. 5 (1999): 504–526; www.microfinance.com/English/Papers/Lessons_from_UISED.pdf.

43 Schreiner, 504.

44 Servon, "Microenterprise Programs in U.S. Inner Cities," 166.

45 Schreiner, "Lessons for Microenterprise Programs."

46 Servon, "Microenterprise Programs in U.S. Inner Cities."

47 Ibid.

48 Ibid., 169.

49 Ibid.

50 Aspen Institute, *1994 Directory of U.S. Microenterprise Programs* (Washington, D.C.: Aspen Institute, 1994); Servon, "Microenterprise Programs in U.S. Inner Cities"; Lisa J. Servon and Timothy Bates, "Microenterprise as an Exit Route from Poverty: Recommendations for Programs and Policy Makers," *Journal of Urban Affairs* 20, no. 4 (1998): 419–441; Schreiner, "Lessons for Microenterprise Programs"; and Mark Schreiner, "Self-employment, Microenterprise, and the Poorest Americans," *Social Service Review* 73, no. 4 (December 1999): 496–523.

51 Schreiner, "Self-employment, Microenterprise, and the Poorest Americans."

52 Schreiner, "Lessons for Microenterprise Programs."

53 Servon, "Microenterprise Programs in U.S. Inner Cities," 175.

54 Lisa J. Servon, "Credit and Social Capital: The Community Development Potential of U.S. Microenterprise Programs," *Housing Policy Debate* 9, no. 1 (1998): 115–149, www.fanniemaefoundation.org/programs/hpd/pdf/hpd_0901_servon.pdf.

55 Servon, "Microenterprise Programs in U.S. Inner Cities."

56 Harrison, *Lean and Mean.*

57 Marlese Durr, Thomas S. Lyons, and Gregg A. Lichtenstein, "Identifying the Unique Needs of Urban Entrepreneurs: African American Skill Set Development," *Race & Society* 3 (2000): 75–90.

58 Servon, "Microenterprise Programs in U.S. Inner Cities."

59 Servon and Bates, "Microenterprise as an Exit Route from Poverty."

60 Mark L. Weinberg, Thomas S. Lyons, and Marsha Shook, "State Government Support of Business Incubators," *Economic Development Commentary* 19, no. 1 (1995): 17–21.

61 This study, funded by a grant from the Aspen Institute, was conducted in the mid-1990s as part of a larger research effort on small-business incubation. Information presented here was gathered during a visit to the CAPsell Center, a business incubation program located in Wautoma, Wisconsin. Center staff, client entrepreneurs, and relevant stakeholders in the community agreed to in-depth interviews as well as observation and recording of center operations.

62 Karl Pnazek, CEO, CAP Services, Inc., telephone interview with authors, February 14, 2001.

63 *Waushara County Book of Facts* (Stevens Point, Wis.: CAP Services, Inc., 1993).

64 Ibid.

65 Joanne Raetz Stuttgen, *Café Wisconsin: A Guide to Wisconsin's Down-Home Cafés* (Minocqua, Wis.: Heartland Press, 1993).

66 Pnazek, interview with authors.

67 Ibid.

68 Ibid.

69 Lichtenstein and Lyons, *Incubating New Enterprises.*

5 High technology, education, and development

Learning objectives

You should be able to:

- Name and describe two theories of how technology leads to economic growth
- Name four factors that are important to high-tech entrepreneurs when they decide where to locate their companies
- Name four factors that contribute to an entrepreneurial climate
- Describe the effects of globalization on the wages of U.S. workers and the strategies of U.S. companies
- Name at least six local government initiatives that can enhance high-tech economic development.

High technology, education, and development

The expression "knowledge is power" dates back to the ancients,[1] and today's information-based, technological economies again prove its truth. Decades ago, in the first postindustrial era, nonmanufacturing service functions—health, education, government, research, finance, insurance, and recreation—began to replace manufacturing in economic importance. Today, in a second postindustrial era driven by globalization, innovation, and information technology, we enjoy improvements in semiconductors, software, fiber optics, digital networks, the Internet, genetics, and the new media—collectively referred to as high technology.

New industries replacing old is a recurring theme in capitalist economies. The long-wave theory of economic development describes how bursts of innovation lead to economic growth.[2] According to the long-wave theory, these bursts of innovation occur at approximately 60-year intervals and spawn major industries. Great innovations in cotton manufacturing, iron smelting, railroads, steel processing, chemical production, automobile manufacturing, and electrical production—taking place after lengthy intervals—are all credited with generating wealth through innovation in the United States.

Technology is still altering the face of the U.S. economy. For example, management expert Peter Drucker says that a new information revolution is replicating earlier economic mutations and predicts that e-commerce (buying and selling over the Internet) will produce profound changes in markets and eventually force all businesses to compete with each other in a global marketplace.[3] Technology allows some people to work "smarter" than others, opens up markets to isolated producers, and permits purchasers to access a broader range of producers. Those who better adapt to the new technologies should enhance their productivity and should be better able to survive in the economic struggle over profits.

How technology leads to economic development

The link between technology and development became very evident after the industrial revolution, when some nations greatly expanded their productive capacities while others that did not adapt to the new technologies lagged behind. The link between technology and development refuted the classic economic view that growth was limited by factors of production such as labor and capital, and over time the association between technological progress and economic prosperity has become widely accepted.[4] It has been estimated that more than 80 percent of the growth in the U.S. economy between 1909 and 1949 was attributable to technology rather than to increases in capital or labor efficiency.[5]

There are several theories about how technology leads to economic development. Chapter 1 described how technology is inextricably linked to capturing profits and economic prosperity. Two specific theories—product-life-cycle theory and agglomeration theory—are particularly relevant for explaining the link between technology and economic development. Both theories are based on the general concept that areas that already have certain advantages will be able to build on those advantages while areas without initial advantages will fall farther behind. Other concepts—of unbalanced growth and "growth poles," for example[6]—also contribute to an understanding of how technology drives development.

The theory of unbalanced growth describes how market forces direct economic activity to leading regions. Leading regions possess comparative advantages because of their location, infrastructure, and other factors. Because of these advantages, leading regions are able to expand their dominance over lagging regions and create what is termed long-term divergence measured as greater wealth and development. The unbalanced-growth theory explains that businesses are initially attracted to one or more regional centers that are well located and offer good infrastructure. Once a critical mass is reached, additional businesses will identify that region as an area of opportunity.

Growth-pole theory hypothesizes that growth depends on one or more "propulsion industries." In growth poles, backward linkages develop when employees set up companies to supply a parent company with material needs, and forward linkages arise when employees set up companies to market products that were originally developed in the parent company. Propulsion industries that depend on backward and forward linkages are often linked to high-quality educational institutions. Major research universities (such as the Massachusetts Institute of Technology [MIT] and Stanford University in California) have assisted high-tech industries in high-growth areas along Route 128 in Massachusetts and in Silicon Valley, California.

Product-life-cycle theory

The product-life-cycle theory introduced in Chapter 1 links technological innovation with high profits and wages. Technologically sophisticated areas create high-value-added goods and services while technologically backward areas are relegated to producing lower-priced goods and paying lower salaries.

According to this theory, technology enhances producers' ability to identify opportunities to make high profits and save on production costs. Products at the early stage of production are unstandardized. For example, automobiles produced before 1910 varied much more than the standardized product of the 1930s. Demand for a new product is not highly dependent upon price, and a "captive market" develops for new, nonstandard, and not easily duplicated products. As demand for a new product expands, a certain degree of standardization usually takes place. Standardization makes possible economies through mass production, and production can take place in areas with less technical expertise. Industries seeking to lower their production costs will be attracted to the technologically backward areas where labor costs are low. For example, the United States exports high-priced products in the early stages of the products' life cycles and imports them later when they have become standardized and less-developed countries offer competitive advantages in terms of labor costs.

Before 1960 in the United States, some standardized industries moved from the more industrialized Northeast to the South where wages were lower. In the textile industry, factories that produced gray goods, cotton sheetings, and men's shirts moved to the South. Producers of high-fashion dresses and other unstandardized items were more reluctant to move. In the electronics industry, mass producers of tubes, resistors, and other standardized high-volume components showed the greatest disposition to move to the South. Custom-built and research-oriented production remained closer to markets and the main industrial complexes. Similar patterns have been identified in printing and chemical production.[7]

The growing interdependence of world markets and a global workforce raises the stakes in the competition for technological supremacy. Those who create cutting-edge technologies and acquire skills that others do not possess reap substantial rewards. But when an area loses its technological advantage and is no longer able to create goods that are at the initial stage of the product cycle, standardized work will be shifted to other areas and plants will close, possibly leading to a downward spiral in wages for workers and profits for owners as well as a decline in real estate values and a loss of population.[8]

Technology is a determinant of wages. Former secretary of labor Robert Reich has noted that the international division of labor will decide the standard of living of citizens in the United States and elsewhere. In 1983 he contended that the United States could not continue to rely on high-volume standardized industries such as automobile and steel production. Reich warned that, for the United States to sustain wages, production would have to shift to high-value-added products such as luxury automobiles, fiber-optic cable, lasers, integrated circuits, and aircraft engines. He saw that high growth was occurring in relatively low-paying service jobs (such as retail sales worker, waiter, janitor, taxi driver, hospital attendant, and security guard) that were immune from transfer to other geographic areas, while higher-paid blue-collar jobs were being eliminated. Those with advanced skills who provide analysis or work in jobs using symbols and who are in fields such as software design, scientific research, engineering, finance, marketing, cinematography, or music could reap large rewards.[9] Research already indicates that declines in U.S. wages are related to the search for lower labor costs outside U.S. borders.

Between 1977 and 1994 there was a sharp upward redistribution of income. Those in the fourth (60 to 80 percentile) and fifth (80 to 100 percentile) quintiles of earnings witnessed large gains in after-tax income. In contrast, the bottom 60 percent of all earners witnessed losses in after-tax incomes. Losses were the greatest (a drop of 16 percent) for the bottom 20 percent of earners.[10] Kevin Phillips has noted that a variety of inequalities grew in the 1990s:

> The worsening dimension of the nineties, especially for low-income and unskilled workers, involved dwindling employee benefits and health coverage. Long perceived as a great equalizer, between 1982 and 1996 they increasingly became part of the architecture of polarization. They were awarded freely—lavishly—in the top echelons and stinted near the bottom, where increasing ratios of employees were temporary or transient and found themselves partially or fully excluded.[11]

The growing split in income between higher and lower earners did not abate in the early 2000s. A 2002 study of full-time workers who were at least 25 years of age found that income inequalities grew in the 1980s and 1990s, until 1996. Inequalities eased between 1996 and 1999 and increased again after 1999. College-educated workers in high-tech fields fared very well while manufacturing workers lost. Declining earnings affected mostly men, a group who tended to be employed in the manufacturing sector. Unequal patterns of earnings growth were not discovered when women's earnings were studied, however. Technology appeared to be only one of a number of explanations for growing inequality; other factors thought to influence income disparities include weaker unions, reluctance of Congress to raise the minimum wage, and tremendous demand for some types of workers.[12]

Fear that America could devolve into a two-tiered society with technologically sophisticated workers above and everyone else below providing low-paying service jobs has led to an increase in protectionist sentiment. George Meany, then president of the AFL-CIO, stated in 1977 that foreign competitors were subsidizing their manufacturing base and taking jobs away from U.S. workers. He speculated that if the United States continued to pursue its free trade philosophies the country could eventually lose its manufacturing base and become dependent on other countries for production. Meany contended that practically every country in the world had some type of restriction, barrier, or subsidy that gave its manufacturers and workers an unfair advantage over U.S. workers.[13]

Others reject the protectionist leanings of organized labor. In a 1999 speech, the Federal Reserve chairman, Alan Greenspan, warned that efforts to erect protectionist barriers were unwise and self-defeating. He noted that protectionist policies could temporarily protect some jobs in noncompetitive industries but would exact a high cost on consumers who would pay higher prices for protected products. As an alternative to protectionism, Greenspan advocated retraining for workers who lost their jobs to foreign competition.[14] Other economists have recommended aggressive investment in research and education to protect competitive advantages in present technology and lead to the creation of new goods and services.

Product-life-cycle theory helps put changes in workforce demand and supply in perspective. It argues that standards of living for residents of the United States (as well as residents in other nations) depend upon the abilities of residents to be innovative and produce goods that are at the initial stages of the product life cycle.

Agglomeration theory

Agglomeration theory puts forward the idea that prosperous areas possess a critical mass of innovative processes and skilled workers. The result is sometimes referred to as the core-periphery effect, with the core experiencing concentrated development and the periphery relegated to accepting the scraps remaining.

Agglomeration occurs because businesses seek geographic proximity with other like-minded businesses. Synergy occurs when firms locate near each other, and among themselves they are able to consult, interact, and respond rapidly. Industrial clusters, which are discussed in the next section, are a variation on the theme of agglomeration economies. Because of the existing strength in a given cluster, new companies feel impelled to operate in the vicinity of the cluster.

Agglomeration theory posits that the rich get richer, and those with location advantages build on those advantages to create further growth. In line with this theory, the market model, and the supply-side economic view discussed in Chapter 1, the belief is that if businesses and people can freely choose where to locate, they will choose areas with comparative advantages. They will be rewarded by these advantages, business will thrive, and the chosen areas will grow. Proponents of agglomeration theory believe that government intervention and taxes for purposes of redistribution can be counterproductive.

Agglomeration has produced concentrations in gun, jewelry, and furniture manufacturing. High-tech concentrations have recently developed in Silicon Valley, along Route 128 near Boston, and in Minneapolis-St. Paul, Houston, and Huntsville, Alabama.[15]

Growth in each of these high-tech areas has been driven by slightly different factors. Research undertaken in major universities—Stanford, Berkeley, MIT, and Harvard—accounted for growth both in Silicon Valley and along Route 128. Private industry—specifically Minnesota Mining and Manufacturing (3M) and Honeywell—propelled the growth of high-tech concentrations in Minneapolis–St. Paul. Government space and rocket programs assisted the emergence of high-tech centers in Houston and Huntsville.

Because of the need for both engineers and production workers, high-technology manufacturing in the United States has remained strongly concentrated. Research validates the principle of agglomeration in high-tech businesses. One leading researcher of technology and economic development has stated that the concentration of R&D favors established regions, especially national capitals. Concentration has also reinforced regional growth in those areas where universities, industrial research, and national government research facilities are plentiful.[16] Agglomeration forces tend to sustain themselves, although some believe the trend can be thwarted at some point by high congestion-related costs, as in New York City.

Local economic development leaders interested in high-tech development should assess where the community or region fits in terms of its knowledge and technology bases. They should evaluate whether they are at the core or on the periphery. Not all localities are equally attractive to high-tech development. The semiconductor-manufacturing industry, for example, is highly concentrated in large-population areas and rarely sets up plants in rural and small-town locations. Later in this chapter, we will see that areas with premier universities and inviting amenities hold distinct advantages in attracting high-tech companies.

Clusters and economic development

An agglomeration of high-tech development often begins with one pioneer technology firm that creates a center of activity. Information needs compel would-be competitors to cluster around that firm, and highly skilled professionals are attracted to the area. Certain addresses begin to acquire prestige value. For example, software firms interviewed in the early 1980s stated that a Silicon Valley, Palo Alto, or San Francisco letterhead was far more valuable than a letterhead from Oakland. Identified clusters of new product activity also sprout their own labor force. Areas such as Silicon Valley draw heavily on engineering graduates from the two nearby universities, the University of California at Berkeley and Stanford.

As predicted by agglomeration theory, industries tend to cluster in the desired area. For example, in the late 1990s vast high-tech corridors with thousands of businesses and hundreds of thousands of employees arose around Washington, D.C. In 1999, those companies (many based on Internet technology, computer services, telecommunications, aerospace, and biotechnology) employed more than 470,000 people, outnumbering the roughly 350,000 people in the Washington area employed by the federal government.[17] Rapidly growing high-tech companies in the Washington, D.C., area actually employed more technology workers than companies in Silicon Valley or the Route 128 technology corridor in Boston.

High-tech clustering grew with the involvement of universities, new business incubators, research parks, and technology licensing programs. Numerous universities were actively involved in developing technology clusters. The University of Texas/Dallas helped to develop the high-technology companies in the area's Telecom Corridor. The University of South Florida helped create a high-tech corridor. The University of Washington

---

Business clusters in the United States

Established clusters can be found in all parts of the United States. New York's financial cluster includes a fully integrated center of banking and other types of financial transactions. It is unlikely that the destruction of the World Trade Center in 2001 will shift financial forces away from New York. Detroit has a network of firms (ranging from engineering to manufacturing and testing) that supports the automobile industry. A large entertainment cluster is located in Los Angeles, California; an insurance cluster exists in Hartford, Connecticut; an amusement cluster in Las Vegas, Nevada; and a microelectronics cluster in Silicon Valley, California. Less familiar clusters also exist in places such as Carlsbad, California (golf equipment); Boise, Idaho (sawmills); Rochester, New York (imaging equipment); and Omaha, Nebraska (telemarketing and credit card processing). Firms located within each cluster area benefit from a critical mass of related companies as each area begins to attract workers and start-ups and becomes known as the "in" place for a given industry.

Source: Michael E. Porter, "Clusters and Competition: New Agendas for Companies, Governments, and Institutions," in *On Competition,* ed. Michael E. Porter (Boston: Harvard Business School Press, 1998), 229.

---

helped spin off companies. Kendall Square in Cambridge, Massachusetts, contains the most concentrated single cluster of biotechnology employers in the world. Most of the biotechnology companies are connected in some way to MIT and Harvard. Biotechnology companies in particular cluster near universities because the research phase that precedes product creation tends to be lengthy, and the companies want access to trained employees and proximity to hospitals that can run clinical trials during this early phase. Institutions of higher learning have generally taken a more active role in job creation and have begun to see themselves as generators of start-ups.[18] The development of cutting-edge businesses near centers of research excellence provides support for the agglomeration theory.

The concept of clusters has recently captured a great deal of attention as an explanation for development.[19] Harvard Business School professor Michael E. Porter notes that clusters—geographic concentrations of interconnected companies—are a feature of virtually every national, regional, state, and metropolitan economy. The vitality of the cluster will determine the vitality of the jurisdiction, and companies have a tangible stake in their jurisdiction. Companies will seek to improve the business environment of their jurisdiction.

Clusters affect competition in three ways: by increasing the productivity of firms, by increasing companies' capacity for innovation and productivity growth, and by stimulating new business formation that supports innovation. The existence of a cluster facilitates personal relations, face-to-face communication, and interaction among networks of individuals and institutions. Clusters also increase productivity by providing superior and sometimes lower-cost access to business inputs. Access reduces inventory needs and lowers import costs. Clusters attract specialized as well as experienced workers, allowing for more efficient matching of jobs to people.

Clusters benefit from technical and specialized information within the area. This allows firms to be more productive and permits sophisticated buyers to gain information that meets their company's needs.

Cluster participants are interdependent. Therefore, poor performance on the part of some in the cluster can undermine the success of others. For example, although hotels, restaurants, and souvenir outlets in Orlando, Florida, rely on the popularity of Walt Disney World, poor service at local restaurants and hotels could negatively impact this popularity. Clusters also create peer pressure to succeed, and comparisons are constant when numerous, similar firms exist in the same area. Cluster participants usually strive for constructive interactions with other members of the regional cluster, and many analysts believe that the presence of multiple rivals operating under similar conditions forces firms to think creatively. Face-to-face contact, direct observation of other firms, the ability to act rapidly, and access to specialized personnel help speed innovation.

New entrepreneurs are attracted to clusters by the success of others and their desire to fill a specific niche. Clustering is related to the concept of social capital—the view that social relationships among individuals can positively influence economic behavior. While technology has diminished the importance of some locations, it has heightened the value of others:

> Paradoxically, then, the enduring competitive advantages in a global economy are often heavily local, arising from concentrations of highly specialized skills and knowledge, institutions, rivals, related businesses, and sophisticated customers in a particular nation or region. Proximity in geographic, cultural, and institutional terms allows special access, special relationships, better information, powerful incentives, and other advantages in productivity and productivity growth that are difficult to tap from a distance.[20]

The concept of clustering is important because it forces jurisdictions to take a hard look at questions that can lead to innovative thinking, a willingness to change, and long-term economic success. Jurisdictions must realistically assess their economic situation and future prospects for growth. By asking simple and to-the-point questions, jurisdictions can begin to develop long-term plans to enhance development. To assess their economic environment, local leaders can ask themselves the following questions:

- Is this jurisdiction competitive in the global marketplace?
- What are the economic strengths and weaknesses of this jurisdiction?
- How can this jurisdiction build upon strengths?
- How can this jurisdiction minimize weaknesses?
- What public policies could assist in creating a cluster?
- What public policies can attract investment?
- What kind of investment can this community most likely attract?

Cluster theory can help localities forge viable strategies because the theory combines a number of concepts such as building upon strength, synergy through mutually supportive linkages, enhancing innovation, and improving productivity. The concept of clustering embraces basic principles of economics and helps communities understand how to compete in the global marketplace.

Higher education and economic development

Higher education, particularly advanced training in scientific fields, has been linked to impressive advances in economic development. For example, one major study investigated the economic impact of MIT, a leading engineering university in the United States.[21] To estimate the economic impact of MIT, the study calculated numbers of employees and gross sales

Table 5–1

MIT-related companies with the largest number of employees

Company	Employment (thousands)	Sales (billions)	Location	Year founded	Founder and MIT class
Hewlett-Packard	102.3	31.5	Calif.	1939	W. Hewlett (1936)
Rockwell International	82.7	13.0	Calif.	1928	W. Rockwell (1908)
Raytheon	76.0	11.7	Mass.	1922	V. Bush (1916)
McDonnell Douglas	63.2	14.3	Mo.	1939	J. McDonnell (1925)
Digital Equipment	61.1	7.6	Mass.	1957	K. Olsen (1950)
Texas Instruments	59.6	13.1	Tex.	1930	C. Green (1923)
Campbell Soup	43.8	7.3	N.J.	1900	J. Dorrance (1895)
Intel	40.0	16.2	Calif.	1968	R. Noyce (1953)
Gillette	32.8	6.8	Mass.	1901	W. Nickerson (1876)
Tyco International	32.0	5.1	N.H.	1961	M. Weinstein (1961)

Source: *MIT: The Impact of Innovation* (Boston: BankBoston Economics Department, March 1997), 8, http://web.mit.edu/newsoffice/founders/Founders2.pdf.

of companies that were related to MIT (founders of the companies were MIT graduates or members of MIT's faculty or staff), spun off from a major MIT lab, or founded on MIT technologies. The study found that in the late 1990s MIT-linked companies employed over one million people and had annual world sales of $232 billion. A total of 1,065 MIT-linked firms employing 353,000 people worldwide and 125,000 people in the state of Massachusetts had headquarters in Massachusetts. Of all workers in the state, 5 percent were linked to MIT, and MIT-linked firms accounted for 25 percent of the sales of all manufacturing firms in the state.

Massachusetts also benefits from the influx of bright young people who come to the state to pursue higher education. Many of the state's "imports" from other states and nations stayed in Massachusetts and opened their own businesses. More than 42 percent of the software, biotech, and electronics companies founded by MIT graduates located in Massachusetts although only 9 percent of MIT undergraduates lived in the state before they attended the university. MIT graduates tend to be at the cutting edge of technology in knowledge-based fields such as software, manufacturing (electronics, biotech, instruments, and machinery), and consulting (architects, business consultants and engineers). Companies specializing in technology are often highly profitable, pay high wages to workers, and export many of their goods and services.

Some of the largest companies in the United States are linked in one way or another to MIT (see Table 5–1). MIT-related high-tech firms were more likely to locate in California or Massachusetts than elsewhere in the United States. These two states accounted for 70 percent of all MIT-related electronics firms, 68 percent of software firms, and 63 percent of drug and medical firms. Silicon Valley and the greater Boston area receive a continuous stream of MIT graduates to either work in existing companies or start new enterprises. Areas other than California that have supported high-tech growth and have attracted MIT graduates include the Washington-Baltimore-Philadelphia region, the Pacific Northwest, the Chicago area, southern Florida, Dallas, Houston, and industrial cities of Ohio, Michigan, and Pennsylvania.

Agglomeration theory explains the clustering of high-tech companies. An MIT survey of 1,300 corporate founders discovered that when they determined the location of new businesses, founders rated quality of life, proximity to key markets, access to skilled professionals, and access to universities as most important. Taxes and the regulatory climate of the area played much smaller roles (see Table 5–2).

Table 5–2 data are consistent with the tenet of the product-life-cycle theory that cost factors are less important for new and innovative types of products. The data also suggest that areas wishing to attract innovative producers must pay greater attention to quality of life, the skill level of the workforce, and the quality of schools. If a company cannot make a profit, the issue of taxation is moot; therefore, finding an environment that can support profit making is of greater initial concern.

The value of higher education has also been identified in studies of the University of California.[22] In FY 1993–1994, every $1 invested in the University of California (UC) generated $3, and in 1993–1994, UC attracted

Table 5–2
Determinants of location of MIT-related companies, by industry

Industry	Quality of life	Proximity of principal markets	Access to Skilled professionals	Skilled labor	Universities	Favorable environment Regulatory	Tax
Electronics	2.97	1.59	3.34	2.27	1.24	.52	.64
Chemicals, materials	2.73	1.20	2.97	1.97	1.10	.33	.17
Aerospace	2.25	2.75	2.38	1.63	1.38	.50	.38
Drugs, medical	2.90	2.26	3.00	1.50	1.59	.94	.81
Software	2.68	2.02	2.84	1.24	1.05	.53	.58
Engineering consulting	2.67	2.30	2.49	1.07	1.42	.60	.58
Management consulting	2.74	2.52	2.55	0.95	1.25	.36	.42
Mean	2.71	2.09	2.80	1.52	1.49	.54	.43

Source: *MIT: The Impact of Innovation* (Boston: BankBoston Economics Department, March 1997), 37, http://web.mit.edu/newsoffice/founders/Founders2.pdf.
Note: 5 = most important, 0 = not important; average for companies by category

more than $2.1 billion in federal funds, which included $1.2 billion for research and education, almost $600 million in health care reimbursements, and $400 million in student financial aid. The university also received annual royalties of more than $63 million from patents for products developed by university scientists (in 1992–1993 UC led the nation in the number of patents produced). In 1993, two California schools (UC and Stanford University) ranked first and second in the nation in terms of royalty income.

University of California graduates started many of the most successful companies in California. UC scientists founded three of the nation's top biotechnology companies—Genentech, Chiron, and Amgen. Students and researchers from Berkeley were the driving force behind the computer companies Intel, Apple, and Sun Microsystems.

Entrepreneurs from California's universities are continuing the region's competitive advantage by making generous gifts to their alma maters. In 1999, Stanford University announced a $150 million gift from James H. Clark, a former member of Stanford's faculty in the department of electrical engineering and founder of both Silicon Graphics, a company based on research he began at Stanford, and the very profitable Netscape Communications Corporation.[23]

Research case 5–1 on page 151 presents additional empirical support for the view that education, particularly scientific and technical education, is linked to economic development. As demonstrated in the case study, larger and wealthier states possess higher-quality education programs, and these states with well-regarded schools have captured the largest shares of technology-based economic growth. Large states appear to be able to capitalize on technological advances that are generated at universities. Smaller states can nevertheless work toward improving their universities and developing technological niches. Local leaders can carefully assess their technical capacities and work to capture markets. For example, the state of Ohio and the University of Akron are developing expertise in the area of polymer technology. The state of New York has established branches of the state university as centers of excellence in separate and distinct technological fields.

The private sector plays the dominant role in applying scientific knowledge to the development of profitable products (see the next section on "Entrepreneurship and development"), but the role of universities in providing a pool of technical talent is very important. Ed Bee, president of a California-based management company, has stated:

> The evidence is conclusive that the private sector is the driver that turns research into useful products and services. The university's role in the process is largely one of supplying technically trained workers for product development and commercialization by private sector companies. Good engineering schools and computer science departments are an excellent resource for attracting technology companies.[24]

To capitalize on scientific knowledge, a complex web of scientists, market researchers, managers, risk takers, and others is needed. Communities need to assess their strengths and weaknesses if they wish to leverage R&D successfully. It appears that, while universities themselves may not generate many patents, start-ups, or licensing fees, they serve as "technology platforms" for established companies. Universities have been recognized for their assistance to established companies, particularly in the areas of chemistry, plastics, and drugs.

The link between education and development is consistent with interrelationships among knowledge, innovation, new products, and profit predicted by the product-life-cycle theory.

Entrepreneurship and development

Advances in the Western world came about not only from academic inquiry that sought to expand the knowledge base but also from the application and diffusion of knowledge. Scientific discovery was a prime mover of capitalist expansion, expansion that rested on three key ideas: invention, innovation, and adoption. Product-life-cycle theory claims that new technologies are discovered, introduced by leading entrepreneurs, and finally adopted by others. Agglomeration theory contributes the observation that innovation arises in core industrial centers (especially centers of research and development) and spreads from those centers to peripheral areas. Those who work with new technology are attracted to and nurtured by core industrial areas.

The concept of entrepreneurship is inextricably linked to technology and economic development. Entrepreneurs have been exalted as problem solvers and engines of development. In the early 1980s, George Gilder stated:

> Whether sorting potatoes or writing software, they [capitalists] are movers and shakers, doers and givers, brimming with visions of creation and opportunity. They are optimists, who see in every patch of sand a potential garden, in every man a potential worker, in every problem a possible profit. Their self-interest succumbs to their deeper interest and engagement in the world beyond themselves, impelled by their curiosity, imagination, and faith....

> Bullheaded, defiant, tenacious, creative entrepreneurs continue to solve the problems of the world even faster than the world could create them. The achievements of enterprise remain the highest testimony to the mysterious strength of the human spirit.[25]

Gilder believes that entrepreneurs "sustain the world," "overthrow establishments rather than establish equilibrium," and represent the "heroes of economic life." Entrepreneurs transcend markets, create their own destinies, make their own markets, develop their own opportunities, evoke their own demand, and create innovative technology. Entrepreneurs do not simply respond to market forces, scout opportunities, use existing technology, or respond to existing demand. Michael Dell of the Dell Computer Corporation is a contemporary example of an individual who made his own market, developed his own opportunities, and created his own innovations. His story is told in Case study 5–1 beginning on page 152.

Educational advances by themselves may have limited commercial application. The presence of entrepreneurs is usually necessary to transform knowledge into commercial products. Orville and Wilbur Wright were the first to fly an airplane, yet others transformed the technology into a profitable industry. Marconi developed wireless communication but innovative applicators developed a profitable radio industry.

Practical application of scientific advances is essential for economic development to occur. Many patents are filed on the basis of basic and applied research; but before patents can be turned into profitable businesses, a prototype, a production method, and a market assessment must be developed. If an invention is identified as a salable product, entrepreneurs need to turn the invention into a profit-making business. At this stage a different set of skills is needed, including an understanding of market opportunities and the costs and risks involved in production as well as the ability to identify executives who could launch the business.

Commercialization is thought to comprise two distinct steps: identifying niche markets and creating mass markets. For example, a research team at

---

What is an entrepreneur?

An entrepreneur is a production innovator who perceives the opportunity to provide a new product or implement a new production method, then organizes the needed production inputs and assumes financial risk to bring the new product or method to the market.

Bell Labs pioneered the transistor. It was first used commercially in the mid-1950s for the niche markets of high-end missile guidance and aircraft electronics systems. In the 1950s, the Dallas-based company, Texas Instruments, placed transistors in radios. In a relatively short period of time the transistor radio became a huge mass-market item, and the price of transistors plunged with the growing worldwide demand.[26]

At the commercialization stage, development requires many more non-scientists and engineers than it did at earlier stages of the process. Universities play a role in the process, yet their role is more important in terms of collaboration with large science-based companies. More than half the nation's basic research (which leads to future opportunities) is performed by universities, and in 1999 more than 100 universities had technology transfer programs to license discoveries. In 1999, however, the university total of licensing fees was less than 1 percent of the more than $78 billion in license fees received by the private sector. Two companies alone (IBM and Texas Instruments) each received in excess of $1 billion a year for patent royalties in the early 1990s. IBM alone received 2,658 patents in 1998, more than all U.S. universities combined.[27]

According to David Birch, the following factors contribute to an entrepreneurial climate that encourages and attracts entrepreneurs:[28]

- Educational resources, especially higher education
- Quality of labor
- Quality of government
- Telecommunications
- Quality of life.

Technology and the global economy

Product-life-cycle and agglomeration perspectives of development suggest that technological advancement is strongly linked to wealth creation. This link has become even stronger and more apparent since some economies have established a global presence. Globalization intensifies competition to create and maintain lucrative markets. Globalization also enlarges the rewards for marketplace winners and increases the pain of market losers. The opening of new markets to trade as well as to advances in technology has accelerated the trend toward globalization.

To survive in the global marketplace, producers will have to identify and enhance their competitive advantages. In general, vested interests that hold a competitive advantage in an area wish to open global markets while those that do not hold an advantage wish to avoid global competition. For example, U.S. workers with minimal skills can be replaced by workers in other countries willing to work for lower wages, so underskilled workers in the United States do not want open markets. Globalization of production also puts U.S. workers in direct competition with workers in countries where environmental and workplace safety standards are low. Some fear that the need to compete may lead to a relaxation of environmental standards in the United States and a more dangerous work environment for U.S. wage earners.

Global hiring already has had an impact on the U.S. economy. In 1999 the number of immigrant workers in the United States rose to 15.7 million, up 17 percent from three years earlier. Nevertheless, in 2000, with the national unemployment rate at about 4 percent (near its lowest point in 40 years), various industries pressured Congress to enact legislation that would admit hundreds of thousands of additional immigrants each year. Among the groups pressuring for more immigration were the National Restaurant Association, the American Hotel and Lodging Association, the agriculture industry, and high-tech companies. Each of these industries was desperate to find adequate numbers of qualified workers. Although Congress in 1998 had expanded the numbers of visas by more than 80 percent, computer and software companies lobbied Congress for more visas to be granted to foreign workers with technology expertise. Labor unions, including the United Farm Workers, opposed the granting of more visas, claiming that immigrants drove down wages and were easy-to-exploit captives of business. Studies show that immigrants—especially illegal, unskilled workers—push down wages for U.S.-born workers who have less than a high school education.[29] American businesses ranging from motels and lettuce farms to high-tech companies have benefited from the influx of immigrants, however.[30] U.S. businesses, evidencing the link between technology and economic development, place a higher value on immigrants with technical skills.

Research case 5–1

Testing the link between education and economic development

This research case attempts to uncover statistical associations between education and economic development.

A comparison of rankings of national universities (as reported in the popular publication, *U.S. News & World Report*) with rankings of state economic development illuminates the link between higher education and economic development.

The national school rankings show a strong agglomeration effect. The more populous states such as California, New York, Massachusetts, Pennsylvania, and Texas claimed many "national" universities, ranked in either the first or second tier of the four tiers reported by *U.S. News & World Report*. The least populous states placed few universities in even the lower tiers.

Agglomeration in topflight technical education, based on rankings of the top 50 graduate programs in the technical fields of engineering, medicine, and business, showed that large states (California, New York, Pennsylvania, Massachusetts, and Illinois) enjoy the most highly regarded educational systems. California claimed four of the top twelve engineering programs (Stanford, ranked 2; University of California, Berkeley, ranked 5; California Institute of Technology, ranked 7; and University of Southern California, ranked 12), but 18 states (Alaska, Arkansas, Hawaii, Idaho, Kansas, Kentucky, Maine, Mississippi, Montana, Nebraska, North Dakota, Oklahoma, Rhode Island, South Carolina, South Dakota, Vermont, West Virginia, and Wyoming) did not place any universities in the top 50 of any of the three technical fields.

Agglomeration theory predicts that educational quality will correlate with measures of development such as gross state product, median income, nonfarm employment, and population. When changes in development instead of aggregate measures of development were considered by the authors, education was related to changes in median income but not to changes in the other development measures. Measures of a state's overall education ranking and technical education ranking in 1991 were compared with the percent change between 1990 and 1997 in gross state product, median income, nonfarm employment, and population. The authors found a statistically significant association (.05 level) between overall education quality in the state and growth of median income; the authors also found a statistically significant association (.01 level) between technical education quality in the state and growth of median income.

Thus growth in the number of jobs was not linked to education, but gains in the income levels of those with jobs were linked to education. The strong increases in median income in the states with better educational systems are consistent with the agglomeration theory.

Data indicate that job growth (in percent) between 1990 and 1997 in low-wage states (such as Arizona, Arkansas, Florida, Georgia, Idaho, Kentucky, Missouri, Nebraska, New Mexico, North Carolina, Tennessee, and Texas) was larger than the percent job growth in the higher-wage states of Alaska, California, Connecticut, Hawaii, Maryland, Massachusetts, New Jersey, Rhode Island, and Vermont. It appears that while median incomes in high-quality-education states were growing, lower-paying jobs were relocating to lower-wage regions of the country. This is consistent with the economic theories presented here that contend that employers will search to reduce their costs and that higher-wage growth will occur in the core and lag in the outlying areas.

Other research has shown that jobs in specific high-tech industries were strongly related to education during the 1990s.[31] As further evidence of agglomeration, high-tech payrolls and growth of those payrolls were concentrated in a few states including California, Texas, New York, Pennsylvania, and Massachusetts. Between 1993 and 1997 the 10 states with the largest growth in high-tech payrolls accounted for 66 percent of payroll growth. Small states had very little activity in high-tech industries. California far surpassed other states in terms of high-tech payroll and growth in high-tech wages.

Case study 5–1   Austin, Texas, and the Dell Computer Company

Not long ago—in the 1960s—Austin, Texas, was a quiet state capital and the home of the University of Texas. If one was not employed by the state government or the university, making a living could be a struggle.[32] In the 1970s, the population was about 250,000. After the collapse of the energy industry in 1987, the office vacancy rate in the city was 48 percent.[33]

But by 2000, Austin was an economic boomtown, with a metropolitan area population of 1 million and an unemployment rate of about 2 percent.[34] At the turn of the twenty-first century, job growth exceeded 4 percent per year.[35] The May 31, 1999, issue of *Forbes* ranked Austin second among the 162 largest metropolitan areas in the United States in the growth of jobs and business activity. The Austin area now adds an estimated 45,000 people to its population every year.[36]

Most of the growth can be attributed to a rapid increase in high-technology activity. The leading industries during the 1990s were software development, semiconductors, and computer hardware.[37] Austin was home to some of the largest computer hardware firms such as IBM and Dell, to more than 350 software manufacturers, and to several computer chip–making firms.[38] The January 12, 1998, issue of *Computerworld* placed Austin seventh among the 25 fastest-growing information technology job markets.[39] In 1999, the Texas Workforce Commission reported a tripling in high-technology employment in Austin since 1989.[40]

Studies have shown, however, that high-technology industrial development per se does not guarantee dynamic economic growth. What is key is the stage of growth of local high-tech businesses. More mature high-tech firms and high-tech branch plants do not necessarily foster rapid growth, but start-ups in these industries do.[41] Austin's boom has come as a result of growth in start-ups, which brought with it more knowledge-intensive jobs.[42]

Certainly the opportunity for backward and forward links created by the presence of large companies such as Advanced Micro Devices, Dell, IBM, Motorola, Samsung, and Texas Instruments has contributed to Austin's economic growth. Although Austin's telecommunications infrastructure has also played a role, one analyst has pointed out that "...having these [telecommunications] facilities will not ensure that development takes place if there is not sufficient entrepreneurial capacity to respond to the opportunities provided by that infrastructure."[43]

Entrepreneurship has been vital to Austin's success, and it is the focus of this case study about the Dell Computer Corporation. Before we explore entrepreneurship's role, however, four other physical and human infrastructure-related factors require discussion: proximity to the University of Texas at Austin, state and local economic development policies that focus on high-technology growth, local leadership, and an entrepreneurial spirit.

The University of Texas at Austin

Cities successful at generating economic development today are accomplishing it by developing high-technology clusters. Because the magnet that creates and holds these clusters is a highly educated workforce,[44] a major engine of development is the local university. Austin enjoys the advantage of being home to the University of Texas (UT), one of the largest institutions of higher education in the country, with approximately 48,000 students and 2,700 faculty.[45] UT is both a source of well-educated talent and a research engine.

Of its 98 degree programs, UT has 49 graduate programs and specialties that rank among the top 10 nationally. These include computer sciences, artificial intelligence, computer engineering, aerospace engineering, electrical/electronic/communications engineering, atomic/molecular physics, and management information systems. The university also boasts top doctoral programs in technology fields: civil engineering, computer science, aerospace engineering, astrophysics/astronomy, and chemical engineering.[46]

UT's graduate programs enroll approximately 11,000 students, and they award approximately 800 doctorates annually (number two in the United States) and 2,500 master's degrees.[47] Thousands of undergraduates also complete their degrees each year. Austin of course also imports some of its well-educated talent. A number of transplants are from California's Silicon Valley and possess degrees from West Coast schools; one example is Joe Liemandt, the founder of Trilogy Development Group, from Stanford University.[48] Thus UT's contribution to an appropriately educated workforce in Austin is substantial, but it cannot be the only source because Austin is having difficulty keeping up with the staggering demand for a technologically competent workforce.

The university's research capacity and efforts have been a deciding factor for a number of high-technology firms that selected Austin as a home. UT has 87 organized research units on campus.[49] It is the residence of a successful high-technology business incubator. The faculty includes Nobel prize winners and members of prestigious research academies such as the National Academy of Engineering, the American Academy of Arts and Sciences, and the National Academy of Sciences.[50] In 1997, UT researchers received $241 million in sponsored research awards.[51] The university actively courts industry. In 1983, it used a pledge of 32 endowed chairs, new buildings, and laboratory space to lure the Microelectronics and Computer Technology Corporation (MCC), the nation's first high-tech R&D consortium, to Austin and, in 1988, led the effort to bring Sematech (a semiconductor manufacturer's consortium) to the city.[52]

All of this research activity is especially attractive to high-tech start-ups that are in the R&D phase of their own growth and that can benefit from access to topflight scientists and their research products. Not only does this create an ideal environment for technology transfer, but it also provides access to R&D expertise and facilities to young firms that might not otherwise be able to secure them in-house.

State and local economic development policies

The presence of a research university is only one factor in the success of a high-technology-based economic development strategy.[53] In Austin, proactive steps by state and local officials also stimulated growth. Since the 1980s, the state of Texas has played an important role in Austin's emergence as a high-technology haven because of its adoption of a number of policies and programs with three major economic development goals:[54]

- Revitalize existing but declining industries, or replace them
- Create growth poles or clusters that will attract other industries and firms
- Diversify state and local industrial mixes.

From the state's perspective, the chief purpose of these policies and programs is to create jobs to replace those lost when industries based on energy and real estate, upon which Texas's economy had been so reliant, went into decline. It could even be said that Texas was forced to switch from selling commodities to selling high-technology products.[55] Overall, the strategy has worked. By 1996, more people in Texas—nearly 250,000 and rising—were employed in high-technology businesses than in energy.[56]

The state of Texas has continued to maintain its focus on high-tech-based growth and development. In September 1996, Governor George W. Bush established the Texas Science and Technology Council, which studied Texas's science and technology industries to learn more about the barriers to continued growth that they face. The council was also charged with recommending strategies for overcoming the barriers they identified.[57]

The city of Austin promotes its own high-technology-based economic development success by, for example, developing telecommunications infrastructure and sponsoring the annual National Summit of Young Technology Leaders (NexTech), a gathering in Austin where the brightest high school mathematics and science students from around the country can learn more about career opportunities in high-tech industries. One purpose of NexTech is to attract this talent to the city to live and work because the shortage of appropriately educated individuals in Austin's labor pool has persisted.[58]

Local leadership

The vision that Austin could be a high-tech center can be traced, at least in part, to Pike Powers, an Austin lawyer and executive assistant to former

Texas governor Mark White. In 1983, when Texas was in the grip of an oil recession, Powers helped lead the effort to land MCC. Powers and Governor White went around the state to raise $23 million to build a home for the consortium, which many credit with starting Austin's high-tech development.

Other public officials contributed greatly to Austin's growth. Government leaders and UT officials collaborated to promote the idea that Austin could serve the high-tech industry. The university changed its curriculum to prepare students to work for high-tech firms. Austin's local government streamlined its permit process and instituted a workforce development program to help draw workers to the city.[59]

The city of Austin developed a strong partnership with the Greater Austin Chamber of Commerce. One of their joint initiatives is the Capital Area Training Foundation (CATF), formed in 1994 and originally funded by a school-to-work grant through the U.S. Department of Education and the U.S. Department of Labor. One of the chief goals of CATF is to build a qualified entry-level workforce for Austin area employers.

Career Pathway, one of CATF's major programs, provides high school students with an opportunity to earn college credits through courses taught by high school teachers and instructors from Austin Community College. Through a partnership with Advanced Micro Devices, CATF provides students with work experience via internships and scholarship opportunities. These educational programs will soon include middle school students, with a goal of heightening interest in mathematics and science and improving skills in these subjects at an earlier age. CATF also provides workshops and seminars to help teachers to stay up-to-date on the latest technological advances.

Together the city and the Chamber of Commerce also undertake business retention and attraction trips. They organized a trip to San Jose, California, in 2002 for local government leaders, the president of the University of Texas, and approximately 40 business leaders to meet with corporations that have production facilities in the Austin area. The delegation urged these companies to move their corporate headquarters to Austin and offered to assist them to expand their facilities already in Austin.[60]

The entrepreneurship factor

Economic development in some cities has been driven by the public sector, accomplished with various incentives to stimulate economic growth, sometimes via business creation. Research universities have attempted to stimulate new enterprise development through the adoption of technology transfer strategies. Although the presence of UT, the policies of the state of Texas and the city of Austin, and the collaboration of local leaders have been important for establishing the infrastructure and environment that have encouraged dynamic growth, the true impetus for this growth has been entrepreneurship itself. Individuals with innovative solutions to problems and the drive to make their visions a reality are the ones who launched Austin's high-tech economy. Thus Austin's high-tech success is driven as much by entrepreneurial spirit as it is by public sector incentives. The public sector sets the stage, but there must be entrepreneurial actors for the show to go on.

Perhaps Austin's most famous high-technology corporate citizen is the homegrown Dell Computer Corporation, a classic example of a large corporation with humble beginnings based in the entrepreneurial skills of one individual. Today it is the world's top-ranked computer systems company, and its share of the global market continues to grow. In 1998, it captured 8.5 percent of that market; in 2001 it was 11.3 percent.[61] Dell, which is headquartered in Round Rock just outside Austin, employs about 38,200 people in the United States and in countries around the world.

Since its founding in 1984, Dell Computer has become something of a symbol of what is possible in the realm of high-tech development. It has also become an individual high-technology growth pole for Austin. Its founder and CEO, Michael Dell, is among the most respected businesspeople in the computer field. His innovative ideas have helped revolutionize the way computers are manufactured and marketed and have played a major role in putting Austin, Texas, on the high-technology map.

Michael Dell is a native of Houston, where his mother, a stockbroker, taught him his first lessons in business. While growing up, Dell excelled in mathematics and computers, joined a mathematics club in junior high school, conversed with other computer enthusiasts via a computer bulletin board he set up, and repaired and modified personal computers. In 1983, he moved to Austin to attend UT and, during his freshman year, began his first business—selling from the trunk of his car upgraded personal computers and add-ons. This turned out to be the forerunner of Dell Computer Corporation, which he formed the following year, after dropping out of UT, with only $1,000 in start-up capital.[62]

Dell's ability to find good, competent technical workers kept him in Austin. In building his company, Dell deliberately sought to hire people who were connected to other people in useful ways. For example, his first president was a venture capitalist who was able to link Dell's company to the venture capital community.[63] He also tried to surround himself with "smart advisers."[64] All of this helped Dell attract strong members to the Dell Computer Corporation board of directors as well. Michael Dell worked at building both internal and external social capital for strengthening and sustaining his firm, a key to strong organizations of any type.[65]

Like most entrepreneurs, Dell created a niche for his company by developing innovative solutions to problems and responding to opportunities presented by the marketplace. At the time Dell Computer entered the market, the accepted way of selling computer hardware was through retail outlets, but this increased the cost of computer equipment and encouraged the production of standardized machines. Dell imagined selling computers directly to customers without retail middlemen and customizing the computers to fit the specific needs of each purchaser.[66]

While making computers to order, Dell from the beginning made it a business practice to maintain close communications with his customers.[67] He calls this strategy virtual integration: the creation of seamless connections between Dell Computer's parts suppliers, Dell itself as the manufacturer, and Dell's customers. The individual pieces of Dell's virtual integration strategy are now common business approaches, and they include "customer focus, supplier partnerships, mass customization, [and] just-in-time manufacturing." Dell's use of customer feedback to drive these links is what is innovative about his approach. Virtual integration gives Dell Computer the control afforded by a traditional vertical hierarchy and the flexibility of a virtual organization.[68]

In his autobiography, *Direct from Dell*, Michael Dell devotes an entire chapter to molding a firm's employees into a team. He believes this practice is essential for a company's success although it is still not widely used by the majority of U.S. corporations. He believes it is important to make all employees feel that they are an important part of a greater whole and to have a company strategy that is widely understood and followed throughout the organization. Dell narrows employees' job responsibilities in order to give them time to innovate, experiment, and grow. The company finds ways to reward employees for working in teams. Finally, Dell emphasizes the value of creating a management team that shares responsibility and permits upper-level management to take an involved, hands-on approach. Michael Dell sees all of this as crucial to "maintain[ing] the entrepreneurial spirit that has characterized Dell."[69]

For high-technology companies in particular, maintaining esprit de corps and an entrepreneurial edge are crucial to survival and success. Talented technology personnel are in great demand, and their relative youth and willingness to take risks make them exceptionally mobile. Thus a competitive salary alone cannot ensure loyalty. Companies must give their employees room to grow by encouraging them to be "intrapreneurs."[70]

Dell also emphasizes the importance of links between his company and its customers and suppliers.[71] When Dell Computer Corporation decided not to build its own computer hardware components but instead purchase components from companies that specialize in making them, thus leveraging the expertise of these firms to facilitate Dell's own rapid growth, it learned that it did not need to own these suppliers to control quality and efficiency.[72] It could instead carefully evaluate, select, and monitor them to ensure that it was getting state-of-the-art components of the highest grade. Dell also found that risk could be pooled by working with multiple suppliers, thereby ensuring access to needed supplies at all times (if one supplier could not meet Dell's needs, another would be available to fill the gap).

Dell's direct relationship with its customers provides additional opportunities for building synergies. Because Dell gets its products to market so quickly, its suppliers do also; and because Dell sells directly to its customers, it can constantly monitor their satisfaction with its products. The feedback Dell gets from its clients is almost immediate and can be routed to suppliers who can use it to make rapid adjustments to correct errors or respond to shifts in consumer tastes or needs. Suppliers are, in effect, forced to become more competitive. Everyone benefits from this relationship—Dell, its customers, and its suppliers.

Despite the advantages of having multiple suppliers for any one component, Dell learned that the ensuing complexity could reach a point of diminishing returns. Today Dell uses fewer than 40 suppliers to meet 90 percent of its needs.[73] Dell has also learned that having its suppliers near its manufacturing facilities yields cost savings, not merely in lower transportation costs but in lower component costs as well. Component prices drop almost weekly, and being near the suppliers means being able to keep inventory very low, allowing Dell to stay ahead of the steady price decline.[74] Dell also shares crucial information with its suppliers about its volume and quality needs.

Lessons for local governments

The Dell experience offers several insights helpful to local government development professionals—some insights reinforce conventional wisdom and some are new. The fact that manufacturers need suppliers in close physical proximity is not new. However, the fact that Dell's inputs are smaller and therefore easier and cheaper to transport than its finished product makes Dell's relationships an untraditional case of economic geography. It suggests, however, that if government seeks to intervene to encourage high-technology growth and development, it should probably enhance the opportunity for local high-tech manufacturers to bring their suppliers nearer to them. This might be accomplished through the creation of research and technology parks, with appropriate space and infrastructure. Maintaining GIS-based databases on available manufacturing space and/or appropriately zoned land can also be effective. Above all, the local government must maintain close contact with its high-tech manufacturers in order to understand their supplier needs, in much the same way that Dell Computer monitors its customers' needs.

Dell's links to its customers and its suppliers reflect new economic relationships. Economic developers must understand this new economic paradigm if their interventions to affect private business behaviors for the benefit of the public good are to have an impact. Regulations to protect consumers are in some ways obsolete in this new scenario because consumers are driving the process. Public incentives to encourage supplier firms to locate in the community are actually unnecessary and serve merely as windfall profits to supplier firms because their customers (Dell, for example) want them there anyway. Public sector efforts to play matchmaker along the supply chain may be equally unnecessary.

Public resources are better spent on initiatives to encourage the creation and growth of entrepreneurial manufacturers like Dell Computer. This might include ensuring that adequate angel and venture capital is available locally, that an appropriately trained workforce is available, that adequate infrastructure (particularly telecommunications) is in place, that adequate and appropriate building space is available, and that public and nonprofit service provision for entrepreneurs is strategically and coherently linked (in other words, that there is satisfactory social capital for new enterprise development).

The retention of employees in today's high-tech job market is largely a matter for each individual private company. Nonetheless, economic developers can assist by undertaking and encouraging activities that build a qualified workforce. By increasing the supply of well-trained workers in the region, some of the demand pressures can be relieved. However, the supply problem cannot be eliminated until the national, and global, supply of high-tech workers equals the demand.

No two communities are the same, and attempting to replicate an Austin or a Silicon Valley elsewhere in the country may not be the most appropriate economic development strategy. It is possible to use high technology as an engine for local and regional economic growth, but a goodly number of ingredients are necessary for success. Some ingredients are the responsibility of the private sector, but state and local governments can do a great deal to foster high-tech economic development:

- Encourage strategic cooperation between state and local governments to assemble the resources for creating an infrastructure and legislative environment that encourages high-technology growth

- Collaborate with local colleges and universities to ensure an adequately skilled workforce and the types of innovation around which new businesses can be created

- Provide assistance to entrepreneurs through the development of business incubation programs, capital provision mechanisms, and other tools discussed in Chapter 4

- Feature local quality-of-life amenities as a way of attracting educated workers from outside the community or region

- Help complementary firms new to the region or new start-ups indigenous to the region find land and buildings

- Look for potential links among local public, private, and nonprofit organizations that assist businesses, and invent ways to enhance those links to ensure efficient and effective assistance to local entrepreneurs

- Strategically enhance public education (K–12 and community colleges), particularly in math, science, and computer technology

A tale of two cities

The experience of Austin, Texas, provides insights into the ingredients for successful high-technology-based development in a metropolitan region. A study of the Johns Hopkins University in Baltimore and economic development in that city notes that having a major research university is not a guarantee of technology-based economic development. Despite the research preeminence of Johns Hopkins, Baltimore has not been particularly successful in building an industrial sector strong in technology. The study of Baltimore concludes that for a research university to be a successful development engine, a "technological infrastructure of innovation" must be in place in the region. This infrastructure includes a cluster of competing firms in a single industry, national headquarters that engage in R&D, specialized business service providers, and an entrepreneurial climate with many small start-ups. These are components that Baltimore did not have in place to foster high-tech development.

Unlike Baltimore, Austin has this full infrastructure at work, with a cluster in the computer hardware and software industries. Austin hosts corporate headquarters, Dell and others. It boasts a strong business service sector. It is home to an active entrepreneurial culture. In this environment, the University of Texas at Austin can act effectively as an economic engine.

Source: M. P. Feldman, "The University and Economic Development: The Case of Johns Hopkins University and Baltimore," *Economic Development Quarterly* 8, no. 1 (1994): 67–76.

- Create R&D parks with appropriate state-of-the-art infrastructure to encourage the attraction, retention, and creation of high-tech firms that complement and enhance the local cluster
- Work closely with local high-tech companies to understand companies' needs and learn what kind of public sector assistance can help companies overcome obstacles that stand in their way.

Summary

After enormous growth in the 1980s and 1990s, technology lost some of its cachet at the turn of the millennium. The technology-laden NASDAQ stock exchange was in sharp decline; between May 2000 and July 2002, the NASDAQ exchange plunged 73 percent. Bankruptcies occurred in new-economy companies such as WorldCom and Global Crossing. Localities at the leading edge of the technology bubble were hardest hit. For example, property appreciation (among the 185 largest U.S. metropolitan areas between 2001 and 2002) was lowest for the high-tech hubs of San Jose, California; Austin, Texas; and San Francisco.[75] Venture-capital companies returning cash to investors was another sign of a bubble burst. In contrast with earlier times, when almost any tech-related idea could attract money, investment companies claimed that a lack of good business opportunities existed.[76]

The economic downturn in 2001 and the sharp drop in the stock market between 2000 and 2002 should not be interpreted as a refutation of long-held economic principles, however. Theories of the product life cycle, agglomeration, and clusters are based on the general concept that certain geographic areas are better than others for high-tech businesses. Areas that already have certain advantages will be able to build on those advantages, and high-tech businesses will multiply in those places. These areas are also home to top-tier educational institutions that can supply an educated workforce for business as well as researchers who innovate for the benefit of business.

To survive in today's increasingly globalized economy, producers must identify and enhance their competitive advantages; and state and local governments must do this as well. Although not every local jurisdiction can be the site of a research university, governments can enhance their attractiveness to high-tech businesses. They can encourage suppliers to locate nearby through the creation of research and technology parks, maintenance of GIS-based databases on available manufacturing space and appropriately zoned land, encouragement of adequate local angel and venture capital, and provision of adequate infrastructure (especially telecommunications). With good business practices, inventions that produce better and cheaper products still lead to profit. Individuals willing to take risks and invest in ideas (in contrast to individuals seeking quick profits) are still needed to build wealth. Business cycles will come and go, but individuals and localities must still position themselves to gain from the next upturn.

Austin, Texas, provides an example for other local governments in their efforts to provide a friendly atmosphere for high-tech businesses.

Study questions

- How can the United States protect future domestic wages?

- How does product-life-cycle theory explain economic development?

- How does agglomeration theory explain economic development?

- What can schools do to enhance economic development in the United States?

- How can a local government official realistically assess the strengths and weaknesses of a jurisdiction in terms of its attractiveness to entrepreneurship?

- Describe how local economies can be enhanced by the presence of a high-quality university with great economic development potential.

- The growth of Michael Dell's high-tech business points out how some of the rules have changed for local governments in their efforts to attract and retain high-tech businesses. What are some of these changes?

- How did the city of Austin and the state of Texas assist the growth of Dell Computer Corporation?

1 Proverbs 24:5.

2 N. D. Kondratieff, "The Long Waves in Economic Life," *Review of Economic Statistics* 17 (1935): 105–115.

3 Peter Drucker, "Beyond the Information Revolution," *Atlantic Monthly,* October 1999, 47–57.

4 A. T. Thwaites and R. P. Oakey, "Editorial Introduction," in *The Regional Economic Impact of Technological Change,* eds. A. T. Thwaites and R. P. Oakey (New York: St. Martin's Press, 1985), 1.

5 Robert Solow, "Technical Change and the Aggregate Production Function," *Review of Economic Statistics* 39 (1957): 312–320.

6 Gunnar Myrdal, *Economic Theory and Under-Developed Regions* (London: G. Duckworth, 1957); Albert Hirschman, *The Strategy of Economic Development* (New Haven: Yale University Press, 1958).

7 Raymond Vernon, "International Investment and International Trade in the Product Cycle," *Quarterly Journal of Economics* 80 (May 1966): 204.

8 Candace Howes and Ann Markusen, "Trade, Industry, and Economic Development," in *Trading Industries: Trading Regions: International Trade, American Industry, and Regional Economic Development,* eds. Helzi Noponen, Julie Graham, and Ann R. Markusen (New York: Guilford Press, 1993): 1–44.

9 Robert Reich, *The Next American Frontier* (New York: Penguin Books, 1983).

10 Kevin Phillips, *Wealth and Democracy* (New York: Broadway Books, 2002), 137.

11 Ibid., 133.

12 Louis Uchitelle, "After Pausing, Income Gap is Growing Again," *New York Times,* 23 June 2002, 3–4.

13 "Amalgamated Clothing and Textile Workers Union Press Conference Transcript," *News from the AFL-CIO* (Washington, D.C.: AFL-CIO, October 31, 1977), 6.

14 Martin Crutsinger, "Greenspan Says Efforts to Erect Trade Barriers 'Unwise, Self-Defeating'," *Louisville Courier Journal,* 17 April 1999, A13.

15 Ann R. Markusen, Peter Hall, and Amy Glasmeier, *High Tech America: The What, How, Where, and Why of the Sunrise Industries* (Boston: Allen & Unwin, 1986).

16 Malecki, *Technology and Economic Development,* 127.

17 Joel Brinkley, "Information Super Highway Is Just Outside the Beltway," *New York Times,* 12 October 1999, 1A.

18 Carey Goldberg, "Across the U.S., Universities Are Fueling High-Tech Economic Booms," *New York Times,* 8 October 1999, A12.

19 Malecki, *Technology and Economic Development;* Michael Porter, *Competitive*

Advantage of Nations (New York: Free Press, 1990); Michael E. Porter, "Location, Competition, and Economic Development: Local Clusters in a Global Economy," *Economic Development Quarterly* 14 (2000): 15–34.

20 Michael E. Porter, "Clusters and Competition: New Agendas for Companies, Governments, and Institutions," in *On Competition,* ed. Michael E. Porter (Boston: Harvard Business School Publishing, 1998), 237.

21 *MIT: The Impact of Innovation* (Boston: BankBoston Economics Department, March 1997), 8, http://web.mit.edu/newsoffice/founders/Founders2.pdf.

22 UC Regents, *UC Means Business: The Economic Impact of the University of California* (Oakland, Calif.: University of California Office of the President, 1996), 2, www.ucop.edu/services/ucmeans.pdf.

23 John Markoff, "Former Professor Gives Stanford $150 Million," *New York Times* 27 October 1999, A14.

24 Ed Bee, "Turning Community Inventions into Sustainable Technology Clusters," *Economic Development Journal* (Spring 2002): 22.

25 George Gilder, *Wealth and Poverty* (New York: Basic Books, 1981), 254.

26 Bee, "Turning Community Inventions into Sustainable Technology Clusters," 16.

27 Ibid., 18.

28 David L. Birch, *Job Creation in America: How Our Smallest Companies Put the Most People to Work* (New York: Free Press, 1987).

29 George J. Borjas, Richard B. Freeman, and Lawrence L. Katz, "Searching for the Effects of Immigration on the Labor Market," *American Economic Review* 86, no. 2 (1996): 246–251; George J. Borjas, Richard B. Freeman, and Lawrence L. Katz, "How Much Do Immigration and Trade Affect Labor Market Outcomes?" *Brookings Papers on Economic Activity* (1997): 1–67; George Borjas, *Friends and Strangers: The Effect of Immigration on the U.S. Economy* (New York: Basic Books, Inc.).

30 Steven Greenhouse, "Foreign Workers at Highest Level in Seven Decades," *New York Times,* 5 September 2000, A1, A12.

31 Daniel Hecker in "High-Technology Employment: A Broader View," *Monthly Labor Review* 122, no. 6 (June 1999), 18, www.bls.gov/opub/mlr/1999/06/art3full.pdf, defined high-tech industries as those with large proportions of technology-oriented occupations as well as a large amount of research and development. Four standard industrial classifications (SICs) defined high-tech industry, including computer and data processing services, engineering and architectural services, research development and testing services, and management and public relations services. Payroll growth in these high-tech industries was strongly related to education.

32 A. Faircloth and E. Brown, "The Best Cities for Business," *Fortune,* 23 November 1998, 142–147.

33 A. R. Myerson, "A New Breed of Wildcatter for the 90's," *New York Times,* 30 November 1997, section 3, 1–10.

34 H. Hylton, "Small Towns Find Ways to Create Their Own Jobs," *Wall Street Journal,* 23 September 1998.

35 C. Solomon and S. Leung, "Boston's Boom Would Be Just a Boomlet Elsewhere," *Wall Street Journal,* 9 September 1998.

36 M. Upstall, "Louisville Group Looks at Austin's Conversion to High-Tech Juggernaut," *Louisville Courier Journal,* 24 September 2000, 1A–2A.

37 J. Battey, "South Texas: Austin Leads High-Tech Job Boom in Southern Part of Lone Star State," *Infoworld,* 22 March 1999.

38 L. Goff and E. Leinfuss, "The Top 25 IS Job Markets," *Computerworld,* 12 January 1998.

39 Ibid.

40 Battey, "South Texas."

41 John P. Campbell, *Comparative High-Technology Industrial Growth: Texas, California, Massachusetts, and North Carolina* (Austin, Tex.: Bureau of Business Research, Graduate School of Business, University of Texas at Austin, 1986).

42 Goff and Leinfuss, "Top 25 IS Job Markets."

43 J. B. Goddard, A. E. Gillespie, J. F. Robinson, and A. T. Thwaites, "The Impact of New Information Technology on Urban and Regional Structure in Europe," in *The Regional Economic Impact of Technological Change,* 218.

44 T. W. Ferguson, "Sun, Fun and Ph.D.s, Too," *Forbes,* 31 May 1999, 220–227.

45 University of Texas at Austin, "Facts [1999]," www.utexas.edu/admin/opa/facts/facts.html.

46 University of Texas at Austin, "Rankings [1999]," www.utexas.edu/ogs/outreach/whyut/rankings.html.

47 University of Texas at Austin, "The Graduate School [1999]," www.utexas.edu/ogs/outreach/whyut/gradschl.html.

48 Myerson, "New Breed of Wildcatter," 10.

49 University of Texas at Austin, "Graduate Research Program-Research [1999]," www.utexas.edu/ogs/outreach/whyut/research.html.

50 University of Texas at Austin, "Rankings [1999]."

51 University of Texas at Austin, "Facts [1999]."

52 Myerson, "New Breed of Wildcatter," 10.

53 M. P. Feldman, "The University and Economic Development: The Case of Johns Hopkins University and Baltimore," *Economic Development Quarterly* 8, no. 1 (1994): 67–76.

54 Campbell, *Comparative High-Technology Industrial Growth,* 1.

55 Myerson, "New Breed of Wildcatter."

56 Ibid.

57 "Bush Announces Creation of Science and Technology Council," www.harc.edu/pressroom/96_0919.html.

58 This has recently been renamed the International Summit of Young Technology Leaders; see www.theinternationalsummit.com/index.html.

59 Upstall, "Louisville Group Looks at Austin's Conversion to High-Tech Juggernaut."

60 John Brier, vice-president for economic development, Greater Austin Chamber of Commerce (telephone interview with author, February 15, 2002).

61 www.dell.com/us/en/gen/corporate/factpack (accessed January 2002).

62 Michael Dell, *Direct from Dell: Strategies That Revolutionized an Industry,* written with Catherine Fredman (New York: Harper-Business, 1999).

63 Ibid., 20–21.

64 Ibid., 17.

65 R. D. Putnam, "The Prosperous Community: Social Capital and Economic Growth," *Current* 346 (1993): 4–9.

66 J. Magretta, "The Power of Virtual Integration: An Interview with Dell Computer's Michael Dell," *Harvard Business Review* 76, no. 2 (1998): 72–86.

67 Dell, *Direct from Dell.*

68 Magretta, "Power of Virtual Integration."

69 Dell, *Direct from Dell,* 107.

70 Gifford Pinchot III, *Intrapreneuring: Why You Don't Have to Leave the Corporation to Become an Entrepreneur* (San Francisco: Berrett-Koehler Publishers, 2000).

71 Dell, *Direct from Dell.*

72 Ibid., 173.

73 Ibid., 177.

74 Ibid., 178.

75 Noam Neusner and Matthew Benjamin, "Shelter from the Storm," *U.S. News & World Report,* 29 July 2002, 31–36.

76 Mara Der Hovanesian, "The VCs Don't Want Your Money Anymore," *Business Week,* 29 July 2002, 81–82.

6 Understanding the local environment

Learning objectives

You should be able to:

- Name at least three factors in a local environment that can constrain economic development choices

- Ask at least four key questions to gauge your community's culture

- Explain the concept of perverse effects

- Name four types of regimes that can characterize American local jurisdictions.

Understanding the local environment

Most local officials recognize the advantages of economic growth. Simply stated, increased levels of economic activity fill tax coffers. Higher levels of economic activity lead to a "virtuous cycle" of increases in property values, greater retail sales, higher personal incomes, larger corporate profits, and increases in other sources of government revenue.

Growth also has favorable secondary consequences for communities. Young people find good jobs at relatively high pay and remain in their communities. Incomes of average citizens in the community rise. Wealth is recycled in a multiplier effect, and further growth occurs as people and businesses are attracted to vibrant communities.

At the other extreme is the "recidivist cycle" of decreasing property values, retail sales, incomes, and profits. Ghost towns—former mining communities—in the Old West are examples of the final stage of the recidivist cycle. They are reminders that localities die once their economic value ceases to exist.

Most localities find themselves between the two extremes of the virtuous and the recidivist cycles. Most communities strive to achieve the former and avoid the latter.

Defining success

The case studies explored in this book suggest that leadership decisions can affect economic development. The United Parcel Service case study in Chapter 3 implies that creative public-private partnerships can be successful in retaining important employers. The case stands as a success in terms of the ability of public leaders to alter market forces to better fit the needs of a large employer. The DaimlerChrysler case study, also in Chapter 3, suggests that financial incentives (tax breaks and other incentives) are influential in bringing manufacturing production to specific localities. The CAPsell incubator case in Chapter 4 demonstrates success in helping local citizens create businesses. This case suggests that economic development strategies do not apply only to massive corporations but that strategies can be formed to help average citizens create and expand small enterprises.

These cases appear to describe successful economic development initiatives. Some analysts, however, compute all the costs associated with providing assistance to large businesses or average citizens and question whether the benefits justify the cost. Some analysts question whether the economic benefits to auto workers or package handlers sufficiently offset the cost of programs to attract or retain those jobs. Analysts also question whether the value added by small-business creation is large enough to justify expenses linked to the public sector programs that support small entrepreneurs.

Numerous studies have compared the costs with the benefits of public sector programs.[1] These studies calculate the costs of a program (such as a mental health program), measure benefits (such as decreased need for subsequent mental health services), and compare the calculated benefits with the calculated costs. A ratio of benefits to costs is computed and used to determine program success. For example, costs of job training programs can be compared with benefits in terms of increases in employment, reductions in transfer payments, reductions in criminal activity, reductions in drug abuse, and other factors. Cost-benefit analysis, however, is dependent on a number of subjective judgments, including which costs and benefits to consider, how costs and benefits should be measured, and how they should be valued. Results can differ considerably depending on these judgments.

The success of local leaders in creating, retaining, and attracting economic opportunities is also determined by how the concept of success is defined. The research case in Chapter 3 demonstrates that jobs can be created through legislative legalization of casinos. If job creation is the only measure, legalization of gambling could be described as a successful strategy. However, other consequences—the flow of revenues to company stockholders rather than to workers, the spread of crime, increases in health care costs—call into question the success of the gambling strategy. Likewise, some communities that have attracted enormous growth find that the effects of that growth undermine the community's quality of life.

National and international factors

Another reality to consider is that local economic development leaders do not control their environments. The fortunes of present-day "company towns" rise and fall with the success of the major employer. Even in the large city of Houston, Texas, government officials could not control the impact of the 2002 Enron Corporation bankruptcy. They could not guarantee that home prices would remain stable in their city, that people would not lose their jobs as a consequence of the private company's bankruptcy, or that individuals would not migrate to other areas in search of better opportunities.

Some communities do not lose their major employer but are negatively impacted by systemic trends such as the movement of people from inner cities to the suburbs to escape crime or congestion. Communities are also affected by larger trends such as the globalization of economic activity; one result of globalization is the migration of jobs to areas of the world that pay lower wages.

The empirical evidence found in the research case and the Austin case study in Chapter 5 suggests that technological innovation and cutting-edge knowledge are associated with economic development. Clearly, however, a small town without a major university can hardly implement a strategy calling for the creation of a major research center in its jurisdiction. In general, the local environment defines the options available to decision makers.

The community

The degree of local economic development can depend on a single employer, skill levels of local workers, existing infrastructure, cultural characteristics, even geography and weather patterns. Each of these factors has a bearing on the choice of economic development strategies.

For example, a small community that depends on a single employer will probably rely heavily on incentives to retain this economic base. Communities with a large supply of scientific and technical workers follow job attraction and job creation strategies different from communities with relatively large numbers of unskilled workers. Communities without a large population base or a state-of-the-art athletic stadium are unlikely to attract a professional sports franchise. Localities steeped in specific norms and values

Figure 6–1

Local environment and
development choices

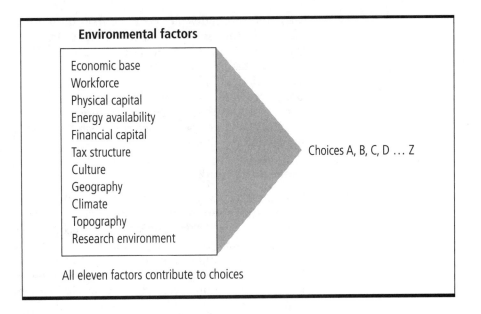

Environmental factors

Economic base
Workforce
Physical capital
Energy availability
Financial capital
Tax structure
Culture
Geography
Climate
Topography
Research environment

Choices A, B, C, D ... Z

All eleven factors contribute to choices

such as risk aversion, resistance to change, and distrust of outsiders may not be able to develop growth based on alternative sets of values. Communities in frigid climates find it difficult to compete for tourism dollars. The state of the local economy itself also influences development decisions: officials in Atlantic City, New Jersey; Tunica, Mississippi; and Detroit, Michigan, accepted casino gaming in part because they were facing dire economic conditions.

To a certain extent, therefore, government officials are constrained by the vicissitudes of their economy and other factors in their local environments. Yet, they cannot afford to permit these factors to hold their communities hostage. To mitigate the negatives and enhance the positives, they must assess environmental factors and then form and adopt economic development strategies based on those factors.

Figure 6–1 does not represent an all-inclusive list of environmental factors, but this list can serve as a starting point. Scoring specific factors will help define a community's current environment. Some factors may be fixed or unlikely to change in the foreseeable future. Climate is a good example of such a factor. Economic development strategies certainly cannot change a community's weather, but climate may dictate which strategies are likely to be more effective. Other factors may be altered, in the short or the long term, by interventions by economic developers. The percentage of the workforce that is skilled in high-technology fields, for example, can be increased through education and training initiatives.

Figure 6–1 provides a visual sketch of the environmental factors that influence the choices made by local leaders. The 11 environmental factors listed describe conditions that leaders can assess in formulating an economic development strategy. Assessments can be somewhat objective and quantitative (as in assigning quantitative scores on dimensions and summing scores) or very subjective. Subjective assessments can take more of a seat-of-the-pants approach. Local leaders can have a feel for their locality in terms of numbers of unskilled workers, price of utilities, availability of energy, taxes, and other factors. A configuration of specific factors should lead to specific choices. For example, leaders in localities with low utility costs and low wages may believe that they can attract companies with high utility needs that normally pay no more than minimum wages. Other configurations of factors should lead to different choices. High scores on research environment and financial capital can lead to technology start-ups. Figure 6–1 indicates that choices may be numerous or limited depending on the characteristics of jurisdictions. Choices are shown as ranging from Choice A to Choice Z but, in reality, choice of development strategy is dependent on factors such as existing local characteristics, willingness of decision makers to try to change those characteristics, ability to enact such change, and willingness to take risks.

Community goals

A community's goals for its economic future must be factored into determining the appropriate economic development strategy. A community dependent on a single company for its economic base may be comfortable with this situation. This community will want to adopt strategies that help to ensure the dominant company's satisfaction with its present location, and the community's focus will be on business retention. On the other hand, if the same community wants to diversify its economy, its economic development interventions will be quite different. It will attempt to attract complementary firms from other places and/or create new businesses that have business cycles that are countercyclical to that of the dominant company. Existing conditions found in the local environment will yield both opportunities and constraints. Local economic goals will guide identification of both opportunities and constraints. The economic development official needs to understand this and act accordingly.

Community culture

Even if all the other factors on the environmental assessment checklist have been addressed with strategies for enhancing and leveraging strengths and mitigating weaknesses, a community's culture may limit its ability to act on these strategies.

The importance of local culture as an environmental factor should not be ignored or underestimated. The best-laid plans of economic development officials can come to naught if they do not reflect the community's collective mind-set. Compellingly rational arguments, innovative strategies, and strong economic leadership together may not be able to counter the inertia of culture. A community that is traditional and risk averse is likely to resist embracing untested strategies of any kind. A community where individuals have been taught that the most desirable approach to economic security is to work for someone else is not likely to respond to an economic development strategy that encourages entrepreneurship. Jurisdictions where many individuals perceive businesses as self-interested as well as poor stewards of community values may resist assisting or cooperating with private firms in any way.

Because local development officials cannot hope to change a community's culture in the short term, culture will help determine the mix of public and private collaboration appropriate to the community. Culture also affects the community's political environment, which in turn further limits economic development choices.

Local officials can assess their cultural environment by asking:

• Is the community generally supportive or antagonistic toward business interests?

• Is the community generally supportive or antagonistic toward government programs and initiatives?

Redistributive and developmental programs

Professor Paul Peterson of Harvard University describes the difference between redistributive and developmental government programs:

Redistributive programs reallocate society's resources from the haves to the have-nots. These programs transfer resources from individuals who have gained the most to individuals who have gained the least. Recipients of transfers include the elderly, the disabled, the unemployed, the sick, the poor, families headed by single parents, and others lacking in material resources. Some analysts assert that redistributive programs contribute to economic development in the long run, but other analysts contend that these policies retard economic development by reducing incentives to work and save.

Most people believe that at least a minimal level of redistribution is justifiable and that the higher the level of economic development, the more a society should redistribute some resources to the needy. It is generally understood that because capital and labor are mobile there are limits to the ability of local governments to redistribute resources. If a locality attempts to place extraordinarily high taxes on its higher-income citizens and heap generous benefits upon the lowest-income citizens, poorer people may enter the locality and the rich may depart. Because the national government can prevent the in-migration of workers from foreign countries and impose some constraints on capital flow, it has the greater capacity to create redistributive programs. Social Security and Medicare (the two largest redistributive programs) are national programs. Localities that engage in large redistribution programs risk alienating their most productive citizens and eviscerating the tax base.

Developmental programs provide the infrastructure to facilitate economic growth. Physical infrastructure includes roads, mass transit systems, sanitation systems, public parks, and basic utilities. Social infrastructure includes organizations that protect persons and property from unlawful activity, organizations that protect the public health, and organizations that educate the next generation. Peterson asserts that local governments are best equipped to design and administer development programs. If local governments do not provide services that meet the needs of local businesses and residents, residents will consider moving to another location. Market forces and political pressures discipline local policy decisions. Peterson states that the national government, on the whole, is the least efficient producer of development policies because signals concerning the effectiveness of national government programs are not as clear or as rapidly conveyed as the signals available to local governments.

Source: Paul E. Peterson, *The Price of Federalism* (Washington, D.C.: Brookings Institution, 1995), 17–27.

- What types of programs are generally supported—redistributive programs or developmental programs?
- Does the community have a history of public-private collaboration?
- Is the community willing to sacrifice some of its quality of life to promote growth?
- Are the elites of the community willing to share power with others?
- Are the citizens generally accepting of change, or do they resist it?

Assessing whether a proper cultural fit exists between community norms and a proposed development strategy can save a great deal of misplaced time and effort. Development officials should carefully consider their environment, not only in terms of natural resources and workforce abilities but also in terms of culture. Understanding the local culture can mean the difference between workable and unworkable economic development strategies.

Perverse effects

Communities should take care to avoid economic development strategies that are well intentioned but have what economists call "perverse effects." Perverse effects refer to unintended consequences of policies. For example, localities can offer inducements to companies that supply employment to low-wage earners. Such a strategy can enhance the local tax base. However, the impact of the new workers in terms of creating a need for additional teachers, social workers, police officers, and other public employees may negate the benefit from increases in local payrolls. Similarly, bringing casinos to a locality may have the perverse effect of changing the nature of a locality; this appears to have happened in Atlantic City. Feelings of neighborhood may be lost, outsiders may change the character of the jurisdiction, and local family establishments (such as bars and restaurants) may not be able to compete with the perquisites offered by the large corporate gambling venues.

Even the virtuous cycle can have uncomfortable consequences. Boom towns and localities benefiting from the growth of very profitable companies may find that some long-time residents cannot afford the higher rents charged by landlords. The elderly on fixed incomes in these towns may be forced to sell their property if they cannot afford the taxes on their homes. Increased market prices (for homes and for taxes) associated with booms will squeeze out those who can no longer afford to live there.

Consequences of development must be evaluated. Trade-offs must be considered. Bringing a new factory to town may be perceived by some as a benefit in terms of jobs and economic base, but it may be perceived by others—retirees, for example, who would like the town to maintain its traditional character—as a cost in terms of quality of life and attractiveness.

Weighing the factors

Although it is helpful to consider individual factors of the local environment in order to understand the impact of each, multiple factors taken together will ultimately guide economic development strategies.

A community may find that it has an economy that ranks high on dominance by a single firm or industry, a tax structure that is conducive to business activity, a good physical infrastructure, and available and affordable energy sources. On the basis of this assessment, it may seek to diversify its economy. However, if it also has a workforce with a low skill level and is in an isolated location, it will need to make some choices. Will it accept its limitations and seek to attract and/or create businesses that require inexpensive, unskilled labor and do not need to be near the source of inputs or markets? Or will the community attempt to mitigate its weaknesses by upgrading the skills of its workforce, enhancing its communications technology, or building an airport to overcome its isolation and thereby expand the range of business activities it might accommodate? These strategies, of course, beg the question of whether the community can find the necessary financial capital.

A community's economic environment plays a major role in determining what it can reasonably expect in the way of development. The economic environment helps to explain why some communities are hotbeds of innovation and high-technology-based growth while others compete for hazardous waste facilities and prisons. Some environmental factors are within a given community's ability to change. Others are more difficult if not impossible to alter.

A framework or model that can be used to assess the environment is a useful place to start. The worksheet on pages 174–177, for example, can help decision makers articulate the defining factors of the milieu in which they operate, a milieu that encompasses the relative positions of a number of variables. Once the local context is defined and articulated, various economic development strategies can be more realistically accepted or rejected.

Politics of economic development

The political economy of development has been well covered by a number of authors, and readers who are interested can seek out their work.[2] Political issues warrant the attention of every economic development professional because the distribution of influence between the private and public sector, the equity of development programs, and the implications of development for governance and citizenship are often controversial.[3]

In general, powerful forces promote growth and development.[4] Those who favor development assume that the rewards of development will benefit everyone. Because some people believe that both jurisdictions and businesses seek to grow, they equate a locality's population growth and its economic growth with forms of business success. Jurisdictions, therefore, are believed to compete with each other for economic value. The more successful jurisdictions enjoy increases in their land values while the less successful lag behind.

At the local level, the political and economic elites of the area often support and advance development policies and encourage collaboration between business and government leaders. Growth-oriented leaders find allies among businesses with vested interests in the area—banks, newspapers, large stores, developers, real estate agencies, property management firms, and utilities. These interests want to attract mobile capital to their area.[5]

Many politicians also promote growth because they believe that economic development will both enhance their constituents' lives and, by extension, improve their own electoral prospects. Scholars in the academic community, however, do not universally embrace promotion of economic development.[6] The current trend toward smart growth sees citizens not as stockholders whose economic position goes up or down in accordance with land-use decisions, but as people who seek social as well as physical shelter in their communities. Land also has value in a qualitative sense—as a place of residence and as a neighborhood setting.[7] Growth may decrease this qualitative value if it produces externalities such as congestion, traffic noise, pollution, school crowding, forced relocation, toxic waste, and flooding.

Public-private relationships

The most recent trend in economic development strategy seems to be toward free-market approaches. Perhaps more precisely, the most recent focus in economic development has been on perfecting markets and encouraging competition. This stems from the widespread recognition that, although the neoclassical model of perfect competition is unrealistic and some government intervention in an effort to perfect markets is deemed acceptable and even desirable, public intervention must be executed carefully because the goal is to perfect markets, not destroy them.[8] This coming together of the

Worksheet 6–1
Checklist for evaluating local business environment

A great many factors shape the local environment. A clear-eyed assessment of a region can provide useful cues to local decision makers who are trying to position a community for increased economic development.

Environmental factors	Low (1)
Economic base	
Dependence on a single firm or industry	
Capacity to diversify	
Will to diversify	
Workforce characteristics	
Size of workforce	
Unemployment rate	
Average wages/salaries	
Skill	
Percent competent in high-technology fields	
Percent competent in other fields	
Percent unskilled	
Land/physical capital	
Vacant land	
Land for redevelopment (underused, brownfields)	
Access to utilities (including communications)	
Access to transportation (highways, airports, ports)	
Energy	
Reliability	
Access	
Prices	

Medium (2)	High (3)

Environmental factors	Low (1)
Financial capital	
Local bank policies on business lending	
Gap financing	
Venture capital	
Angel capital	
Tax structure	
Business-related taxes	
General tax rates	
Community culture	
Supportive of business values	
Willing to innovate and risk personal capital	
Willing to accept externalities	
Willing to alter status quo	
Geography	
Climate	
Topography	
Distance from economic centers	
Distance from complementary clusters of business/industry	
Access to global markets	
Research environment	
Major university nearby	
College nearby	
Internet access	

Medium (2)	High (3)

roles of government and private business in the quest for economic development is the impetus for the public-private partnership approach offered throughout this book.

As we have seen, local governments still do provide financial incentives to large businesses. Given the footloose nature of investment, private companies are still able to extract benefits from government when they promise to build or expand plants because many public leaders want to see quick results, even at the expense of long-term improvement to the economic base.

Nevertheless, in recent years public officials have become involved in economic activities beyond conventional financial and tax incentives. Officials recognize that if they want growth, they must market their communities and pursue strategies to assure growth. Aggressive public sector intervention flies in the face of a cultural predisposition toward individualism and limited government that acts as a powerful constraint on expansion of public sector activities. However, economic development initiatives such as grants, loans, technical assistance for small entrepreneurs, business incubators, tourism, research, and investment in higher education are consistent with a market-oriented approach to wealth creation. The thrust of these initiatives contrasts sharply with direct transfer payments that came under sharp attack during welfare reform.

Supported by studies that show that small businesses, in total, actually employ larger numbers of new workers than do major corporations,[9] a newer, alternative model of development focuses on entrepreneurs and how they benefit the local economy. Small-business creation finds wide acceptance because it conforms to the American values of individualism, hard work, and opportunity. Public programs designed to help private entrepreneurs survive and flourish promote a broader participation in the economy and a wider economic base than do the generous tax concessions from state and local jurisdictions to large corporations.

Public-private collaborations will continue to evolve. Working relationships between government and private business can encourage new startups, support the growth of small businesses, buttress large job generators, encourage very limited government intervention, and take on even more forms. Government can become the employer of last resort if labor shortages give way to high unemployment. The direction that public-private collaboration will take in the future will undoubtedly be influenced by the distribution of political power.

Regime theory

The political issues surrounding economic development depend partly on what kind of regime—an informal collaboration between public and private interests—makes and carries out governing decisions for a given jurisdiction. Under some regimes, political power is broadly distributed; under other regimes, power is closely guarded. How power is distributed will determine public policies in regard to who gets what, when, and how.

Regime literature in the United States identifies two groups as key participants in most local policymaking: elected officials and businesses. A variety of other interests, however, may also be brought into the regime. Regime theory addresses the politics of coalition building in order to gain certain kinds of outcomes. Regime formation seeks to achieve some shared sense of purpose and direction among actors. American cities can be grouped into four distinct types:[10]

- **Maintenance regimes** seek to preserve the status quo; government officials and nongovernmental actors develop relatively straightforward relationships

- **Development regimes** take positive steps to promote growth or counter decline
- **Middle-class progressive regimes** seek environmental protection and control over growth; this type of regime focuses on regulation as a core responsibility of government
- **Lower-class opportunity regimes** are grass roots–oriented and require substantial mass mobilization.

Depending on regime type, different kinds of economic development strategies are viable. For example, maintenance regimes that are committed to preserving the status quo can develop policies that benefit existing leaders within the community. Louisville, Kentucky's effort to satisfy the demands of United Parcel Service is an example. Development regimes are usually more proactive than reactive in attracting business. Government officials in Alabama did not wait until they were discovered by the large German corporation, Daimler Benz AG; instead, Alabama governor Jim Folsom and the head of the state's development office, Billy Joe Camp, aggressively courted the automobile manufacturer (see Case study 3–2). These officials were not willing to simply maintain; they were willing to take risks in an effort to promote growth. Still another type of private-public collaboration can be found in Wautoma, Wisconsin's small-business incubator that assisted low-income individuals (Case study 4–1). This is an example of a lower-class opportunity regime.

Cases in this book describe how the priorities of government leaders influence the type of policies pursued. Policies that focus on assistance to low-income residents (as in Wautoma) are less likely to evolve in localities historically captive to business interests. A maintenance-type regime is likely to support established business interests and is not likely to upset the status quo. A development-type regime may look at big-ticket items (convention centers, sports arenas, global companies) that can provide an immediate stimulus for development. Middle-class progressive regimes may shun growth that is oriented to providing benefits to big businesses. Environmentally conscious groups may fear that growth will stain the beauty of their surroundings. For example, many citizens and leaders in Virginia successfully resisted a major new attraction when Disney proposed a large establishment in the Virginia suburbs west of Washington, D.C. They did not want miles of new hotels and fast food restaurants replacing the Virginia countryside and its historical sites. Local leaders should carefully assess the type of regime that appears to be in place in their community before they adopt a specific strategy.

Regimes influence the type of policy that is pursued, yet regimes do not exist in perpetuity. At some point in the past, leaders in Alabama might not have wanted "foreigners" such as Northerners or others coming into their state, even if it might have meant additional jobs and tax revenue. Although Alabama and other states seemed to have a maintenance-regime posture for many years, at some point they shed that posture in favor of development. Such a change may be caused by a change of heart in existing leaders or by the replacement of old leaders with new people who possess different mind-sets.

The type of regime in favor can shift with the electoral winds. At the national level, electoral realignments have ushered in periods of significant policy change. The presidential election of 1932 marked a rejection of the status quo regime of Herbert Hoover and the greater acceptance of the lower-class opportunity regime of Franklin Roosevelt. The election of 1980 to a lesser extent marked another change, a change back to maintenance and development priorities.

Regime change can be identified at the local level as well. In many cities, mass mobilization and redistribution marked the 1960s. The change in leadership in New York City in 1973—from John Lindsay to Abraham Beame—represented a significant change in ideas toward governance. While Lindsay was viewed as a redistribution crusader, Beame represented a return to "clubhouse," or traditional, politics.[11] Cleveland, Ohio, offers another example of regime fluidity. The election of Dennis Kucinich as mayor in 1977 was viewed as a victory for grassroots groups. Kucinich's defeat in the 1979 election was interpreted as a reassertion of traditional business priorities,[12] more attuned to maintenance and development. Electoral change occurs in small localities as well. Sometimes grassroots interests find a champion and prevail in the electoral process; at other times, other interests prevail.

Regime theory describes the fusing of public and private resources for the good of the jurisdiction and the good of citizens.[13] It explores the idea that partnerships between public and private entities or actors to pursue an economic objective do not arise out of thin air but are the product of distinct political contexts. According to regime theory, the capacity and legitimacy of a partnership are derived from the legitimacy of the regime; this legitimacy either sustains or undermines the philosophy of joint public-private action.

Summary

The focus of this book is economic development policy. Various theories of development have been presented. These classic theories are based on different sets of assumptions and make use of different views of the world to explain the phenomena of economic growth and decline. Although no one perspective can fully explain economic growth and decline, the theories introduced in this book provide a basic understanding of economic development themes.

The tools of development identified in this book are available to most policymakers who wish to promote development in their communities. Some tools, such as grants, loans, and tax relief, are traditional in the United States. Others, such as equity financing, are novel. Some tools involve financial incentives; some, such as site development and training, provide nonfinancial incentives.

Government officials who want to address pressing economic needs must be equipped with tools of the trade. But officials must consider the local environment as well. Tools must be carefully chosen to suit the situation and the setting. Explanations for and details of development successes and failures can be found in detailed case studies such as those in this book. Empirical research also sheds light on economic development, supporting or undermining the credibility of theoretical perspectives. For example, research data presented in Chapter 5 suggest a strong link between education and economic development.

The proper role of government in economic development remains an unresolved question. Case studies such as CAPsell illustrate that the public sector can assist individuals at the grassroots level to develop their own businesses. Governments and private businesses can collaborate to alter economic factors, as in the UPS example. Public officials can amend morality legislation to permit previously banned activities such as gaming and casinos. Public officials can also foster a general environment for economic growth as they did for the Dell Computer Corporation. Governments can invest in high-quality scientific research and education. Public officials can lure high-profile manufacturers with large tax incentives and regulatory relief; the case of Alabama and DaimlerChrysler is one example. Finally, government can minimize its role in the economy and let market forces work (following Adam Smith and the classical economic perspective).

Clearly no one of these strategies is workable in every environment. The role of government in economic development is influenced largely by the environment in which decisions are made, and the environment has cultural, political, and economic dimensions. The environmental-factor worksheet on pages 174–177 can help decision makers select strategies that are feasible within their local environments. Identifying early the more workable strategies will save both time and money. Then, instead of having to work harder, economic development leaders will be able to work smarter for their communities.

Study questions

- What is a virtuous cycle? What is a recidivist cycle?

- What are some common criticisms of cost-benefit analyses?

- How do national and international trends affect local economic situations?

- Which factors affecting development choices in the local environment cannot be changed?

- Which factors affecting development choices in the local environment can be changed?

- Why is the culture of a community important?

- Describe the difference between redistributive programs and developmental programs.

- What are perverse effects? Give examples.

- Why are perverse effects important?

- In what way does land have more than one kind of value?

- What is the definition of a regime in regime theory?

- Describe four regimes; give examples of how regime choice has determined types of development projects.

1 James E. Kee, "Benefit-Cost Analysis in Program Evaluation," in *Handbook of Practical Program Evaluation,* eds. J. Wholey, H. Hatry, and K. Newcomer, 483–485 (San Francisco: Jossey-Bass, 1994); Emil Posavac and Raymond Carey, *Program Evaluation Methods and Case Studies,* 5th ed. (Upper Saddle River, N.J.: Prentice-Hall, 1997), 199–201; Jeanette Jerrell and The-Wei Hu, "Estimating the Cost Impact of Three Dual Diagnosis Treatment Programs," *Evaluation Review* 20, no. 2 (1996): 160–180.

2 John L. Logan and Harvey L. Molotch, *Urban Fortunes: The Political Economy of Place* (Berkeley, Calif.: University of California Press, 1987); Paul E. Peterson, *City Limits* (Chicago: University of Chicago Press, 1981); Clarence N. Stone, *Regime Politics: Governing Atlanta, 1946–1988* (Lawrence, Kans.: University Press of Kansas, 1989); David R. Imbroscio, *Reconstructing City Politics: Alternative Economic Development and Urban Regimes* (Thousand Oaks, Calif.: Sage Publications, 1997).

3 Stephen L. Elkin, *City and Regime in the American Republic* (Chicago: University of

Chicago Press, 1987); Clarence N. Stone and Heywood T. Sanders, eds., *The Politics of Urban Development* (Lawrence, Kans.: University Press of Kansas, 1987); Todd Swanstrom, *The Crisis of Growth Politics: Cleveland, Kucinich, and the Challenge of Urban Populism* (Philadelphia: Temple University Press, 1985); Pauline Vaillancourt Rosenau, ed., *Public-Private Policy Partnerships* (Cambridge: MIT Press, 2000); David Imbroscio, *Reconstructing City Politics;* Harold Wolman, "The Politics of Local Economic Development," *Economic Development Quarterly* 10 (1996): 115–150.

4 Elaine B. Sharp, *Urban Politics and Administration: From Service Delivery to Economic Development* (New York: Longman, 1990); Harvey L. Molotch, "The City as Growth Machine," *American Journal of Sociology* 82 (1976): 309–330; David Imbroscio, "Economic Development," in *Handbook of Research on Urban Politics and Policy in the United States,* ed. R. Vogel, 261–271 (Westport, Conn.: Greenwood Press, 1997); Laura A. Reese and Raymond A. Rosenfeld, *The Civic Culture of Local Economic Development* (Thousand Oaks,

Calif.: Sage Publications, 2002); Bryan D.
Jones and Lynn W. Bachelor, *The Sustaining
Hand*, 2d ed. (Lawrence, Kans.: University
Press of Kansas, 1993).

5 Elkin, *City and Regime in the American
Republic*, 14.

6 Bryan D. Jones and Lynn W. Bachelor, with
Carter Wilson, *The Sustaining Hand:
Community Leadership and Corporate Power*
(Lawrence, Kans.: University Press of
Kansas, 1986); Elkin, *City and Regime in the
American Republic*.

7 Peter Dreier, "Sprawl's Invisible Hand," *The
Nation* 270, no. 7 (21 February 2000): 6–7;
Ellen Romano, "Living Smarter: Better
Communities for the New Millennium,"
Journal of Property Management 65, no. 1
(January-February 2000): 30–35.

8 Roger E. Hamlin and Thomas S. Lyons,
*Economy Without Walls: Managing Local
Development in a Restructuring World*
(Westport, Conn.: Praeger, 1996).

9 David L. Birch, *Job Generation in America*
(New York: Free Press, 1987); John Case,
*From Ground Up: The Resurgence of American
Entrepreneurship* (New York: Simon &
Schuster, 1992).

10 Clarence N. Stone, "Urban Regimes and the
Capacity to Govern: A Political Economy
Approach," *Journal of Urban Affairs* 15, no. 1
(1993): 1–28.

11 Charles R. Morris, *The Cost of Good
Intentions: New York City and the Liberal
Experiment, 1960–1975* (New York: McGraw-
Hill, 1980).

12 Todd Swanstrom, *The Crisis of Growth
Politics: Cleveland, Kucinich, and the
Challenge of Urban Population* (Philadelphia:
Temple University Press, 1985).

13 Jon Pierre, "Local Industrial Partnerships:
Exploring the Logics of Public-Private
Partnerships," in *Partnerships in Urban
Governance: European and American
Experience*, ed. Jon Pierre (New York: St.
Martin's Press, 1998), 112.

Glossary

Accelerated depreciation   Method of altering tax payments whereby companies are able to write down the cost of plant and equipment more quickly; can allow for more frequent investment in plant and equipment.

Affiliates program   Services offered by some incubators to clients whose companies do not reside in the incubator; businesses that do not reside in the incubator can have access on a prearranged fee basis to many of the services offered by the incubator. *See also* **Business incubator.**

Agglomeration theory   Explanation of economic growth that states that areas with relatively strong existing cores will continue to grow at the expense of outlying areas.

Agri-tourism   Economic development tactic that uses a region's agricultural activities as a tourist draw.

Angel capitalist   Wealthy individual who provides financial capital to entrepreneurs; usually does not substantially participate in the management of the business and typically demands a relatively small equity share of the business.

Backward and forward linkages   Economic connections among companies; backward linkages involve the purchase of inputs by a given firm from another, and forward linkages involve the sale of the given firm's outputs to another company.

Balloon payment   Minimal repayment of loans is required until a specified time when the remainder of the principal is due in one large lump sum.

Bootstrap   Belief that the poor can get ahead mostly by their own efforts, i.e., pick themselves up by their bootstraps.

Business attraction   Efforts by local economic development organizations to encourage firms from outside their communities to locate headquarters or other operations within their jurisdictions.

Business climate   Environment of a given community that is relevant to the operation of a business; usually includes tax rates, attitudes of government toward business, and availability of capital.

Business creation   Local economic development strategy that focuses on encouraging the formation of new companies that are locally based and will remain in the community and grow.

Business incubator   Building that houses several start-ups; provides them with space, shared business services, management training and assistance, financial assistance, and an opportunity to network with each other.

Business information center (BIC)   Outlet that provides information and assistance to small businesses; supported by the U.S. Small Business Administration.

Business plan   Guide for the growth and development of a company; usually takes into account the nature of the product or service to be sold, the structure of the business, its markets and competition for those markets, and its financing.

Business retention   Efforts by local economic developers to keep existing businesses in the community and to encourage them to expand their operations on their present sites.

Center of excellence   Group of specialists who perform research of high quality with market potential; such a group can be identified or assembled by a university and formalized into a center whose activity is linked to economic development.

Certified and Preferred Lenders Program   U.S. Small Business Administration program that encourages highly active and expert lenders to provide funds to borrowers.

Certified Development Companies   U.S. Small Business Administration program that uses nonprofit entities to provide long-term, fixed-asset financing to small businesses.

Chip chasing   Pursuit of high-tech businesses by local economic development organizations.

Circuit breaker   Mechanism of property tax relief targeted to those with low income relative to property tax obligations.

Classification   Tax strategy of categorizing properties according to their use; it is assumed that owners of some categories of property have a superior ability to pay.

Clean industries   Desirable industries that do not pollute and usually employ white-collar workers.

Clusters   Colocation of firms in the same or similar industries to foster interaction as a means of strengthening each other and enhancing the community's competitive advantage.

Collective good   Something that is used simultaneously by many people, and no one can be excluded from enjoying it; the marketplace is not able to supply this because its consumption cannot be limited on the basis of such factors as ability to pay. Also known as a public good; contrast with **Individual good.**

Colonized neighborhood   Area where corporations locate branches or chains; corporate profits typically return to corporate headquarters instead of stay in the neighborhood.

Common stock   Part ownership with voting rights.

Community development theories   Generally associated with community organizing and antipoverty efforts that grew during the 1960s; housing rehabilitation and construction are concerns of community organizations.

Community development venture capital   Capital made available through funds created by local communities for the purpose of making venture capital accessible to entrepreneurs in low-income areas.

Comparative advantage   Ability of one nation, region, or individual to produce a commodity at a lower opportunity cost than another nation, region, or individual; nations, regions, and individuals will focus on producing products if a comparative advantage exists.

Convertible debt   Permits the conversion of loans to common stock.

Corporate welfare   Government subsidies targeted to large corporations.

Creative destruction   Term coined by economist Joseph Schumpeter that refers to the displacement of the obsolete by the novel, the more efficient, and the new in the system of capitalism.

Customized training   Learning designed to meet the needs of a given employer; used by local governments to attract or retain major employers.

Demand-side theory of development   Explanation of economic development that focuses on discovering, expanding, and creating new markets; forming new businesses; nurturing indigenous resources; and involving government in the economy.

Development credit corporation   Publicly chartered, privately funded enterprises established to pool resources of various lenders; these corporations may also sell stock to financial institutions and other corporations.

Doughnut metropolitan area   Metropolitan area in which the dough—the area of wealth—surrounds a central economic void.

Eco-industrial park   Industrial park designed to encourage business interaction in ways that foster the reuse of waste streams, the recycling of inputs, and other mechanisms.

Ecological amenities   Natural environmental assets (e.g., forests, wetlands, barrier islands) that a community can protect and use to attract tourism.

E-commerce   The buying and selling of goods and services via the Internet.

Eco-tourism   Tourist activity that is ecologically sensitive; the focus is on human interaction with the ecosystem being visited, with an emphasis on educating people about the ecosystem's value and importance and thereby fostering appreciation for its preservation.

Empowerment incubator   Program located in minority or economically disadvantaged community that helps entrepreneurs overcome obstacles to success. *See* **Business incubator.**

Enterprise development   Assistance to entrepreneurs in support of the creation, growth, and survival of their businesses.

Enterprise zone   Area in which taxes and regulation could be lowered; these areas are usually set up in depressed areas, with the goal of encouraging investment and job creation.

Entrepreneur   Production innovator who perceives the opportunity to provide a new product or implement a new production method, organizes the needed production inputs, and assumes financial risk.

Entrepreneurship forum   Event that brings venture capitalists and small-business owners together.

Equity financing   Investments are typically secured in this type of financial support in return for partial ownership of an enterprise; three mechanisms can be used for receiving an equity position in a firm: common stock, preferred stock, and convertible debt.

Export-base theory   Explanation of development that links regional growth to regional exports.

First wave   Strategic paradigm of economic development that focuses on business attraction tactics.

Gap financing   Debt capital made available to entrepreneurs to help them reach the point where their businesses are considered suitable for commercial bank loans. *See also* **Mezzanine capital.**

General obligation bond   Traditional form of borrowing for state and local government; secured by full faith and credit of jurisdiction.

Grants   Public monies given to an entity; recipient is not obligated to repay.

Growth machine theory   Belief that community elites such as local bankers, real estate developers, builders, owners of retail stores, attorneys, and owners of utility companies have a vested interest in growth that adds value to community property.

Growth pole theory   Belief that growth depends on propulsion industries that are fast growing, large, innovative, and linked to suppliers as well as to markets.

High technology, high-tech   Reference to products or businesses that produce products that require substantial intellectual capital in their creation (e.g., computer chips, biomedical products, and computer software).

Home-based business   Small company operated out of an entrepreneur's home or garage.

Home-grown business   Business created by a resident of a given community.

Incubator-without-walls   Form of business incubation that does not take place in a single building but instead comprises a network of entrepreneurs and entrepreneurship service providers throughout a community or region.

Individual good   Something that can be consumed by a single person, and others can be excluded from enjoying it; the marketplace is able to supply this because its consumption can be limited on the basis of factors such as ability to pay. Also known as a private good; contrast with **Collective good.**

Industrial development bond   Certificate of indebtedness issued by a public entity to finance private economic development activity; allows private entities to borrow money at below-market rates.

Industrial park   Parcel of land purchased by a local government for the purpose of subdividing it into lots for use by manufacturing businesses; the government usually provides the necessary physical infrastructure as well as the land and, in some cases, may put speculative industrial buildings on the lots. *See also* **Research park; Smart park.**

Industry-focused incubator   Program that brings together companies that are in the same business but not necessarily competitors; designed to support the development of microindustry.

Information asymmetry   Information is not equally distributed between buyers and sellers; a form of market failure.

Invisible hand   Refers to pursuit of individual self-interest in the marketplace; first named by Adam Smith.

Jobs-housing imbalance   Spatial mismatch between where people live and where they work.

Just-in-time inventorying   Cost-saving approach by a manufacturer that involves maintaining no inventory of product inputs on-site; instead the inputs are delivered from the supplier(s) at the time they are needed in the production process.

Labor-force theory of development   Explanation of development that stresses the importance of an educated, skilled, and dependable workforce for attracting and growing businesses; accepts the concept that the public sector has a responsibility to fit human resources to the needs of the business community.

Laissez-faire   Economic principle that emphasizes a policy of leaving the private sector alone.

Land banking   Acquiring and improving contiguous parcels of land in an effort to create a unified site for development.

Land write-down   Providing land to developers at a price that is below public sector expenses for improvements.

190 Economic Development: Strategies for State and Local Practice

Loan Monies given to recipients with an expectation of repayment; public sector loans generally permit firms that have trouble obtaining loans through normal channels to secure financing at either market rates or below-market rates.

Loan guaranty program Government initiative that guarantees that a percentage of loans are given to private companies; these programs enhance a private company's ability to secure loans.

Loan pooling Two or more lenders contribute to a fund from which loans are made to applicants; publicly chartered, privately funded corporations can be established to pool resources.

Location theory of development Explanation of economic development that emphasizes factors such as transportation, access to raw materials and labor, taxes, business climate, and quality of life as they relate to industrial location.

Long-wave theory of development Explanation of economic development that contends that bursts of innovation lead to economic growth.

Market failure Situation in which the free market fails to take into account the true cost of a good or a service, for example, a paper mill that pollutes a river to the disadvantage of local citizens and the environment but does not price its paper to reflect the cost of cleaning up the river; market failure is commonly cited as a reason for government intervention in free markets.

Mature industry Industry in which the technology has become standardized.

Mezzanine capital Funds or goods used to bridge the gap in resources from one stage of business to another. *See also* **Gap financing.**

Microenterprise program Undertaking that makes very small loans to entrepreneurs in a local community; loans are usually made from a revolving fund that is managed by a peer group of small entrepreneurs. These programs also provide technical training. *See also* **Microloan program.**

Microloan program Program that makes very small loans, ranging from $500 up to $25,000, from a revolving fund to very small businesses. *See also* **Microenterprise program.**

Minority business development center Small-business development center that targets minority-owned businesses. *See also* **Small-business development center.**

Mixed-use incubator Business incubator that permits clients from more than one economic sector; typically a mix of service and light-manufacturing businesses.

Mom-and-pop business Small business typically owned by neighborhood residents.

Multiplier effect   Situation in which jobs or income have a larger effect on the overall economy of an area because money that is generated from those jobs or income will be spent within the area; keeping the money in a local area produces a total effect that is a multiple of the income itself.

Natural monopoly   Situation in which a single firm can take advantage of increasing returns to scale and attain a monopoly position; a form of market failure.

Negative externality   Instance of an individual's actions imposing a cost on others.

Opportunity cost   The cost of using resources for a certain purpose; the cost is measured by the benefit given up by not using the resources in their best alternative use.

Payments in lieu of taxes (PILOT)   Payments typically made in tax abatement schemes on the value of the predeveloped land.

Positive externality   Instance of an individual's action conferring a benefit on others.

Preferred stock   Part ownership of a company; does not carry voting rights but carries a higher-priority claim than common stock on company assets in case of bankruptcy.

Product-life-cycle theory   Explanation that the technological sophistication of a product and its stage in a life cycle determine its price in the free market.

Purpose-built incubator   Business incubator facilitator constructed exclusively for being an incubator.

Quality of life   Term used to connote a bundle of amenities that may have an influence on attraction and retention of companies.

Research park   Industrial parks that focus on research and development activities; as economic developers provide high-tech communications to these operations, they have come to be known as smart parks. *See also* **Industrial park; Smart park.**

Residential incubator   The most common form of business incubation, in which several small businesses are housed together in a single building.

Revenue bond   Bond backed by anticipated revenue stream from specific project.

Reverse foreign investment   Foreign corporations or other interests take equity positions in U.S. firms, acquire U.S. real estate, or locate plants or other facilities in the United States.

Revolving loan fund   Collection of funds from which repayments of outstanding loans are continuously recycled and used to make loans to other businesses.

Royalty agreement   Investment made in return for a promise of a proportion of future sales.

Second wave   Strategic paradigm of economic development that focuses on retaining firms already in the community and on creating new businesses.

Sense of place   Identity of a neighborhood or a community; a feeling among residents regarding the identity of their community.

Server farm   Large collection of computer servers in a single location with the purpose of providing service to multiple companies that would otherwise have to purchase and maintain their own servers.

Service Corps of Retired Executives (SCORE)   Involves former businesspeople who volunteer their expertise in a range of management specialties; operated by the U.S. Small Business Administration.

Shared services   Collection of business services offered by business incubators; can include phone answering, security, parking, janitorial services, meeting facilities, and other services.

Small-business development center   Facility that provides business development, information, and assistance in one location; administered by the U.S. Small Business Administration.

Smart park   Latest version of the industrial park concept; high-tech information is provided to technology-oriented firms. See also **Industrial park; Research park.**

Smokestack chasing   Pursuit of traditional manufacturing businesses by local economic development organizations.

Social capital   In economic development, linkages between and among business development service providers and the companies they assist; these linkages are both internal, within a given service provider organization, and external, between an organization (and its clients) and external service providers and businesses.

Start-up   Company in the first stage of the evolution of a business.

Start-up capital   Funds that help nascent enterprises acquire space, equipment, supplies, and other inputs needed to launch a business.

Supply-side theory of development   Explanation of economic development that focuses on efforts to reduce costs of production in order to lure capital to a new location; typical strategies include tax abatements, reductions, and exemptions; guaranteed loans; direct loans; and reduced regulation.

Sustainable development   Economic improvement that makes use of resources in a manner to insure the ability of future generations to also use those resources.

Tax abatement   Contracts between a government entity and a holder of real estate that stipulate that some share of assessed value will not be taxed for an agreed time period; a typical goal of tax abatement is to encourage economic development.

Tax credit   Amount of money directly subtracted from a tax bill after a tax liability has been incurred.

Tax deferral   Policy that permits individuals whose property values have risen dramatically through no fault of their own to pay taxes on the basis of old values.

Tax-exempt bond   Obligation that does not require recipients of interest payments to pay taxes on the interest revenue; although revenue bonds may be a form of tax-exempt bonds, not all revenue bonds qualify for a tax exemption (e.g., stadium projects, parking facilities, and nongovernment office buildings lost their tax-exempt status in 1986).

Tax exemption   Policy that reduces the base from which property is assessed; accomplished by subtracting a given amount of money from the assessed market rate. Tax exemptions are often granted to individuals, institutions, or types of property.

Tax expenditure   Deductions to taxable income that one would normally be required to pay under corporate or income taxes.

Tax increment financing (TIF)   Tool of economic development in which taxes that can be traced to a specific development are used to repay bonds that were issued to finance that development. When bonds are fully paid, the jurisdiction can begin to receive the additional tax revenue produced by the development.

Tax stabilization agreement   Agreement to not raise taxes significantly; used to assure potential investors of a stable tax environment.

Third wave   Strategic paradigm of economic development that aims to create a local or regional environment that is supportive of growth and development.

Value added   Revenue created by the processing of resources; the amount of revenue is greater because those resources have been processed.

Venture capitalist   Wealthy individual who provides financial capital to entrepreneurs; often participates in the management of the business and demands a relatively large equity share of the business.

Virtual incubator   *See* **Incubator-without-walls.**

Voucher   Coupon that allows customers to acquire market goods at reduced prices or a fixed quantity of goods for free.

Warrant   Contract giving the investor the option to purchase a certain number of a company's shares at a fixed price for a certain period of time.

Working capital   Funds or goods used to meet day-to-day operating needs of a business.

Worthy good   A commodity determined to be so valuable or so important that its consumption is encouraged regardless of an individual's ability to pay for it.

Select Bibliography

Birch, David L. *Job Creation in America: How Our Smallest Companies Put the Most People to Work.* New York: Free Press, 1987.

Blakely, Edward J., and Ted K. Bradshaw. *Planning Local Economic Development: Theory and Practice.* 3d ed. Thousand Oaks, Calif.: Sage, 2002.

Bluestone, Barry, and Bennett Harrison. *The Deindustrialization of America: Plant Closings, Community Abandonment, and the Dismantling of Basic Industry.* New York: Basic Books, 1982.

Eisinger, Peter K. *The Rise of the Entrepreneurial State: State and Local Economic Development Policy in the United States.* Madison: University of Wisconsin Press, 1988.

Leicht, Kevin T., and J. Craig Jenkins. "Three Strategies of State Economic Development: Entrepreneurial, Industrial Recruitment, and Deregulation Policies in the American States." *Economic Development Quarterly* 8, no. 3 (1994): 256–269.

Lichtenstein, Gregg A., and Thomas S. Lyons. "The Entrepreneurial Development System: Transforming Business Talent and Community Economies." *Economic Development Quarterly* 15, no. 1 (2001): 3–20. www.newamericancommunities.org/resources/Lichtenstein_-_EDS.pdf.

Logan, John R., and Harvey L. Molotch. *Urban Fortunes: The Political Economy of Place.* Berkeley: University of California Press, 1987.

Luke, Jeffrey S., Curtiss Ventriss, B. J. Reed, and Christine Reed. *Managing Economic Development: A Guide to State and Local Leadership Strategies.* San Francisco: Jossey-Bass, 1988.

Malecki, Edward J. *Technology and Economic Development: The Dynamics of Local, Regional, and National Competitiveness.* 2d ed. Essex, England: Longman, 1997.

Markusen, Ann, Peter Hall, and Amy Glasmeier. *High Tech America: The What, How, Where, and Why of the Sunrise Industries.* Boston: Allen & Unwin, 1986.

Pinchot, Gifford, III. *Intrapreneuring: Why You Don't Have to Leave the Corporation to Become an Entrepreneur.* San Francisco: Berrett-Koehler, 2000.

Porter, Michael E. *The Competitive Advantage of Nations.* New York: Free Press, 1990.

Porter, Michael E. "New Strategies for Inner-City Economic Development." *Economic Development Quarterly* 11, no. 1 (1997): 11–27. http://home.furb.br/wilhelm/COMPETIV/Porter_Sistemico.doc.

Putnam, Robert D. *Bowling Alone: The Collapse and Revival of American Community.* New York: Simon & Schuster, 2000.

Reich, Robert B. *The Work of Nations: Preparing Ourselves for 21st-Century Capitalism.* New York: A. A. Knopf, 1991.

Rice, Mark P., and Jana B. Matthews. *Growing New Ventures, Creating New Jobs: Principles and Practices of Successful Business Incubation.* Westport, Conn.: Quorom, 1995.

Savas, E. S. *Privatization and Public-Private Partnerships.* New York: Chatham House, 2000.

Saxenian, AnnaLee. *Regional Advantage: Culture and Competition in Silicon Valley and Route 128.* Cambridge: Harvard University Press, 1994.

Servon, Lisa J. "Credit and Social Capital: The Community Development Potential of U.S. Microenterprise Programs." *Housing Policy Debate* 9, no. 1 (1998): 115–149. www.fanniemaefoundation.org/programs/hpd/pdf/hpd_0901_servon.pdf.

Tiebout, Charles M. "A Pure Theory of Local Expenditures." *Journal of Political Economy* 64 (1956): 416–424.

Vernon, Raymond. "International Investment and International Trade in the Product Cycle." *Quarterly Journal of Economics* (May 1966): 190–207.

Weinstein, Bernard L., Harold T. Gross, and John Rees. *Regional Growth and Decline in the United States.* 2d ed. New York: Praeger, 1985.

Index